UNDE
PAUI

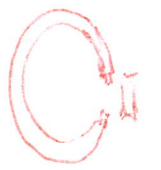

Understanding Contemporary American Literature
Matthew J. Bruccoli, Series Editor

Volumes on

Edward Albee • Sherman Alexie • Paul Auster
Nicholson Baker • John Barth • Donald Barthelme
The Beats • Thomas Berger • The Black Mountain Poets
Robert Bly • T. C. Boyle • Raymond Carver • Fred Chappell
Chicano Literature • Contemporary American Drama
Contemporary American Horror Fiction
Contemporary American Literary Theory
Contemporary American Science Fiction, 1926–1970
Contemporary American Science Fiction, 1970–2000
Contemporary Chicana Literature • Robert Coover
James Dickey • E. L. Doctorow • Rita Dove • John Gardner
George Garrett • Tim Gautreaux • John Hawkes • Joseph Heller
Lillian Hellman • Beth Henley • John Irving • Randall Jarrell
Charles Johnson • Adrienne Kennedy • William Kennedy
Jack Kerouac • Jamaica Kincaid • Tony Kushner
Ursula K. Le Guin • Denise Levertov • Bernard Malamud
Bobbie Ann Mason • Cormac McCarthy • Jill McCorkle
Carson McCullers • W. S. Merwin • Arthur Miller • Lorrie Moore
Toni Morrison's Fiction • Vladimir Nabokov • Gloria Naylor
Joyce Carol Oates • Tim O'Brien • Flannery O'Connor
Cynthia Ozick • Walker Percy • Katherine Anne Porter
Richard Powers • Reynolds Price • Annie Proulx
Thomas Pynchon • Theodore Roethke • Philip Roth
May Sarton • Hubert Selby, Jr. • Mary Lee Settle • Neil Simon
Isaac Bashevis Singer • Jane Smiley • Gary Snyder • William Stafford
Anne Tyler • Gerald Vizenor • Kurt Vonnegut • David Foster Wallace
Robert Penn Warren • James Welch • Eudora Welty
Tennessee Williams • August Wilson • Charles Wright

UNDERSTANDING
PAUL AUSTER

James Peacock

The University of South Carolina Press

© 2010 University of South Carolina

Cloth edition published by the University of South Carolina Press, 2010
Paperback edition published in Columbia, South Carolina,
by the University of South Carolina Press, 2016

www.sc.edu/uscpress

Manufactured in the United States of America

25 24 23 22 21 20 19 18 17 16
10 9 8 7 6 5 4 3 2 1

The Library of Congress has cataloged the cloth edition as follows:

Peacock, James, 1970–
  Understanding Paul Auster / James Peacock.
    p. cm.— (Understanding contemporary American literature)
  Includes bibliographical references and index.
  ISBN 978-1-57003-864-8 (cloth : alk. paper)
  1. Auster, Paul, 1947—Criticism and interpretation. 2. American
 literature—20th century—History and criticism. I. Title.
  PS3551.U77Z75 2010
  813'.54—dc22   2009034324

ISBN 978-1-61117-052-8 (paperback)

For Sheena, Bonnie, and Ruby

Contents

Series Editor's Preface / ix
Acknowledgments / xi

Chapter 1
  Understanding Paul Auster / 1
Chapter 2
  The Invention of Solitude / 15
Chapter 3
  The New York Trilogy / 42
Chapter 4
  Last Chances: *In the Country of Last Things*
  and *The Music of Chance* / 84
Chapter 5
  Auster's Frontier Novels: *Moon Palace* and
  Mr. Vertigo / 116
Chapter 6
  The Book of Illusions / 146
Chapter 7
  Other Works / 168

Notes / 193
Bibliography / 207
Index / 227

Series Editor's Preface

The volumes of *Understanding Contemporary American Literature* (UCAL) have been planned as guides or companions for students as well as good nonacademic readers. The editor and publisher perceive a need for these volumes because much of the influential contemporary literature makes special demands. Uninitiated readers encounter difficulty in approaching works that depart from the traditional forms and techniques of prose and poetry. Literature relies on conventions, but the conventions keep evolving; new writers form their own conventions—which in time may become familiar. Put simply, *UCAL* provides instruction in how to read certain contemporary writers—identifying and explicating their material, themes, use of language, point of view, structures, symbolism, and responses to experience.

The word "understanding" in the titles was deliberately chosen. Many willing readers lack an adequate understanding of how contemporary literature works—that is, what the author is attempting to express and the means by which it is conveyed. Although the criticism and analysis in the series have been aimed at a level of general accessibility, these introductory volumes are meant to be applied in conjunction with the works they cover. They do not provide a substitute for the works and authors they introduce, but rather prepare the reader for more profitable literary experiences.

M. J. B.

Acknowledgments

I would like to thank Kenneth Millard for his expert supervision at the University of Edinburgh. This book would not have been possible without it, and Dr. Millard's guidance, support, praise, patience, and friendship have always been exemplary. I would also like to thank Aliki Varvogli at Dundee University, who read my first articles on Paul Auster and provided astute and detailed comment. More recently, the readers of the first draft of this book offered warm encouragement and thoroughly constructive criticism of the work: many thanks to them.

Paul Auster was kind enough to grant me an interview at his Brooklyn home in March 2005. It must be an odd experience for a writer having a stranger come into one's house, claiming to know everything about one's work. For his time, his appreciation of my ideas, and his suggestions for new research areas, I would like to offer Mr. Auster my gratitude. He also kindly gave me permission to consult his manuscripts in the Berg Collection of the New York Public Library in summer 2008. Many thanks once again for giving me that invaluable opportunity. Thanks also to the Berg Collection staff for all their fetching, carrying, and advice on time management.

Colleagues at Keele University have been kind enough to read sections of the manuscript and give detailed feedback. I am indebted to them for taking on this extra work when they are already so busy.

Finally, my wife, Sheena Kalayil, deserves special mention, not only because she is the best proofreader and reference checker around, but also because she has been unflagging in her encouragement and optimism since I started. It should also be said that if anyone understands Paul Auster, it is she.

UNDERSTANDING
PAUL AUSTER

CHAPTER 1

Introduction

Paul Auster was born on 3 February 1947 in Newark, New Jersey, the son of Samuel and Queenie Auster. After attending school in Maplewood, New Jersey, he studied English and comparative literature at Columbia College, graduating with a B.A. in 1969 and an M.A. in 1970, after a fragmentary career that saw him travel to Europe, quit, and then reenroll. Auster traveled to France in 1971 with his girlfriend, writer Lydia Davis. They returned to the States and were married in 1974. In 1978 they separated, and they divorced in 1982, the year he married his current wife, novelist Siri Hustvedt.

Career

The formative influence of the years in France can be seen not only in Auster's translations of French poets like Stéphane Mallarmé and Jacques Dupin but also in Auster's novels. He describes in the 1997 memoir *Hand to Mouth* how he existed on the edge of poverty in France, eking out a living doing translations and tutoring while writing poetry and essays. Poverty's effect on the creative individual is an important theme in novels such as *The New York Trilogy* and *Moon Palace*.

Perhaps the most influential event, however, is the death of Auster's father on 15 January 1979. Auster began *The Invention of Solitude* immediately after Sam's death. In it he introduces many of the ideas that have become familiar in his novels and movies—mortality, the difficulty of knowing another person, the importance of chance, father-son relationships—and uses Sam as the central "character." In the book's second part Auster also quotes liberally from philosophical and literary antecedents, starting a trend for allusiveness that has continued throughout his career. As *The Invention of Solitude* demonstrates, major influences include Samuel Beckett, Franz Kafka, the Bible, philosophers such as Gottfried Wilhelm von Leibniz, Jewish writers such as Edmond Jabès, and Freudian psychoanalysis. In later works Auster openly references his nineteenth-century American antecedents, particularly Nathaniel Hawthorne, Edgar Allan Poe, and Henry David Thoreau. This combination of European and American influences gives Auster's work its unique flavor, at once inward-looking, speculating on the big mysteries of personal existence, and expansive, engaging with America's grand foundational myths.

In 2007 Paul Auster turned sixty. The preceding years had witnessed a significant raising of his international profile. In the December 2005 edition of *Esquire* magazine, celebrity fans and friends of Paul Auster, including actor Harvey Keitel and musician David Byrne, offered their fond opinions of the man and his work. A year later Auster was awarded the prestigious Prince of Asturias Prize for Literature.[1] Given his current popular and academic appeal and his status as "a literary giant,"[2] it may be surprising to learn that the manuscript for *City of Glass,* the first part of *The New York Trilogy,* was rejected by seventeen publishers between 1982 and 1984.

Auster had been busy as a writer long before then, however. Throughout the 1970s he wrote plays and published five poetry collections. He even produced a conventional detective novel called *Squeeze Play* in 1978, which did not find a publisher until 1982 and therefore failed to help achieve its author's ambition "to turn it into cash and pay off as many bills as I could."[3]

Since the publication of the trilogy Auster has had fewer problems paying the bills. He has published fourteen novels, three memoirs, several collections of essays, translations of French poetry, and four screenplays. Translated into thirty languages, Auster's work has sold consistently well in Europe. In France, in particular, he has achieved iconic status and sustains an intellectual industry all his own. For example, 1996 saw the publication of four French scholarly texts devoted entirely to *Moon Palace*.[4]

Although the novels have garnered the majority of scholarly attention, it may well be the movies, particularly *Smoke* (1995) and *Blue in the Face* (1995), that have cemented Auster's reputation as a significant cultural figure in the United States, not simply a purveyor of belles lettres. Not only do these movies offer a beguiling portrait of a Brooklyn populated by eccentric individuals, but their collaborative nature has promoted an image of Auster as metropolitan and sophisticated, yet generous and open-minded. In short, the Auster who wrote the screenplay for *Smoke,* codirected its ramshackle sequel with Wayne Wang, and elicited inspired, improvised performances from everyday Brooklyn citizens and stars such as Lou Reed, is generally considered "cool." Despite declaring in 1994 that he had no desire to direct again, Auster has since gone on to write and direct *Lulu on the Bridge* (1998), a love story centered on a mysterious stone with magical properties, and *The Inner Life of Martin Frost* (2007), the plot of which first appeared in *The Book of Illusions* (2002).[5]

Overview

The movies are significant not only for the celebrity status they have conferred upon Auster but also because they constitute a distillation of his main preoccupations in a medium accessible to a wider audience. These concerns, despite his experimentation with a wide variety of media as well as literary forms, have remained remarkably consistent, from the pithy, enigmatic, and somewhat difficult poetry of his early career, to the apparently more open, inclusive, and optimistic imaginings of *Smoke*, *Blue in the Face*, *Timbuktu* (1999), and *The Brooklyn Follies* (2005).

A useful starting point is Auster's analysis of *Smoke*'s title: "Smoke is something that is never fixed, that is constantly changing shape. In the same way that the characters in the film keep changing as their lives intersect. Smoke signals . . . smoke screens . . . smoke drifting through the air. In small ways and large ways, each character is continually changed by the other characters around him" (3F 16). Clearly *Smoke* is primarily about human relationships and the mutability of the individual within social interactions. While "smoke screens" connotes deception, the difficulty of perception, and the invisible barriers we throw up between ourselves and others, the phrase "smoke signals" reaffirms the primacy of communication, even if that communication might at times seem to be in code. At heart the message here is similar to E. M. Forster's famous formulation: "Live in fragments no longer. Only connect."[6] The means of connection may be obscured, but nonetheless the need remains.

If Forster's statement implies, in addition to its ethical imperative, despair at humankind's inability to connect, then Auster's work makes this a constant. A typical Auster protagonist is male, a storyteller, and, for a variety of reasons, in a state of isolation from his loved ones and wider society. This isolation is often self-enforced, and although not all the characters' attempts are successful, the narrative of an Auster text tends to describe their attempt to break free of this enervating isolation and find reinvigoration in relationships with others. Paul Benjamin, the protagonist of *Smoke*, has lost his wife and unborn child in a random shooting incident outside the neighborhood cigar shop that forms the central location of the story. Suffering from writer's block, and with his professional solitude amplified by personal suffering, Paul lives in self-imposed exile in his apartment. He only begins an at times painful rehabilitation when he meets young runaway Rashid Cole and becomes involved in the attempt to reunite Rashid with his estranged father.

Another crucial figure is Auggie Wren, proprietor of the cigar shop. Through his conversations with Auggie, and through close scrutiny of the photographs Auggie has taken of the shop every day since stealing his first camera, Paul learns to pay attention to Brooklyn itself as a possible balm for his emotional wounds. Part of Auster's intention in scripting the movie was to "work against some of the stereotypes that people carry around about this place [New York City, and Brooklyn in particular]." Of his neighborhood, Park Slope, he says, "It has to be one of the most democratic and tolerant places on the planet. Everyone lives there, every race and religion and economic class, and everyone pretty much gets along. Given the climate in the country today, I would say that qualifies as a miracle" (3F 18). Whether or not this is romanticization, it is evident that geographic and demographic factors participate in the escape from isolation almost as much as the formation of individual friendships. This is particularly true of *The Brooklyn Follies,* in which Brooklyn helps cure the narrator of his misanthropy.

One has to be careful when studying Auster's work to distinguish between isolation—an essentially uncreative and solipsistic state of withdrawal from contact—and solitude. The latter condition, specifically the "productive kind of solitude, the solitude of a vicar or an artist," enables a sympathetic outlook from the individual through immersion in the lives of others.[7] While acknowledging the paradoxical nature of this idea, Auster, in an interview with Larry McCaffery and Sinda Gregory, attempts to explain it: "You don't begin to understand your connection to others until you are alone. And the more intensely you are alone, the more deeply you plunge into a state of solitude, the more deeply you feel that connection." Ultimately, he continues, "it isn't possible for a person to isolate himself from other people. No matter how apart you might find yourself in a physical sense . . . you discover that you are inhabited by others." In another important paradox, Auster stresses that "your language, your memories, even your sense of isolation—every thought in your head has been born from your connection with others."[8] The question is whether a particular character is inclined to accept this fact or hide from it.

Art, particularly writing, has an important role to play. To write literature and to read a book require a person to enter into dialogue with others. Despite their both being solitary acts in the physical sense, Auster stresses that ethically and psychologically, reading and writing are collective endeavors: "It's the only time we really go into the mind of a stranger, and we find our common humanity doing this. So the book doesn't only belong to the writer, it belongs to the reader as well, and then together you make it what it is."[9]

This is why so many of his novels portray writers or people who, sometimes inadvertently, become writers by changing their attitudes to language. For Auster, the precise point at which an individual begins to think and feel artistically—that is, to break free of an outlook in which precedence is given to sense perceptions or factual knowledge—is the point at which he or she becomes truly human. There are numerous examples throughout his work. Most influential is *The Invention of Solitude* (1982).

Inspired by the death of his father, the book is divided into two distinct parts. In the first section, called "Portrait of an Invisible Man," Auster reflects in the first person on his bereavement and attempts to piece together an accurate portrait of Sam from memories, photographs, possessions, and newspaper clippings. That he fails to do this is testament both to the coldness and reticence of his father and to the futility of biographical investigation itself. In recognizing that "the essence of this project is failure," Auster comes to regard his father as emblematic of one's inability really to "know" another person.[10]

A possible solution is explored in part two, "The Book of Memory." Here Auster is reconfigured as "A." and writes in the third person, at one remove from himself. Rather than biography, what is attempted here is an extended, more abstract meditation on memory, authorship, and fatherhood, one that includes a wealth of quotations from literary antecedents such as Friedrich Hölderlin and Anne Frank. Auster explains, "I wanted it to be a collective work. . . . These are the voices that I live with and I wanted them to come out and share the work with me."[11] Drawing on literature—allowing the writing itself to become more literary, ambiguous, and dialogic—enables Auster to come closer to an understanding of human experience based not on factual or material evidence, but rather on a communal sharing of ideas. "Truth" lies somewhere among the various voices.

Time and again in Auster's novels one sees this transition from fact to fictionalization, from documentary to art. For instance, Blue, the protagonist of *Ghosts* (1986)—the second part of *The New York Trilogy*—has been accustomed to writing reports that "stick to outward facts." Yet the protracted observation of his mysterious quarry, Black, renders such reports increasingly problematic, until he realizes that "words do not necessarily work."

At this point his reports are transformed into speculative works of fiction.[12] Through this fictionalization he achieves a clearer understanding of his situation.

Blue's realization is crucial to understanding Auster's entire oeuvre. Far from being an unequivocally liberating or reassuring experience, the shift into a more literary mode depends on accepting that all language misbehaves: it is subjective, endlessly nuanced, open to interpretation, and, to quote one of Auster's major influences, Ralph Waldo Emerson, "vehicular and transitive."[13] To put it another way, before one can fix a word to an object or person, its meaning shifts. For human beings who crave control and security, such a concept can rock the very foundations of existence, because one must understand that the inability to know another person, or indeed the world in general, is for Auster bound up in this slipperiness of language. It is a constitutive paradox of his work: artistic expression, which is necessary because language cannot be tied to a documentary recording of the world, ends up talking about its own inadequacy to express the world. Most of Auster's early poetry wrestles with this paradox: "if we speak of the world it is only to leave the world."[14] Later, in *Moon Palace* (1989), Marco Stanley Fogg attempts to describe his surroundings to his blind employer, Thomas Effing. The difficulty this task poses leads Fogg to muse philosophically on language's relationship to perception. "What do you see?" he asks. "And if you see, how do you put it into words? The world enters us through our eyes, but we cannot make sense of it until it descends into our mouths. I began to appreciate how great that distance was." Eventually he appreciates that "the more air I left around a thing, the happier the results, for that allowed Effing to do the crucial work on his own . . . to feel his own mind traveling toward the thing I was describing for him."[15] Once again, then, meaning is not objective. It stems from a tacit contract between individuals and is produced in the space between their subjective interpretations.

The evacuation of objectivity from language has important consequences for "reality." If one cannot state with any confidence what is objectively real, can reality be said to exist? And if reality ceases to exist, is all that remains at best subjective, at worst a total fiction? This has significant implications for Auster's work, both thematically and formally. First, the recession of reality only increases the importance of *stories*. With objective reality unavailable, stories become the primary means of conveying truths of an altogether more psychological, emotional, and, ultimately, profound nature. Viewed negatively, this can of course lead to imprisonment in a world of words, with no escape to reality.

Alternatively, if one welcomes other people's narratives, then a kind of democracy of storytelling ensues. This is best illustrated by the *National Story Project,* which Auster edited and published as *I Thought My Father Was God, and Other True Tales of American Life from NPR's National Story Project* (2001). Assuming a single, knowable reality to be unavailable, the best approach is to build reality collectively, as an exercise in storytelling. As Auster expresses it, "People would be exploring their own lives and experiences, but at the same time they would be part of a collective effort, something bigger than just themselves. With their help, I said, I was hoping to put together an archive of facts, a museum of American reality."[16] Any "facts" are of course open to interpretation, but the relationships between the stories create communal truths that are more accurate representations of our experience as social beings.

Formally Auster employs several characteristic techniques to reflect this experience. Since the second part of *The Invention of Solitude,* Auster has been fond of utilizing direct allusions to his literary forbears. To cite just a few examples: Daniel Quinn's pen name in *City of Glass* is William Wilson, which is the name of an Edgar Allan Poe story of 1839 about a case of doubled identity. Both *Leviathan* (1992) and *The Brooklyn Follies* are presided over by the spirit of Henry David Thoreau. *The Book of Illusions* (2002) expands and updates Nathaniel Hawthorne's tale "The Birth-mark" (1843). One could argue that such allusiveness makes the work "too obsessively literary."[17] However, it can also be viewed as recognition that stories, like identities, are created collectively, that there is a community of storytellers transcending individual authority and historical eras.

Originality, in consequence, is never achievable in any pristine manner, only in the way a writer refocuses and reapplies a story to a new context. If this would seem to undermine the writer's authority, then Auster is always willing to allow this to happen. Another way of doing this is to dissolve the barrier between writer and character, biography and fiction. From the moment Daniel Quinn, in *City of Glass,* receives a series of phone calls from a stranger asking for "Paul Auster" (7), Auster enthusiastically inserts himself into his work. Sometimes he appears in anagrammatical form, as the writer John Trause in *Oracle Night;* sometimes pseudonymously, as Paul Benjamin in *Smoke* (Benjamin being Auster's middle name); and sometimes as a vague memory: "a guy named Anster, Omster, something like that."[18]

Moreover, Auster has always used autobiographical elements in his fiction. *Leviathan* is a supreme example of this tendency. The narrator, Peter Aaron, shares initials with Paul Auster, falls in love at first sight with a woman named Iris (Auster's wife is Siri), and has a writing retreat in Vermont, like Auster. Despite inviting dismissal as, in one critic's words, "intellectual gamesmanship,"[19] it should first be noted that many other writers (such as Philip Roth) indulge in such biographical teasing. Second, if Auster takes it to extremes, it serves as consolidation of the idea that "real" lives are the sum of the multiple stories told about them, and therefore lack an objective, authoritative center.

Another formal symptom of this lack is the characteristic Russian-doll construction of Auster's narratives. Auster is fond of building layer upon layer of narration to the extent that an inattentive reader might forget which character is actually speaking. For some critics, the technique becomes wearisome. D. T. Max asks, "At one point in *The Book of Illusions* Auster narrates Zimmer narrating Mann narrating Frost narrating his story. What are we to make of this?"[20] One might respond that readerly frustration is part of the point. Rejection of the traditional, omniscient narrator in favor of this multivocal approach is a more accurate reflection of how one's clamorous reality is textured, and it can indeed be frustrating for those who seek definitive answers. An Auster reader, like his characters, must learn not to seek them.

Life will always remain resistant to the imposition of order. In fact for Auster life's only certainty is chance. His narratives invariably contain outrageous coincidences, chance meetings, seemingly impossible connections. An underlying tension in his work is that an artist is someone who creates an ordered universe, yet has a responsibility to incorporate random incidents. In such a structured environment, however, nothing is ever truly random. "From an aesthetic point of view, the introduction of chance elements in fiction probably creates as many problems as it solves. I've come in for a lot of abuse from critics because of it," Auster admits. Yet chance cannot be avoided: "In the strictest sense of the word, I consider myself a realist. Chance is a part of reality: we are continually shaped by the forces of coincidence. . . . What I am after, I suppose, is to write fiction as strange as the world I live in" (AH 287–88). The problem for some of Auster's characters is that they cannot accept the unexpected, and instead succumb to a belief that every single event happens for a reason and specifically implicates them. Part of Auster's project is to repudiate this notion.

The ultimate in meaningless occurrences is death itself. When Auster was fourteen, he witnessed a friend being struck dead by lightning only yards in front of him. After the tragedy, he speculated on his own proximity to death and declared, "Life would never feel the same to me again."[21] This ethical and aesthetic epiphany is repeated when his father passes away. *The Invention of Solitude* stems from "death without warning" (IOS 5). (It was also, as Auster has admitted, made possible by the inheritance he received when his father died.) Death, in other words, is frequently the inspiration for creativity. The end becomes the beginning.

All of Auster's concerns, including the meaninglessness of death, can be viewed through the prism of his Jewish background. His grandparents, Anna and Harry, were Jews from Stanislav in present-day Lithuania who emigrated to the States in the late nineteenth century. Like many of his generation, he considers himself "Americanized": he was "brought up as an American boy, who knew less about my ancestors than I did about Hopalong Cassidy's hat" (IOS 28). Nonetheless, there are important ways in which his work has a recognizably Jewish sensibility. Unlike Philip Roth, say, Auster rarely tackles overtly "Jewish" themes: it is more a question of aesthetic practice. Reference is made to the Holocaust in *Oracle Night* (2003), for example, and Auster has stated that *In the Country of Last Things* (1987) allegorizes the Warsaw ghetto (AH 321), yet neither is

Understanding Paul Auster / 13

made the explicit *theme*. Instead, they function as cataclysmic events that summon the writer to deal with them, but constantly frustrate his efforts because their sheer magnitude and horror expose the redundancy of language. The gap between reality and the possible representation of that reality widens when one takes into account Jewish historical experience.

What results is something the author dubs "exile." This is, for the Jewish American writer, not simply a condition of outsiderness; it is a complex state of being both inside and outside simultaneously. In his essay on Charles Reznikoff called "The Decisive Moment," Auster articulates this state: "Reznikoff's poems are what Reznikoff is: the poems of an American Jew, or, if you will, of a hyphenated American, a Jewish-American, with the two terms standing not so much on equal footing as combining to form a third and wholly different term: the condition of being in two places at the same time, or, quite simply, the condition of being nowhere" (AH 44). This is Auster's condition: it explains his ambivalence over national and literary identity. His tendency to mine his Jewish familial and literary heritage in texts like *The Invention of Solitude* is combined with a fascination for American mythologies such as the Wild West. Similarly, Auster balances the numerous references to nineteenth-century American writers with allusions to European antecedents such as Franz Kafka. Being nowhere is the artist's condition, because the artist is both involved in and distant from the event he or she describes, as well as being alienated from the language he or she employs—hence the Russian-doll narrative form already alluded to: stories are constructed like parables, in Hebrew *mishral*, with the final cohesive lesson, the *nimshal*, missing in the layers of narration. The reader, then, finds himself or herself exiled from any definitive meaning. And finally, being nowhere is the condition of many of Auster's itinerant and homeless protagonists (for example, Walter Rawley in *Mr. Vertigo* [1994]): perpetual movement, the sense that one is only at home when mobile, stems from a Jewish inheritance of dispersion and exile.

Thus there is an endless oscillation in Auster's work between confinement (in locked rooms or the author's own psyche) and freedom in open spaces (western landscapes or the streets of Brooklyn). Of course, the two are not mutually exclusive: an individual can be as free in his or her mind and soul as any wanderer if he or she chooses to acknowledge the plurality of others' experience.

It is intriguing, however, to speculate on Auster's next move. His previous two novels were markedly contrasting. *The Brooklyn Follies* takes Auster out of his customary locked room and into a thriving community. It is in many ways the most open and generous of all his works, despite ending on 11 September 2001. *Travels in the Scriptorium* (2006), on the other hand, takes place metaphorically within the writer's head. An aging author, Mr. Blank, wakes up inside a room with no recollection of his arrival and where, periodically, he is visited by characters from his books. The novel got a hostile critical reception. Angel Gurria-Quintana, for example, dismisses it as "self-indulgent" and "an elaborate in-joke."[22] It seems that Auster's future reputation depends on his willingness to step outside into the world once more. *Man in the Dark* (2008), his latest, may offer a suitable compromise. Despite taking place largely within the head of another aging writer, August Brill, it paints its stories on a broader historical canvas, offering a vision of an alternative America that descends into civil war after the 2000 election. At once inward and outward looking, it marks at least a tentative step into new political territories.

CHAPTER TWO

The Invention of Solitude

In 2003, when *The Invention of Solitude* appeared in Paul Auster's *Collected Prose,* readers familiar only with celebrated novels such as *The New York Trilogy* had a second context in which to read what the author regards as "a bridge" between his poetry and prose, and "the meat of what I have done since."[1] Such a revisiting feels appropriate. Not only does each subsequent novel reprise and extend themes and ideas first addressed explicitly in *The Invention of Solitude,* but that book is also an exercise in revisitation. Inspired by the sudden death of Auster's father, Sam, in 1979, and first published in 1982, it is divided into two parts. The first, "Portrait of an Invisible Man," is a kind of biography written in the first person and examines the life of Sam Auster (and Sam's parents) in order to try to explain his enigmatic absences, his "distance from life" (7). Part two, "The Book of Memory," implicitly addresses the inevitable failure of part one. It goes back to the work of Auster's literary and philosophical antecedents in order to elucidate the pressing questions of memory, fatherhood, relationships, and life's essential meaninglessness raised in the "Portrait."

Unsurprisingly, given the considerable shifts in form and tone between parts one and two, critics tended to discuss them almost separately, often with quite distinct opinions of each. W. S. Merwin, writing in the *New York Times,* praises "Portrait of an Invisible Man" for having "the virtues and rawness of letters written under stress." The best sections, Merwin believes, "are direct and immediate and seem to have emerged more or less as they are out of the guiding impulse." In attempting urgently to convey the material of his father's biography in language, Auster exposes "one of the abiding and essential delusions of writers," that "there is in fact a relatively solid body of material that exists on its own and can really be put into words." In marked contrast, "The Book of Memory" lacks immediacy and power, and is for Merwin "marred . . . by recurrent pointless mannerisms apparently suggested by contemporary French 'experimental' writing." Among these he includes Auster's decision to refer to himself in the third person and "the author's urge to supply a final weighty generalization" to his observations.[2]

Auster has very specific reasons for adopting the third person. Ironically, after failing to traverse the distance between him and his father, he requires rhetorical distance to explore the issues at stake: "What it came down to was creating a distance between myself and myself. If you're too close to the thing you're trying to write about, the perspective vanishes, and you begin to smother. I had to objectify myself in order to explore my own subjectivity. . . . It's . . . a way of watching yourself think" (AH 319). Michael Walters's review in the *Times Literary Supplement* shows more understanding of this process than Merwin's. Admiring both the metaphorical and experimental aspects of the text, Walter recognizes the necessity of Auster's self-distancing, given that this is as much a book about "the procedures of recall" as what there is to be recalled. Like Jacqueline Austan, writing in *American Book Review,* Walters appreciates that the form reflects the ethical content, in his words the oscillation between "A part" and "Apart," recurring throughout *The Invention of Solitude* and Auster's subsequent writing.[3]

Adam Begley puts it this way: "First, there is the upper case 'I': Auster's life is broken in two, and the crisis that marks the break is the quintessential Auster story."[4] This move from first to third person in *The Invention of Solitude* is repeated throughout the work that follows. It is the moment when chance tragedy invades life, when the writer is forced out of cozy assurances and into intense scrutiny of reality and self. It is also the moment of greatest despair, when art provides the greatest hope of salvation. In 1979, the year "everything changed" in Auster's life, Auster "was suffering. . . . He was really inside of that solitude, that loneliness, and I don't think he knew at all how he was going to make it through other than by working."[5] *The Invention of Solitude* is testament both to the loneliness and to the consolations of the work. What distinguishes it from Auster's other prose is the degree to which the *processes* of writing are laid so bare. To read both parts is to watch a fiction-making consciousness evolve.

"Portrait of an Invisible Man"

The plain prose of the opening sentences of "Portrait of an Invisible Man" reflects the starkness of the defining event. "One day there is life," writes Auster, "everything is as it was, as it will always be. . . . And then, suddenly, it happens there is death." In the case of Sam Auster, this is neither "accidental death" nor "death after a long illness," both of which might allow for simple "resignation" or a belief in "fate," but death from "no apparent cause" (5). A man in perfect health has simply ceased to live. Consequently, all that one can do is accept that the unexpected happens, which is to say "life stops. And it can stop at any moment." It is clear from the beginning of the text that

Sam's death is emblematic of randomness itself and of the collapse of certainties. The "boundary between life and death" has become more fragile, and "we no longer know which side we are on." In fact it is "as if this death has owned this life all along" (5). If one cannot rely on the most fundamental of oppositions, that between life and death, one cannot rely on anything.

Rather than grief, the son's predominant feeling is a sense of urgency, the need to engage immediately in the recuperation and preservation of his father's biography through writing. "If I do not act quickly," Auster speculates, "his entire life will vanish along with him" (6). As is so often the case in the novels, writing is not simply an aesthetic activity, but one that answers a desperate need. It is quite literally a matter of life and death.

That the need is particularly great here has to do with the peculiarities of Sam Auster's situation and character. What worries Auster is "the realization that my father had left no traces." Without dependant family, without anyone "whose life would be altered by his absence," Sam will rapidly fade into distant memory: "Eventually, it would be as though he had never lived at all" (6). Most important, Auster's fears are exacerbated by the knowledge that the physical death of his father is simply a continuation of the distancing process Sam started in life. Here was a man "devoid of passion, either for a thing, a person, or an idea, incapable or unwilling to reveal himself under any circumstances." By revealing that his father managed "to avoid immersion in the quick of things," to eschew meaningful human relationships, Auster further breaks down the boundary between life and death: Sam's life was "a kind of death by anticipation" (7). Once again this is an idea revisited throughout Auster's writing: to cast oneself adrift from the network of human interactions is effectively to be dead. The implications for the "Portrait" are deeply ironic. The writing of this text can only be a failure because of the limitations of the material. It becomes, rather than a biography, "a kind of meditation on how you *might* write a biography,"6 and poses the questions: How can one know someone who refuses to be known? How can one *know* anyone? Auster hints at awareness of his failure early on when he acknowledges that "death has not changed anything. The only difference is that I have run out of time" (7).

Yet the lack of time and material, combined with Sam's elusiveness, only makes the process more imperative. As William Dow puts it, Auster "places a new value on the elusive and discloses a longing for a stable self."7 In other words, Sam becomes representative of the inscrutability of selfhood and highlights the need to try to write a coherent life narrative through the linking together of the fragmentary evidence available. These fragments assume many forms in the "Portrait"—memories, snippets of dialogue, newspaper clippings—but perhaps the most evocative fragments are the physical objects directly associated with Sam, including the "shabby, depressing" house (10) that stands as "the metaphor of my father's life" (9). They have a material solidity that holds out the possibility of a tangible narrative, but are so disembodied after his death that in the end they serve chiefly to emphasize Sam's remoteness. Going through his father's possessions, Auster reflects on this irony: "Things are inert: they have meaning only in function of the life that makes use of them. When that life ends, the things change, even though they remain the same. They are there and yet not there: tangible ghosts" (10). When Auster throws away "more than a hundred" of his father's ties, objects particularly evocative of their relationship, he fully recognizes that his father is now no more than a ghost: "The act of throwing away these ties seemed to embody for me the idea of burial. I finally understood that my father was dead" (13).

The physical objects that assume the greatest significance are the many family photographs described throughout the text, objects that yet again destabilize the relationship between life and death. In the bedroom closet Auster finds "several hundred photographs" of his father (13). He senses that they may "reveal some previously hidden truth," partly because they seem to "reaffirm my father's physical presence in the world, to give me the illusion that he was still there." Studying them intently, it is "as though he were still alive, even in death. Or if not alive, at least not dead. Or rather, somehow suspended, locked in a universe that had nothing to do with death, in which death could never make an entrance" (14). Photographs carry special weight for Auster because the undead status they impart to the subject provides a fitting model of the task in which he is engaged. He is attempting to keep Sam alive while confirming his absence, so that the father becomes both alive and dead, and therefore neither. In this way Auster's attitude to the photographs recalls Susan Sontag's famous formulation: "All photographs are *memento mori*. To take a photograph is to participate in another person's (or thing's) mortality, vulnerability, mutability."[8] They imply mortality, but also a strange continuity.

Sontag's further description of a photograph as "a token of absence" is entirely fitting for one of the images Auster finds.[9] The image's fundamental importance is reflected in its inclusion on the book's cover and in the fact that Auster uses the phrase "portrait of an invisible man" for the first time in analyzing it. It is, he explains, "a trick photograph taken in an Atlantic City studio sometime during the Forties." In it, shots of Sam Auster have been multiplied such that "at first you think it must be a group of several different men. Because of the gloom that surrounds them, because of the utter stillness of their poses, it looks as if they have gathered there to conduct a seance. And then, as you study the picture, you begin to realize that all these men are the same man." Characteristically, Auster extends his "séance" analogy to read the image as one of withdrawal, absence, and death: "The seance becomes a real seance, and it is as if he has come there only to invoke himself, to bring himself back from the dead, as if, by multiplying himself, he had inadvertently made himself disappear." The photo becomes symbolic of his father's inability to connect with the world: "There are five of him there, and yet the nature of the trick photography denies the possibility of eye contact among the various selves. Each one is condemned to go on staring into space, as if under the gaze of others, but seeing nothing, never able to see anything. It is a picture of death, a portrait of an invisible man" (31).

As a visual representation of what Auster elsewhere dubs "the multiplicity of the singular" (AH 319), the photograph reveals another of the major difficulties in tracking down Sam Auster. As well as by his aloofness, the impression he gives of "want[ing] so little from others" (20), Auster is thwarted by his father's surprisingly chameleon-like personality, to the extent that he eventually declares, "I have the feeling that I am writing about three or four different men" (61). The narrative provides numerous examples. There is the Sam Auster who is unable to accept his daughter's psychiatric problems. He continues to insist there is "nothing wrong with her" despite all evidence to the contrary, yet treats her instinctively as "an angel" rather than "an autonomous being" (25), thus effectively worsening her condition. Even when he begins to accept her situation and falls into despair, it is a solipsistic despair: "She was merely the *site* where the battle would take place, which meant that everything that was happening did not really affect *her*" (26–27). In other words, Sam is unable to see beyond his own closed world. In contrast, there is the "crazy, tensed-up" Sam Auster who expresses "bizarre opinions" and is happy to "play devil's advocate" with people. At such times he comes across almost as playful: "Teasing people put him in buoyant spirits, and after a particularly inane remark he would often squeeze that person's leg—in a spot that always tickled. He literally liked to pull your leg" (30). The suggestion is that in such situations, Sam is not called upon to invest too much of himself in his verbal games. There is no danger of touching on deeper emotions, if indeed he has any.

In addition, there is the Sam whose "reluctance to spend money was so great it almost resembled a disease." Auster attributes his father's obsessive need to buy the cheapest and most functional things not simply to meanness but to "a permanent state of sensory deprivation"; it is an attempt to "cut himself off from the possibility of experiencing aesthetic pleasure" and to deny himself "intimate contact with the shapes and textures of the world" (53). It is just another symptom of his isolation. Yet he is also capable of extreme generosity. As a slum landlord he comes into contact with some of the most impoverished people in northern New Jersey. His work is "a perpetual assault" (56), but Auster notes his father's ability to be "soft-hearted with the tenants—granting them delays in paying their rent, giving clothes to their children, helping them to find work" (57). This aspect of Sam's character is confirmed when Auster finds a letter from one of the tenants addressed to "Mr. Sam" and expressing gratitude for his kindness (57).

The trick photo, along with these examples, demonstrates that Sam is unknowable partly because he is plural. (Of course,

Auster's decision to distance himself from himself in "The Book of Memory" by becoming "A." is recognition that he is also plural.) By glancing briefly at further examples of multiple selves in subsequent novels, one can see that the father has in fact taught the son a valuable lesson about identity. Maria Turner, the conceptual artist in *Leviathan,* transforms her life into art by assuming playful and occasionally dangerous new identities— the detective, the voyeur, the prey under surveillance. Likewise in *The Book of Illusions* Hector Mann's whole life is a series of adopted roles, disguises, and unreliable biographies. The implication is clear: nobody possesses a unified identity. We are all split, changeable, and unpredictable precisely because, as the trick photograph implies, we are subject to the gazes and the interpretations of others.

As well as highlighting the aspects of Sam's personality that make it virtually impossible for Auster ever to understand him, the trick photo also highlights the drawbacks of reading and interpretation as activities in themselves. The very fact that it is a *trick* photo is revealing. Of all visual art forms, photography seems to have, in the French theorist Roland Barthes's terms, "special credibility."[10] The cliché "the camera never lies" stems from the widely held belief that photography is somehow realistic, honest, and easy to read. But from its earliest inception, and especially now with the possibilities offered by digital technology, photography has always allowed for tampering, special effects, and selectivity. It might give the illusion of impartiality, but even the initial choice of subject matter is necessarily subjective and exclusive. What appears to be an uncomplicated statement is in fact heavily "coded,"[11] a fiction rather than reality, and this is true of all photos, not just trick shots. For Auster, looking at the trick photo of his father brings home the futility of what he is attempting because photography is a lot like biography. Both promise objectivity but turn out to be selective fictions, representations that obscure knowledge. In turn, the act of reading the evidence becomes much more complicated, and in the end much less fruitful, than Auster originally anticipated.

Nowhere is this connection between biography and photography made more brutally apparent than in the photo of Sam as a small boy with his family in Kenosha, Wisconsin (again, reproduced at the beginning of the book). On first viewing the picture seems to portray an almost idyllic familial past: "My father, no more than a year old, is sitting on his mother's lap, and the other four are standing around her in the tall, uncut grass. There are two trees behind them and a large wooden house behind the trees." Auster perceives "a distinct time, a distinct place, an indestructible sense of the past"—that is, the graspable presence he has been seeking throughout (33). Even the clumsy tear on the right-hand side of the picture he attributes to a simple accident. But when he begins to notice certain details—"a man's fingertips grasping the torso of one of my uncles," another of his uncles resting his hand on "a chair that was not there"—he realizes with horror that his grandfather has been deliberately cut out of the photograph. Continuing the theme of exile and ghostly in-betweenness, Auster observes, "Only his fingertips remained: as if he were trying to crawl back into the picture from some hole deep in time, as if he had been exiled to another dimension" (34). Like the adult Sam Auster, though for quite different reasons, Harry Auster is both there and not there, suspended in an undead state.[12]

The story that results in this excision is an extraordinary one and provides justification for Auster's desire to portray in his fiction "the real world that I live in, no matter how fantastic or crazy or uncontrollable it might seem."[13] Auster hears the story from a cousin, who found it out during a chance conversation with a Kenosha resident on a plane. Once again, therefore, chance is the catalyst for outlandish events and revelations. From the beginning of the extended narrative, Auster makes it clear that it is not the facts themselves that horrify him: "I am not even afraid to say it. My grandmother murdered my grandfather. On January 23, 1919, precisely sixty years before my father died, his mother shot and killed his father in the kitchen of their house on Fremont Avenue, Kenosha, Wisconsin" (35).

What unsettles is the facts' existence as textual artifacts. They are yet another version of the undead—"unburied, so to speak, from the realm of secrets and turned into a public event" (35). In reproducing some of the "more than twenty articles" about the case (35), Auster continues to gain a deeper understanding of the complexities of his quest to decipher his father's, and by implication his own, identity. First, he learns that when an individual has an emotional investment in past events, history blends with personal obsessions and ceases to be an accepted truth but rather, like the altered photographs, a subjective reading of events. As Auster explains, "I read these articles as history. But also as a cave drawing discovered on the inner walls of my own skull." It is impossible to view them dispassionately, and they come to dwarf all other contemporary events: "Perspective is lost in favor of proportion—which is dictated not by the eye but by the demands of the mind" (37).

Second, Auster realizes that the past exists only in the form of texts anyway. "The facts seem to be there" in these articles, but the word "seem" is the operative one (36). Because these texts have been written by *someone,* what facts there are must inevitably be colored and incomplete, just as Auster's reading of them is. He describes these articles as "a mixture of scandal-mongering and sentimentality, heightened by the fact that the people involved were Jews—and therefore strange, almost by definition" (36). (The outsider status of the Jewish community is cursorily referred to here, but it becomes central to the ideas and the aesthetics of "The Book of Memory.") Even though the events outlined in the article—the grandparents' separation and imminent divorce (37), the inquest (39), Anna's headline-grabbing "TEARLESS" appearance at the murdered Harry's graveside (39), her confession (41), Harry's brother's failed attempt to carry out a revenge shooting (43), and the startling not guilty verdict (47)—"explain a great deal" about Sam Auster's adult behavior (36), there lingers the sense that when events are only available through multiple representations in writing, they cannot be relied upon.

Indeed it is not just Sam Auster's elusive character that condemns the work to failure, it is also, ironically, the very process of writing necessary to memorialize him. "Never before have I been so aware of the rift between thinking and writing," Auster reflects, acknowledging that language is imprecise and unequal to the task of exactly transcribing mental processes. More than this, his attempt to identify and pin Sam down turns out to be fundamentally "incompatible with language" (32). He craves a singular understanding of his father, but is thwarted by words, which are pluralistic, ambiguous, open to different interpretations. The attempt to pull together the fragmentary evidence into a coherent picture results only in further diffusion and vagueness, so that Auster is never quite able to say exactly what he means: "the degree to which it resists language is an exact measure of how closely I have come to saying something important ... when the moment arrives for me to say the one truly important thing (assuming it exists), I will not be able to say it" (32).

If the majority of the "Portrait" chronicles Auster's attempts to trawl through and interpret the evidence—the photos, the objects, the newspaper clippings—the last ten pages or so see a distinct change in emphasis and tone brought about by the author's increased awareness that language simply does not allow a documentary understanding of his father. Having tried to overcome the distance between them through the narrating of anecdotes and the reading of texts, Auster is no closer to Sam, who remains a textual ghost, neither fully dead nor fully alive. Auster's writing becomes, correspondingly, more fragmented, more reflective, and more abstract in an attempt to fashion a new approach to the problem. One aspect of this approach is its scrutiny of the writing processes and of meaning in general, rather than the specific subject matter. For example, Auster muses on "the rampant, totally mystifying force of contradiction. I understand now that each fact is nullified by the next fact, that each thought engenders an equal and opposite thought. Impossible to say anything without reservation. . . . Fragments. Or the anecdote as a form of knowledge. / Yes" (61). Such sentences, with their choppy, broken syntax, mirror the inevitable breakdown in coherence when one attempts to write about another person. And yet, Auster realizes, the alternative to writing is too frightening. He keeps on writing because "I want to postpone the moment of ending. . . . No matter how useless these words might seem to be, they have nevertheless stood between me and a silence that continues to terrify me. When I step into this silence, it will mean that my father has vanished forever" (65). Precisely because language is so ambiguous, it can effectively keep the questions open and keep the father virtually alive.

Integral to the development of Auster's new approach, and to the postponement of the silence, are the quotations from other writers that begin to enter the text in between the personal reflections. By quoting, among others, the Soviet Jewish writer Isaac Babel and the French novelist and essayist Marcel Proust (60), Auster seems to acknowledge that if texts are all that one has in order to think about the past and about identity, then it is necessary to find a new way to use them. Rather than trying to locate certainties in documentary sources, one can call upon more literary, deliberately abstract sources to shed light on one's experiences. Auster has realized that his own sense of self and his own acts of interpretation constantly obscure the "truth" he is looking for: the wisdom of others may offer a clearer vision.

These literary allusions signpost Auster's future aesthetic practice, and it is no coincidence that many of them concern father-son relationships. At the very end Auster's attention is transferred from Sam to Daniel, his own son, and hence from a murky, inaccessible past to a sign of an optimistic future. "Portrait of an Invisible Man" ends with "An image of Daniel now, as he lies upstairs in his crib asleep. To end with this. To wonder what he will make of these pages when he is old enough to read them. And the image of his sweet and ferocious little body, as he lies upstairs in his crib asleep. To end with this" (69). Auster knows of course that even if he would like to, he cannot end with this: in terms of literary practice, this is really another momentous beginning.

"The Book of Memory"

The struggle to decide whether the past can be confined *to* the past is carried over into the second part of the book. It opens with this: "He lays out a piece of blank paper on the table before him and writes these words with his pen. It was. It will never be again" (75). Now writing in the third person, Auster makes it clear that "The Book of Memory" will tackle the question of the past from a more abstract perspective. To what extent does memory keep things alive? Is writing itself a form of memory? And if words survive after people die, can anything truly "never be again"?

One of the most significant features of "Portrait of an Invisible Man" is the increase toward its conclusion in the number of literary and philosophical quotations. Marcel Proust is summoned to remind the reader that "children have always a tendency either to depreciate or exalt their parents," after which Auster concludes that he "must have been a bad son" (60). Auster is also haunted by lines from Maurice Blanchot: "I have said nothing extraordinary or even surprising. What is extraordinary begins at the moment I stop. But I am no longer able to speak of it" (63). Language, biography, objective knowledge—their inadequacies are fully brought home to Auster through his musings on Blanchot. His conclusion appears bleak; he notes "the vanity of trying to say anything about anyone" (63). Yet in the words of the Danish philosopher Søren Kierkegaard there resides at least some justification for the writer's efforts: "he who is willing to work gives birth to his own father" (68).

Such allusiveness is expanded in "The Book of Memory" and becomes its structural and ethical principle. Aliki Varvogli calls the transition from part one to part two "the passage from the personal to the public,"[14] an acceptance that the words of others can provide inspiration, justification for the individual's ideas and emotions, and a sharing of tragedy and solitude, which prevents descent into private despair. Carsten Springer neatly sums up the somewhat paradoxical nature of this situation when he refers to it as the state of being "alone and not alone."[15] A. opens "The Book of Memory" "alone in his little room at 6 Varick

Street" (76–77), virtually penniless and estranged from his wife and son. It is unsurprising, therefore, that many of his literary and philosophical allusions are to artists—Vincent Van Gogh (143), the German poet Friedrich Hölderlin (98–100)—whose experiences were, for a variety of reasons, equally bleak and from whom he can therefore gain sympathetic understanding. Of particular significance is the emotional epiphany that inspires "The Book of Memory" and happens on a visit to Anne Frank's room in Amsterdam. While A. weeps, "as if purely in response to the world," he begins to imagine, and to be inspired by, "a solitude so crushing, so unconsolable, that one stops breathing for hundreds of years." Clearly he is writing, metaphorically, "in the shadow of Anne Frank's room" (83). This will go on to have specific formal consequences for *In the Country of Last Things.*

Memory, trauma, solitude, and creativity come together in the image of the room; this is why Auster puts the word "Room" at the center of his topographical plan in the manuscript of "The Book of Memory."[16] Perhaps the single most resonant quotation in *The Invention of Solitude* comes from Blaise Pascal in his *Pensées* of 1670: "All the unhappiness of man stems from one thing only: that he is incapable of staying quietly in his room" (IOS 76, 83). If there is any narrative trajectory to "The Book of Memory," it describes the mental and literary processes A. undergoes in order to learn to stay quietly and be happy in his room. (It should be noted that several of Auster's later protagonists, notably David Zimmer in *The Book of Illusions*[17] and Sidney Orr in *Oracle Night,* follow the same path.) The question is: why should it be so difficult for a person to do so?

One obvious answer for A. is that the Varick Street room in which he writes "The Book of Memory" is so unremittingly bleak. A former electrician's workshop that reinforces A.'s isolation by having someone else's name on the door, it is "a room meant for machines, cuspidors, and sweat" rather than intellectual endeavor (77). But there is a more profound answer, which is nonetheless connected to this postindustrial bleakness. Quite simply, a room is never just a room for the writer, a point illustrated in the opening remarks: "By staying in this room for long stretches at a time, he can usually manage to fill it with his thoughts, and this in turn seems to dispel the dreariness, or at least make him unaware of it" (77). The suggestion is that the room functions something like the writer's head, as a generator of ideas. To some extent this is comforting and makes the space inhabitable, yet each return promises a renewal of creative agony: "During his absence the room gradually empties of his efforts to inhabit it. When he returns, he has to begin the process all over again, and that takes work, real spiritual work. Considering his physical condition after the climb (chest heaving like a bellows, legs as tight and heavy as tree trunks), this inner struggle takes all that much longer to get started." Thus the room becomes a site of existential as well as physical anguish where A. risks becoming as thoroughly absent as his father was: "In the void between the moment he opens the door and the moment he begins to reconquer the emptiness, his mind flails in a wordless panic. It is as if he were being forced to watch his own disappearance, as if, by crossing the threshold of his room, he were entering another dimension, taking up residence inside a black hole" (77).

A.'s very state of being is therefore symbolized by his room. It is, he acknowledges, tantamount to existence itself: "The world has shrunk to the size of this room for him, and for as long as it takes him to understand it, he must stay where he is. Only one thing is certain: he cannot be anywhere until he is here" (79). And the best way to *be* there is to write about it, it seems. The "wordless panic" A. feels when he reenters his room results from his inability to construct his experience linguistically, to translate his thoughts and memories into words. It is as if life itself fades away without the words to express it even if, as "Portrait of an Invisible Man" demonstrates, one's words alone are seldom equal to such a task. As Auster puts it in an early notebook, "The transformation from experience to word is taken for granted. It is never totally successful."[18]

What one must try to do, as a result, is make thought or experience and the *recording* of thought or experience as close to simultaneous as possible. For "The Book of Memory," this has specific consequences in terms of literary form. Whereas "Portrait" is written predominantly in the past tense, implying a distance between event and word, its successor reads like a diary or a commonplace book, written in the present and giving the impression of immediacy. Frequently entries are little more than hastily transcribed mental notes, with reminders to embellish in the future. For example, the first paragraph on Jonah and the whale ends with "Initial statement of these themes. Further installments to follow" (79). In choosing such an approach, A./Auster attempts to marry the idea and the representation of the idea in the same instant. The reader can add yet another layer of complexity to the central image: the room stands for language itself and, inevitably, for the writer's worry that there will always be an unbridgeable gap between language and experience.

As the title would imply, memory is also strongly linked to language. A. explains that when "a word becomes another word, a thing becomes another thing," then the connecting process "works in the same way that memory does" (136). In fact one presupposes the other, so that "as soon as there is more than one thing, there is memory, and because of memory there is language" (AH 39). In other words, as soon as there are things to remember, language is required to call them up. As "Portrait" shows, however, memory is at best unreliable or intangible, at worst a total fiction. Like language, it is a representation or reconstruction in the present moment, "an artificial structure for ordering the historical past" (116). It is not synonymous with the event being recalled. For this reason it must be treated metaphorically rather than as fact. Much of the text is devoted, as A. recalls haunting events from his own life and the lives of others, to reflections on the numerous metaphorical ways of visualizing memory itself. Unsurprisingly, many of them are spatial and return to the image of the room. Memory is "a place, a building" (82); it is "the space in which a thing happens for the second time" (83). A. sees memory "as a room, as a body, as a skull, as a skull that encloses the room in which a body sits" (88).

Then again, "memory sometimes comes to him as a voice. It is a voice that speaks inside him, and it is not necessarily his own" (123). Although the idea that the voice of one's memory can be someone else's is a counterintuitive one, it serves here to reinforce the notion first that memory is an unreliable representation, but second that memory is best viewed as something collective, a shared space of reflection rather than a locked, private room. In effect Auster picks up on the image of the plural self, so problematic in "Portrait," and turns it into something creative and therefore positive.

So Auster's "Book of Memory" is a compilation of his and other writers' memories rendered in writing. Its effect is aggregative rather than strictly narrative, in the sense that it builds toward understanding by piling quotation upon quotation. In this it closely resembles the work from which its name is derived, the Egyptian-born French writer Edmond Jabès's *The Book of Questions* (1963). Auster describes Jabès's work as "a mosaic of fragments, aphorisms, dialogues, songs, and commentaries that endlessly move around the central question of the book: how to speak what cannot be spoken" (AH 107). He also observes that it demands the reader read it "by fits and starts—just as it was written." In so doing one realizes that "what happens in *The Book of Questions,* then, is the writing of *The Book of Questions* —or rather, the attempt to write it" (AH 111). This is certainly true of Auster's text, too. Another very important similarity lies in Auster's and Jabès's shared Jewish background. The "central question" is for Jabès "the Jewish Holocaust, but it is also the question of literature itself. By a startling leap of the imagination, Jabès treats them as one and the same." To support his assertion, Auster then quotes from Jabès: "I talked to you about the difficulty of being Jewish, which is the same as the difficulty of writing. For Judaism and writing are but the same waiting, the same hope, the same wearing out" (AH 107). Jabès even goes as far as to say that the book "has become my true place . . . practically my only place."[19]

Auster describes Jabès's work as "a poetics of absence." This is a phrase applicable to all of Auster's work, in that it explains the condition of exile, of being in-between, as well as the struggle with language and the use of ghostly literary allusions to dead writers. Auster explains: "If language is to be pushed to the limit, then the writer must condemn himself to an exile of doubt, to a desert of uncertainty. What he must do, in effect, is create a poetics of absence. The dead cannot be brought back to life. But they can be heard, and their voices live in the book" (AH 114).

This "poetics of absence," which for Auster is a characteristically Jewish mode of expression, underpins the choice of quotations in "The Book of Memory." It means that this part is, more than the "Portrait," a cultural meditation on broader themes pertaining to "the Jewish people as a whole"[20] as well as an exploration of family relationships. As Derek Rubin explains, "the importance of Scripture—of specific texts from the Old Testament," along with "the concept of the Book itself, and . . . the act of commentary or interpretation," is "central to Jewish life, religion, and culture."[21] Auster's achievement is to link these textual concerns, like Jabès, with his personal experiences, which in "The Book of Memory" include his first visit to Paris in 1965 to visit the composer S. in his tiny room (89–93); the death of his maternal grandfather (102–6, 113–14, 117–18, 119–21); his son Daniel's pneumonia and the negative effect it has on his marriage (106–8); and his thoughts on the way Daniel plays (164–65). He links the textual and the personal in order not just to work out a theory of prose practice but also to reconcile himself to the past and make contact with the world again by fully engaging himself in the book. One of the ironies of this process is best exemplified by the Russian poet Marina Tsvetayeva's famous quotation: "In this most Christian of worlds / All poets are Jews" (95). Jews and writers are in exile, both inside and outside, here and there, everywhere and nowhere. Only by fully committing himself to this exile and immersing himself in his and others' expressions of solitude can Auster be in the world.

One of the most important reference points in "The Book of Memory" is the Book of Jonah and its "parallel text," *Pinocchio* (79). His commentaries on these texts provide a good example of how Auster develops an idea by mapping textual interpretation onto personal history, and vice versa. First, it is clear that the belly of the whale stands as another version of the writer's locked room. In the Bible, God's (the father's) displeasure at Jonah's refusal to proclaim judgment against Nineveh leads to Jonah's incarceration. One could argue that A.'s spell of confinement in his room is also brought about by the ongoing biographical and philosophical debate with his father, whose absence casts doubt on the very possibility of meaning and authority. *Pinocchio,* however, inverts the situation and gives the son power and authority: "Gepetto in the belly of the shark (whale in the Disney version), and the story of how Pinocchio rescues him. Is it true that one must dive to the depths of the sea and save one's father to become a real boy?" (79). In effect, roles are reversed, and the son becomes the father in the act of rescue. Likewise Auster as a "real" prose writer only emerges through the symbolic, if unsuccessful, act of rescuing his father in the "Portrait."

It is significant that A. reads *Pinocchio* to his son and decides that "it is the image of Pinocchio saving Gepetto (swimming away with the old man on his back) that gives the story meaning for him" (133). Enchanted by the dream of becoming an adult, the young boy responds to the idea of rescuing his father just as the father frequently "saves his little boy from harm" (134). Yet the implication is also that Daniel has already saved him, first by urging him to read the story and start the necessary chain of literary and religious associations in his head (133), and second by pointing ahead to the future rather than constantly back at the past and his loss.

Throughout "The Book of Memory" Auster returns to Jonah. His importance lies in the way he both parallels Auster's experience and provides a model for understanding and moving on from this experience. Jonah's story has obvious formal qualities in common with Auster's text: "This brief work, the only one to be written in the third person, is more dramatically a story of solitude than anything else in the Bible, and yet it is told as if from outside that solitude, as if, by plunging into the darkness of that solitude, the 'I' has vanished from itself" (124). This is exactly what Auster is attempting—a view on to his own solitude. Moreover there is a recognition that the closeness of death is inspirational for Jonah in the same way it is for Auster. "And when the fish then vomits Jonah onto dry land," Auster comments, "Jonah is given back to life, as if the death he had found in the belly of the fish were a preparation for new life, a life that has passed through death, and therefore a life that can at last speak" (125). Seen in this way, Jonah experiences a kind of resurrection. Having come so close to the end, he is able to find his voice and begin again. Once again it is possible to understand Auster's experience as he moves from part one to part two of *Solitude* in the same way. "The Book of Memory" is a resurrection in the form of a blossoming literary awareness, a newfound creativity and understanding, but Auster has had to plunge into darkness for it to come about, "for it is only in the darkness of solitude that the work of memory begins" (164). One sees the possibility of resurrection repeated throughout Auster's novels, particularly *The Book of Illusions*.

It is possible to extrapolate from Jonah's moment of resurrection to include the Jewish people as a whole. From Jonah's terrible suffering and apparent injustice comes understanding of God's purpose, as well as a prophetic voice. Likewise, one could argue, the unfathomable darkness of the Holocaust inspires beauty in the form of work by artists such as Edmond Jabès and Paul Auster. But Auster does not read Jonah unequivocally as a story of suffering or persecution. Instead he reads it as a story of fledgling democracy. Jonah's anger at God's sparing of the Ninevites prompts this response: "And should I not spare Nineveh, that great city, wherein are more than sixscore thousand persons that cannot distinguish between their right hand and their left hand; and also much cattle?" The implications of this statement Auster finds "startling and original," that "these sinners, these heathen—and even the beasts that belong to them—are as much God's creatures as the Hebrews.... If there is to be any justice at all, it must be a justice for everyone" (159). It is but a short step to "liberty and justice for all." Auster has made clear elsewhere that he reads Jonah as the basis of democracy,[22] and it is characteristic of "The Book of Memory" that Jewish theology influences and is deliberately merged with American culture and politics as part of the writer's process of finding his place in the world. More lightheartedly, for example, A. remembers confusing "the last words of the Passover Seder, 'Next year in Jerusalem,'" with the "refrain" of disappointed baseball fans, "Wait till next year." Thus, Auster reflects, "baseball had somehow become entangled in his mind with the religious experience" (117). Elsewhere in Auster's novels, especially in the wilderness trials of Marco Stanley Fogg and Walter Rawley, one sees a meeting between Jewish exile and American mythologies of the frontier and the Wild West.

The analysis of Jonah progresses from a series of speculations on father-son relationships, through a portrait of the suffering individual, to a much broader understanding of equality and democracy. Through extended close reading of the story, Auster is able to reach the following startling though potentially liberating conclusion: "Everything, as has been noted before, is connected to everything else. And if there is everything, then it follows there is everyone" (159). To read a particular text is to become involved in an endless network of connections and associations with other texts and ideas: this is how "The Book of Memory" is structured. It is also, crucially, how language is structured. Language is not "a list of separate things to be added up and whose sum total is equal to the world"; it is "an infinitely complex organism, all of whose elements—cells and sinews, corpuscles and bones, digits and fluids—are present in the world simultaneously, none of which can exist on its own." Because of the "network of rhymes, assonances and overlapping meanings" at the heart of language, each word comes to be "defined by other words, which means that to enter any part of language is to enter the whole of it" (160).

Language is central to our experience as humans. It is "the way we exist in the world" because it reveals the workings of the mind. Auster's boldest and most invigorating move in "The Book of Memory" is his suggestion that our collective experience as humans is also based on rhymes, assonance (similarity of sounds), and a complete "grammar of existence." The world "is not just the sum of the things that are in it. It is the infinitely complex network of connections among them." Instances of coincidence reveal these connections most clearly: "A young man rents a room in Paris and then discovers that his father hid out in the same room during the war. If these two events were to be considered separately, there would be little to say about either of them. The rhyme they create when looked at together alters the reality of each." At such "rare moments . . . the mind can leap out of itself and serve as a bridge for things across time and space, across seeing and memory" (161). This is why so many anecdotal commentaries "on the nature of chance" are included in "The Book of Memory" (80, 88, 94, 134, 143). They remind Auster and the reader that moments of coincidence mean we are all connected to everyone else. This, then, is the way out of isolation into productive solitude; this is why "The Book of Memory" takes the form of a set of autobiographical and textual coincidences and connections. "Wherever his eye or mind seems to stop," writes Auster, "he discovers another connection, another bridge to carry him to yet another place, and even in the solitude of his room, the world has been rushing in on him at a dizzying speed, as if it were all suddenly converging in him and happening to him at once" (162). Coincidence, this convergence of like ideas, allows the individual to be happy in his room. He is in solitude, but if he speaks about or writes about that solitude, he becomes "more than just himself" (139) because he enters into other people's discussions of solitude and thereby learns more about it.

However, Auster is keen to emphasize that coincidences have no meaning *in themselves*. They may be uncanny and haunting (to use a Freudian idea discussed elsewhere [148]), but they do not suggest an underlying system or pattern in the world. They merely demonstrate that individuals do not live in a vacuum any more than events happen in isolation. It is tempting, though, for the individual to search for a pattern: "Like everyone else, he craves a meaning. Like everyone else, his life is so fragmented that each time he sees a connection between two fragments he is tempted to look for a meaning in that connection. The connection exists. But to give it a meaning, to look beyond the bare fact of its existence, would be to build an imaginary world inside the real world, and he knows it would not stand" (147). One could call the building of this imaginary world in the individual's head "paranoia," a belief in patterns and conspiracies that somehow center on the individual. Several Auster characters (notably Jack Pozzi in *The Music of Chance* and Benjamin Sachs in *Leviathan*) display the symptoms of paranoia. In "The Book of Memory" Auster highlights the temptation to seek significance in every tiny event,[23] but ultimately insists that "life has no meaning" and that one must embrace "meaninglessness as the first principle"

(147). It is enough to know that coincidences happen, that cha affects our lives. If one accepts this, then one moves closer to others and understands, paradoxically, that the world cannot be understood, only appreciated in all its strangeness.

To some critics, this conclusion feels like a cop-out. Carsten Springer, for example, appreciates that in "The Book of Memory" Auster participates in a Jewish tradition of storytelling as a means of passing on memories and hence of survival. However, Springer says that the Jewish tradition is obscured in "associative free play." Auster loses control of his material, in Springer's opinion, and in a story that "begins with death" (149), the reprise at the very end of the opening words—"It was. It will never be again" (172)—illustrates that Auster has failed fully to integrate with his tradition, to find his identity, or to move beyond his loss.[24] This seems harsh. In this most paradoxical of texts, Auster shows that his success lies in his failure. He understands now that he can never understand, but, crucially, his allusions to the writing of others have shown him that none of us will ever understand. We fail to understand *together*. The addition of one word to the final line—"Remember" (172)—actually makes the ending and beginning very different. It is an ethical injunction that encapsulates all "The Book of Memory" stands for. Writing is a way of entering the network of human relations. Writing is a means of remembering, listening, and passing on, of saving and preserving, and hence of looking to the future with hope.

CHAPTER THREE

The New York Trilogy

A recurring motif in Paul Auster's work is the missing person. All his novels rehearse, in Charles Baxter's words, "the drama of lost-and-found personalities."[1] Apart from the more conventional narrative threads involving missing persons—Anna Blume's search for her brother in *In the Country of Last Things* is one example—Auster fills his pages with figures missing in more complex emotional or existential ways. For instance, Sam Auster's refusal of sympathy with his friends and family betrays his profound detachment from *himself*. It is this trait that renders him, in effect, unrecoverable. He becomes emblematic of life's essential meaninglessness, of the lack at the heart of all human relations. That the son persists in searching for meaning in the father's life attests to the human craving for certainties and solutions in the face of all-encompassing mystery.

Antidetective Fiction

The first part of *The Invention of Solitude* is, therefore, a kind of biographical detective story, and it was not surprising that the next major work, *The New York Trilogy*, played more self-consciously with detective narratives. After all, the pseudonymous writing of *Squeeze Play* (1982) indicated that Auster had some respect for hard-boiled detective writers such as Dashiel Hammett and Raymond Chandler. In *Hand to Mouth* he comments: "The best ones were humble, no-nonsense writers who not only had more to say about American life than most so-called serious writers, but often seemed to write smarter, crisper sentences as well" (124). Such a view is evident in the trilogy: Daniel Quinn, the protagonist of *City of Glass*, sees in the genre a "plenitude and economy" lacking in the wasteful chaos of life. In the good mystery "there is nothing wasted," and the world of the book constitutes a reassuring internal closure, with all questions answered and nothing extraneous allowed (CG 8).

Squeeze Play, despite unexpectedly hinging on a suicide disguised as a murder, largely adheres to this satisfying pattern. The case is cracked, the femme fatale is banished, and the detective is consigned once again to his solitary, cynical existence. *The New York Trilogy*, however, allows no such satisfactions. Before the omnibus came out in 1987, its three parts were published separately by Sun and Moon Press as *City of Glass* (1985), *Ghosts* (1986), and *The Locked Room* (1986). What provides the trilogy with its sense of unity is not only its strong geographical sense, implied by the title, but also the way each part raises certain expectations of detective fiction, only to thwart these expectations in the unfolding story.

In *City of Glass* a man named Daniel Quinn impersonates a detective named Paul Auster, and is hired by a Peter Stillman Jr. to follow Stillman's father because he fears the father is insane and may come after him. One expects the father, therefore, to be the "villain" and for a specific crime to be committed. None of this transpires. Instead the "case" simply fades into insignificance, if it ever existed, and it becomes apparent that the main source of interest is Quinn's increasingly obsessive behavior, his almost pathological need to establish meaning in events, to work out in fact what the case *is* and what role he plays in it. Thus, where the focus of the traditional detective novel might be said to be knowledge, meaning, or comprehension, the emphasis here is on the existential questions of identity and one's relation to the world.

Similarly the plot of *Ghosts* is decidedly insubstantial in conventional investigative terms. A detective named Blue is hired to watch a man called Black from a room in Brooklyn. He has no idea why, and as the days turn into weeks and nothing much happens, the emphasis shifts to Blue's psychology, his increasingly introspective musings, and the working out of his relationship with his quarry. Whereas traditional detective fiction tends to work toward endings that answer questions, the endings of both these tales are open and inconclusive. They leave numerous questions unanswered and resist the conventional need to find a scapegoat for a criminal act, and to administer judgment or punishment. *Ghosts,* in particular, explicitly disallows the reader the comforts of knowledge: its last words are: "And from this moment on, we know nothing" (192).

The "we" in this sentence implies a self-conscious relationship between writer and reader. Such a deliberate constructedness in the writing is one characteristic of what has become known as "antidetective" (sometimes "metaphysical" or "postmodern" detective) fiction. This term is useful for understanding what Auster is attempting in the trilogy. Critics such as Dennis Porter and Stefano Tani have identified sets of tendencies in postwar literature that, taken as a whole and despite their destabilization of traditional genres, can be seen to comprise a recognizable genre of their own. To declare "we know nothing" is not simply to mock the reader, but to draw attention to the fact that these antidetective texts are predominantly about the *process* of reading, rather than a single explanation, and that multiple interpretations are always possible. A text like *Ghosts* reminds us much more deliberately than, say, a Mickey Spillane thriller of the 1950s that the reader is engaged in, and is bound to fail at, the same activities as the detective: looking for clues and seeking answers.

Another characteristic of the antidetective story is its refusal to see order restored. If traditional detective stories, particularly so-called country house tales written by Agatha Christie and Dorothy L. Sayers, work to reinstate what is morally permissible, insist on social cohesion, and reaffirm the familiar, antidetective fiction does the opposite. As Dennis Porter puts it: "much of the serious fiction of our time has been committed to the task of defamiliarization, often by means of a more or less explicit parody of the detective genre."[2] The alien becomes part of the normal, and, by extension, reality itself becomes unfathomable. Once again twentieth-century history and culture provide diagnoses for these literary symptoms. Faced with incomprehensible brutalities like war, the Holocaust, and the atomic bomb, how can a writer produce in good faith a text that promotes neat, rational explanations? Moreover in a cold war political climate, and in a post-9/11 environment of suspicion and surveillance, how can anyone trust those in positions of authority who lay claim to logic or reason? Too many actions remain unexplained and too many secrets hidden for political, religious, economic, or military reasons. Antidetective literature also undermines the notion of authority, then, rejecting the idea that any individual or institution (including the writer, the detective, and the reader) can hold the monopoly on truth.

Another reason the truth becomes more elusive is the proliferation of representations brought about by mass media and advertising. Put simply, we now live in a world saturated with signs and media messages. In such a world, where any single event can be subject to, potentially, an infinite number of variant retellings in different media, it becomes increasingly difficult to state with any certainty what reality or the truth is. Much anti-detective fiction proceeds from this unsettling proposition: an influential example is Thomas Pynchon's 1967 novel, *The Crying of Lot 49*. Similarly, as the title of *City of Glass* suggests, the urban space itself promises transparency, yet ends up endlessly reflecting and refracting messages and signs like a hall of mirrors. In fact, in Auster's original notes for "New York Spleen," the story that eventually became *City of Glass,* the final item in the plot summary notes that Daniel Quinn (here known as D.Q.) "begins all over again. Investigates the case—in old newspapers." Having failed to crack the case in "reality," his only recourse is to texts. To reinforce the point further, much of "New York Spleen" is devoted to the reports of various "commentators," all of whom offer contradictory versions of what happened to the mysterious D.Q.[3]

Given these frustrations, and the resultant questioning of identities, it is no surprise that the detective finds it impossible to remain aloof like Sherlock Holmes. Or to cite another example: "The detective of the anti-detective story no longer has the detachment of a M. Dupin [Edgar Allan Poe's detective in 'The Murders in the Rue Morgue']. Unwillingly, he gets emotionally caught in the net of his detecting effort and is torn apart between the upsurge of feelings and the necessity for rationality."[4]

This is especially true of *The Locked Room,* the final part of *The New York Trilogy.* Here the unnamed narrator searches obsessively for clues to the whereabouts of his childhood friend Fanshawe. In effect, he is searching nostalgically for that same childhood relationship—"the Fanshawe I had known" (277)—so that the detective-style quest has more to do with the narrator's emotional frailties than a desire to establish truth.

Contemporary reviews of the trilogy tended to agree on its antidetective qualities. Marcel Berlins, writing in the *Sunday Times,* acknowledges the debts to the "traditional private eye" such as Raymond Chandler's Philip Marlowe, but decides that "it's more Kafka than Chandler, full of unnamed characters, never explained events, disturbing coincidences, and intangible fears." Rather than a concrete "case," Berlin wryly observes that "we are dealing with our old friend the search for inner self and identity."[5] Dennis Drabelle, reviewing the first two parts, again evokes Franz Kafka and also compares Auster's "post-existential private eye" narratives to the work of Vladimir Nabokov. In a familiar refrain, Drabelle argues that Auster's preoccupations are more European than American. "The syndrome of being obsessed with and paralysed by an idea you've talked yourself into," he says, "seems a particularly European one, not viable on a continent where you can easily pick up and desert your past." Yet, he concludes, Auster "has provided a striking version of contemporary American stasis."[6] Toby Olson in the *New York Times* notes that *City of Glass* reveals a nightmarish new world "in which fact and fiction become increasingly difficult to separate."[7]

Such responses are typical and have been expanded upon in an impressive number of scholarly articles and books. Indeed such has been the critical and popular success of *The New York Trilogy* that subsequent works have tended to be overshadowed by it. As recently as 2008 Brendan Martin declared: "It is my intention to examine Auster's main body of writing and the ways in which this has been influenced, and determined by the subject matter of Auster's first, and best known postmodern novel. The similarities between *The New York Trilogy* and Auster's other writings, ensure that Auster remains a self-consciously and self-deprecating [sic] postmodern author."⁸ Aside from the fact that one should cite (as the author does) *The Invention of Solitude* as the wellspring of Auster's concerns, Martin's comments risk mistaking consistency with homogeneity. Though certain themes and ideas do of course recur, there are always significant shifts in emphasis from text to text. Martin also makes too much of chronology: just because the trilogy was published earlier than, say, *In the Country of Last Things* or *Moon Palace* does not mean that it represents the definitive inception of certain ideas. (Indeed parts of *Last Things* were published as early as 1969 in the *Columbia Review Magazine* as "Letters from the City.") It is best to view Auster's work not in linear terms, as Martin implies, but as an amorphous set of ideas that constellate in new forms at appropriate moments in time. Finally, Martin is somewhat too eager to treat the trilogy itself as homogenous. There is unity of place and narration, but each part has a different focus and tone and requires subtle shifts in loyalty on the part of the reader.

City of Glass

"It was a wrong number that started it" (3): these are possibly the most famous words Auster has ever written. Like the opening lines of *The Invention of Solitude,* they remind the reader that chance is the presiding power in life and fiction. And once again they are based on real-life experience. As Auster explains in *The Red Notebook,* a collection of true stories all sharing the theme of coincidence, he was called twice in the spring of 1980 by a man asking for the Pinkerton Detective Agency. After putting the caller straight, Auster begins to wonder, "What if I had actually taken on the case?" These speculations are the genesis of *City of Glass,* a story about "detectives who [are] not detectives, about impersonation, about mysteries that cannot be solved." Auster's decision to name his detective "Paul Auster," the subject of much critical conjecture, stems first from a desire "to remain faithful to my original impulse," to include himself in some way simply because it happened to him.[9]

Unlike Auster, Daniel Quinn gets a third opportunity, and this time does pretend to be the detective. Even though "much later, when he was able to think about the things that happened to him, he would conclude that nothing was real except chance" (3), it would be misleading to attribute his actions entirely to random impulse at this stage. Enough biographical information is provided to suggest a different motivation. "We know that he had once been married, had once been a father, and that both his wife and son were now dead," the narrator explains (3). As a result of this tragedy, he has withdrawn into himself, to the extent that "he no longer exists for anyone but himself" and "no longer [has] any friends" (4, 5). He is, like Sam Auster, effectively "living a posthumous life" (5): even his frequent random walks around New York City aim to inspire the feeling of "leaving himself behind." Rather than an opportunity to immerse himself in the flow of metropolitan life, these outings merely let him "feel that he [is] nowhere" (4). Indeed Manhattan functions here as "an incomprehensible labyrinth where individual spaces are indistinguishable, which provides little in the way of coordinates for the individual to navigate by."[10] For someone who does not want to be seen, it is the perfect setting.

Given Quinn's almost total isolation, then, it is likely that his decision to become "Paul Auster" the private detective, at least for the duration of the phone call, is prompted by a reawakening of his desire for human contact. Now, five years after the death of his family, he "no longer wish[es] to be dead" (5): the case offers the hope that he can be a somebody, somewhere, rather than a nobody, nowhere.

But who is he? Names are never randomly assigned in Auster's work, and they carry great significance. Quinn has at least four, and they all suggest distinct personalities. His real name, "Daniel Quinn," represents his reclusive self and is "no longer that part of him that could write books" (4). This he leaves to "William Wilson," who, appropriately enough, takes his name from an 1839 Edgar Allan Poe story about a doppelganger, and Quinn adopts this moniker for his detective fiction. Never having emerged "from behind the mask of his pseudonym," he has come to regard "Quinn" and "Wilson" as completely separate people (5). Then there is "Max Work." Max is Quinn's fictional detective and, as his name implies, a man of action who continues "to live in the world of others" and is everything Quinn is not—"aggressive, quick-tongued, at home in whatever spot he happens to find himself." Quinn admires Work for his ability to get out there and do things, to the extent that Quinn pretends to be him while writing (9). Finally, of course, there is "Paul Auster," whom Quinn becomes in a bid to be more like Max Work. As *The Invention of Solitude* suggests, every writer becomes someone else when he or she writes, but Quinn takes this idea to unnerving extremes. His multiple roles have nothing to do with the ethical demand that writing try to connect empathetically with others; they are simply a way to avoid being found, to disappear from the world.

When he accepts the case, Quinn suddenly confronts the possibility of encountering real "death and murder," as the mysterious caller phrases it (11). Up to now, despite being a writer of crime novels, he has "never met a private detective" and "never spoken to a criminal." His sources are "books, films, and newspapers" rather than life experience or empirical research. Moreover "what interested him about the stories he wrote was not their relation to the world but their relation to other stories" (7). Quinn's various names can be seen as textual identities, and it is clear from this last quotation that he chooses to remain in a world of texts rather than venturing into the world outside his room. As "The Book of Memory" demonstrates, stories and texts *are* vital for Auster, but only as long as they promote a keener understanding of the world in all its unpredictability and strangeness. For all their "plenitude and economy" (8), detective mysteries do not reflect the world. Because "everything becomes essence" and there is "no word that is not significant" (8), such tales fail to adhere to "meaninglessness as the first principle." Meaning, order, and rationality take precedence over chance. Therefore Quinn finds solace in them because they pretend to explain random events such as the death of his family. The detective—the private "eye" or "I"—is for Quinn "the man who looks out from himself into the world and demands that the world reveal itself to him" (8). If *The Invention of Solitude* proves anything, it is that the world will never reveal or explain itself. The detective, then, is a fantasy figure, another means of escape from the world. Quite simply, Quinn has been reading and writing the wrong books.

Virginia Stillman arrives straight from the pages of a Raymond Chandler novel: "hips a touch wide, or else voluptuous, depending on your point of view; dark hair, dark eyes, and a look in those eyes that was at once self-contained and vaguely seductive. She wore a black dress and very red lipstick" (13). Quinn cannot help but imagine "what she looked like without any clothes on" (14). She is the femme fatale in his noir detective fantasy, yet her name gestures toward the more complex historical and linguistic issues of the narrative. "Virginia" connects her with early America as an unsullied Eden (softening her dangerous, sexualized image), and "Stillman" connotes the arrested development of her husband, Peter Stillman Jr.

Peter's arrival immediately confirms that the reader should expect a radical departure from tradition. His clumsy movements lead Quinn to compare him to "a marionette trying to walk without strings" (15), which is appropriate given his role as "puppet boy" in his father's experiments (22). And his "almost transparent" paleness (15) identifies him as one of Auster's recurring character types—the living ghost, cut off from normal human interaction and exiled to a dimension somewhere between life and death, reality and the imagination. His fragmented, aphasic speech,[11] punctuated by nonsense words such as "wimble click crumblechaw beloo" (17), is the legacy of the horrific story he has to tell. After the mother's death, his father locked him in a room for nine years because he "wanted to know if God had a language" that the boy, unexposed to human speech, would learn to speak (20). Peter Stillman Sr. was judged insane and sent away for thirteen years but is about to be released and, Peter Stillman Jr. insists, will return to kill his son (18). It is Quinn's task, as Virginia later informs him, to watch the father and "find out what he's up to" (29). Quinn takes a check "made out to Paul Auster" and is "reassured" by the fact that he will never be able to cash it. Not only can he not be "held accountable for impersonating a private detective without a license," but the lack of financial motivation keeps the whole job, at this stage, theoretical, experimental, and somehow unreal (31).

It is unsurprising, then, that his initial investigations and observations take place only in books. The first third of *City of*

Glass is largely taken up with a series of stories-within-the-story, culminating in Quinn's reading of Stillman Sr.'s thesis in chapter 6. These stories emphasize the importance of language to Quinn's investigation, but also the fact that life is comprised of an endless number of competing texts and interpretations, suggesting that his efforts to find the truth are unlikely to succeed. First, Quinn recalls other historical cases in which "cranks and ideologues" experimented on children in order to discover "man's true 'natural language'" (33). Examples he cites include the Holy Roman Emperor Frederick II (33) and the famous case of Kasper Hauser, "who appeared one afternoon in Nuremberg in 1828, dressed in an outlandish costume and barely able to utter an intelligible sound" (34). These recollections do not reveal anything new about Stillman Sr.'s motivations, however. Instead they betray Quinn's emotional investment in the case: "He knew he could not bring his own son back to life, but at least he could prevent another from dying.... He thought of the little coffin that held his son's body and how he had seen it on the day of the funeral being lowered into the ground. That was isolation, he said to himself. That was silence. It did not help, perhaps, that his son's name had also been Peter" (35). Evidently Quinn will not be able to achieve the detachment required of the traditional detective. He sees the case as a personal drama of guilt and salvation.

This perception is why the first entries in his notebook are a curious mixture of straightforward observations on the case and metaphorical speculations on identity and existence that could have come straight from "The Book of Memory." Starting with an analysis of Stillman Sr.'s photograph, Quinn abruptly shifts to a much darker mode: "Little Peter. Is it necessary for me to imagine it, or can I accept it on faith? The darkness. To think of myself in that room, screaming" (39–40). These are important questions for the (anti-) detective. Should he empathize or remain detached? Despite making reference to Dupin, Poe's most detached of detectives, Quinn ends up echoing Little Peter's own words: "Who are you? And if you think you know, why do you keep lying about it? I have no answer. All I can say is this: listen to me. My name is Paul Auster. That is not my real name" (40). These scribblings hint at what lies ahead: fragmentary identities, the breakdown of rationality, and a crisis of confidence in the ability to understand the world. As William Wilson, Quinn can write neat detective stories in which everything is wrapped up and nothing wasted. Now detection is no longer a story but "something happening in the world" (40), but his writing risks becoming abstract and introspective. Certainties are being destroyed.

The next key text is Stillman's book, *The Garden and the Tower: Early Visions of the New World* (41). In it he outlines the various strands of "utopian thought" associated with the discovery of America and the opposing conceptions of Native Americans as either innocents or savages (42). Of particular relevance to *City of Glass* are the sections on the "fall of man." Stillman argues that "the story of the Garden . . . records not only the fall of man, but the fall of language." This happens because Adam's "prelapsarian use" of words "was free of moral connotations" (he simply named what he saw and thus revealed the "essences" of things) whereas after the fall words such as "serpentine" acquired moral connotations. So names "became detached from things; words devolved into a collection of arbitrary signs." The Tower of Babel story from Genesis 11 Stillman regards as "an exact recapitulation of what happened in the Garden—only expanded, made general in its significance for all mankind" (43).

When the people are scattered and made to speak, as God's punishment for their pride, a variety of tongues, words are further separated from things by the need for translation. The final part of Stillman's thesis outlines the work of Henry Dark, supposedly John Milton's private secretary but really Stillman's invention, who foresaw the construction of a new Babel in the New World. America would be the place where humankind learned to speak "God's language" again (49). The new tower would be "a symbol of the resurrection of the human spirit. What had fallen would be raised up; what had been broken would be made whole" (48). Paradise would return when humanity was united by one common tongue, and words and things were once again tied together. Dark predicted that work would begin in 1960, the year Stillman locked up his son (49).

It is clear that *City of Glass* takes the concern with language and meaning from *The Invention of Solitude* and connects it more explicitly with the mythological ideas underpinning American identity—paradise, new beginnings, individual transcendence. As Aliki Varvogli explains, debates about the possibility of reclaiming a purer language, and thus a purer spiritual connection with the world, were prominent during the nineteenth-century American Renaissance in the work of writers such as Ralph Waldo Emerson.[12] The question that *City of Glass* poses is: attractive though these ideas are, do they make any sense in the contemporary world, or are they simply insane? New York City is the perfect place to look for an answer, first because it is a place where many languages are spoken. Auster's essay on the writer Louis Wolfson is called "New York Babel" (AH 26–34), and *Squeeze Play* stars a detective who has nine reproductions of Brueghel's *The Tower of Babel* on his walls because it reminds him of New York.[13] Diverse and cacophonous, New York on the one hand stands for an American ideal of unity-in-diversity, and on the other hand for the possibility of fragmentation and mutual incomprehensibility. As Stillman later tells Quinn, "I have come to New York because it is the most forlorn of places, the most abject. The brokenness is everywhere, the disarray is universal" (77). For Auster, as for Quinn, New York is both inspiring and terrifying in terms of its physical size and its embodiment of the author's main linguistic concerns.

Having digested Stillman's book, Quinn heads to Grand Central Station to meet the man himself. In the dazzlingly diverse crowd of people, "each one different from all the others, each one irreducibly himself" (54), he spies someone "broken down and disconnected from his surroundings" (56). Like Quinn, this individual appears to have given up on human interaction, and so, understandably, Quinn thinks he has got his man. But in the narrative's most uncanny moment, an identical Stillman appears, only this time expensively dressed and with the look of "a man of the world." Quinn realizes that the whole case now rests on "a submission to chance. Uncertainty [will] haunt him to the end" (56). This is a crucial moment because it demonstrates perfectly how the world will not bend to the will of the detective. Some things are simply inexplicable. It is telling, however, that Quinn, himself so isolated, chooses to follow the disconnected Stillman rather than the "man of the world." Whether or not he has got the "right" man, and subsequent events suggest he has, he will never know for sure, and his choice is not necessarily a rational one, more a result of his own situation and state of mind.

The case never amounts to anything. Quinn follows Stillman every day, "dutifully" recording his quarry's movements in his notebook (58). Stillman collects apparently random objects, "clumps of flotsam" and rubbish from the streets (59), and makes no attempt to contact his son. Finding it difficult to prevent his mind from wandering, Stillman tries to immerse himself fully in the persona of "Paul Auster," and then decides "to record every detail about Stillman he possibly could" (62). Precisely because there appears to be no meaning, Quinn begins to gather empirical evidence more obsessively, in the vain hope of finding meaning. Still "there seems to be no substance to the case" (64), and our detective grows "deeply disillusioned" (65). "He had always imagined that the key to good detective work was a close observation of details," we are told: "The implication was that human behavior could be understood" (65). However, the more closely he follows Stillman, the more he feels "the man's impenetrability" (66).

What he does next smacks of desperation. Tracing Stillman's daily wanderings in his notebook, he finds that he is drawing what appear to be a series of letters, and that the letters seem to spell "Tower of Babel" (70). As the narrator points out, Quinn is "looking for a sign" because he continues "to disbelieve the arbitrariness of Stillman's actions" (68). Refusing to accept "meaninglessness as the first principle," Quinn is becoming increasingly paranoid and "allowing himself to deny the facts" of the case (68)—which are that there is no case. Although momentarily he suspects that the whole thing may be "a hoax he has perpetrated on himself," he goes to sleep still believing that Stillman is sending him a "message" (71).

This scene exemplifies a link between physical space, textual space, and mental space, which proves fruitful throughout Auster's work, particularly *In the Country of Last Things*. One way to understand Stillman's movements and Quinn's reading of them is as a pun on the word "plot." As the old man plots a course through Manhattan, so Quinn plots his movements into the notebook and, most significantly, searches for a plot, in the sense of a story or conspiracy. All these meanings of "plot" merge together in the squiggly hieroglyphs that may or may not spell "Tower of Babel." As Auster says in *Invention of Solitude*: "what we are really doing when we walk through a city is thinking, and thinking in such a way that our thoughts compose a journey" (122). So to walk through space is to think a sequence of thoughts that create a mental journey or story. Whether or not there is any intrinsic meaning to Stillman's walks, it is inevitable that Quinn will *read* them and interpret them textually because, in effect, these walks are a form of writing. Another connotation of plotting, then, is the work readers do: we plot a course through the textual space just as Quinn does. The implication—and it is a common one in antidetective fiction—is that reading can itself be a paranoid process, a constant search for meaningful patterns and answers where in fact there may be none. As the place where this search happens, the page functions like the city.

Breaching the terms of his contract with Virginia, Quinn contrives a series of face-to-face meetings with Stillman. Again they achieve little. The old man confirms at the first meeting that his grand aim is the reunion of things and words. Yet the pathetic nature of his task—the coining of new names for broken objects (76)—also confirms his insanity, his complete estrangement from reality. At the second meeting yet another web of literary allusions is opened up when Stillman discusses *Alice through the Looking Glass* and proclaims that Humpty Dumpty is "the purest embodiment of the human condition" by virtue of his unfulfilled potential and his recognition of the need for humankind to become "masters of the words we speak" (80). Quinn pretends to be Stillman Jr. at the third meeting, and without shock, fear, or even suspicion, the father wishes him well, says he is proud of him, tells him not to lie (84), and stresses the importance of filial inheritance (85). It is a sad, yet in itself curiously unemotional, parody of a father-son reunion. Like words and objects, some things are not meant to be put back together, and yet Stillman Sr. treats it as conclusive. He says to Quinn, "I'll be able to die happily now, Peter," and promptly disappears from Quinn's life (85).

Bereft of ideas, Quinn visits the "real" Paul Auster, who turns out of course not to be a detective after all, but a writer. Their conversation represents, from several perspectives, a pivotal moment in Quinn's life and in Auster's work. The writer claims that *City of Glass* is a "love letter" to his wife, Siri, and Quinn a model of "what would have happened to me if I hadn't met her" (AH 306). Certainly the domestic contentment of Auster's life offers Quinn a glimpse of what he might have had and serves as a painful reminder of what he has lost. Yet if the Auster he meets appears quite smug, this in itself proves to be a joke at the author's expense when they arrive at the main topic of conversation—Miguel de Cervantes's 1605 novel *Don Quixote*. Cervantes's protagonist is addicted to chivalric romances to such an extent that he believes he is living one, and Auster's assertion that the novel is "an attack on the dangers of the make-believe" (97) and an experiment "to test the gullibility" of readers (98) is a veiled warning to Quinn about his detective fantasies. It is also a warning to the reader, however, and a reminder to Auster himself about the complexities of his prose practice, particularly the question of authorship. Just as Cervantes "goes to great lengths to convince the reader that he is not the author" (96), so Auster's presence as a character is a trick designed to undermine his authority. The extended discussion about the authorship of *Don*

Quixote (who shares his initials with Daniel Quinn) shows that authorship, in a world full of competing narratives, is a delicate and problematic thing. With all its literary allusions, one could argue that *City of Glass,* like "The Book of Memory," is a collective work authored by Auster, Poe, Cervantes, Carroll, and any number of other antecedents. The work is like a mosaic; it is not the uniform creation of the God-like author figure. In fact the *Don Quixote* discussion hints at what turns out to be the biggest mystery in *City of Glass:* Who actually narrates it? Is he or she the real villain, setting traps for readers and characters alike?

In Auster's antidetective tales, protagonists need to be "cured of investigative impulses."[14] That is, they need to extricate themselves from their obsessive search for an overarching explanation. One way of doing this, as the *Don Quixote* scene illustrates, is to listen to other voices, to accept that one is not the author of everything that happens but that each person is, as it were, authored by everyone else in a complex web of interaction. When he leaves Auster's apartment, Quinn is not completely cured, but there are signs of a change in outlook. Walking through Manhattan, he begins to see "many things that day he had never noticed before" (104). Consequently he writes passages in his notebook that, for the first time, have "nothing to do with the Stillman case." He writes about harsh economic realities, and about the diversity of human experience, including "the tramps, the down-and-outs, the shopping-bag ladies" (106). He writes about street performers and beggars, "the elite of the fallen," but also about the mentally ill, "locked inside madness—unable to exit to the world that stands at the threshold of their bodies" (107). Given that this has been precisely his problem, it is tempting to see detection as a kind of madness, too. Finally, he quotes Baudelaire:

"Wherever I am not is the place where I am myself" (108). From the obsessive plotting of his notes on Stillman, he has progressed to more open, poetic, and reflective observations on the need to exist not within oneself, but beyond oneself, in the mass of individuals comprising society.

With this in mind, Quinn's protracted vigil in the alleyway opposite the Stillmans' apartment could be viewed as a kind of empathy, an attempt to live like the homeless people he has for the first time noticed. It is also the first example in Auster's fiction of certain key ideas—how to survive on as little as possible; what one learns about oneself when thrown into poverty; and also how best to delay the final moment when all resources run out. Quinn has only three hundred dollars, and so sets about limiting what he eats (112), reducing his sleep (113), and making do with a trashcan for accommodation (114). Unfortunately none of this has to do with true empathy for the destitute, or even with romantic notions of poetic poverty. All of these deprivations are suffered with a look to "keeping the case uppermost in his thoughts" (112). Even though Quinn realizes he is "falling," he cannot relinquish his detective fantasy (115). Only when he has "less than a dollar" does he leave the alleyway (116). Rapidly his life falls apart. He calls Auster, who tells him that Stillman Sr. jumped off the Brooklyn Bridge months earlier and that Virginia's check bounced (120). He returns to his flat to find it occupied by a new tenant and all his possessions thrown out (123). He truly has nothing now.

The final scene, in which Quinn spends his days in the now deserted Stillman apartment, writing in his notebook, is highly ambiguous. Given that plates of food miraculously appear beside him (126), giving the whole episode a hallucinogenic atmosphere, it is unclear whether any of it "really" happens or whether it is all inside Quinn's head. What is clear is that Quinn achieves some measure of peace. He starts off writing "marginal questions concerning the Stillman case" (127) in the notebook but soon realizes that this is all behind him and therefore a waste of time and paper. At this point "Quinn no longer [has] any interest in himself," and his words have become "part of the world at large" (128). His language, as a consequence, becomes much more metaphorical and poetic (the opposite, it should be noted, of what Stillman proposed): "He remembered the moment of his birth and how he had been pulled gently from his mother's womb. He remembered the infinite kindnesses of the world and all the people he had ever loved. Nothing mattered now but the beauty of all this. He wanted to go on writing about it, and it pained him to know that this would not be possible" (128–29). Like A., Quinn has hit the bottom and emerged into a productive solitude, which allows him to reach out beyond himself to the world. He is no longer a detective plotter but a true writer who embraces the fact that words cannot record the world, but can do so much more.

However, *City of Glass* has one last surprise for us. In a move intended to recall *Don Quixote,* we discover that the narrator is a friend of Paul Auster's (at least, the fictional character) who was actually away in Africa when most of the action took place. The two men have since fallen out, the narrator blaming Auster for Quinn's decline (130). This sudden revelation casts doubt on everything that has gone before. "I have followed the red notebook as closely as I could," the narrator declares, "and any inaccuracies in the story should be blamed on me." This seems honest enough, but then he claims to have "refrained from any interpretation," something the entire narrative has shown to be impossible (130). Quinn's final entries in the notebook appear so abstract, so dreamy, that surely interpretation is all that could be attempted. The narrator's appearance forces the reader to revisit *City of Glass* and check its reliability. There are references to "diligent research," "investigations," and "evidence" (116), which suggest that the narrator has not even learned the lessons Quinn apparently has and still considers himself to be a detective on a case. Ultimately this only reinforces the main point: detection is a form of paranoid reading aiming to explain the world in all its complexity. In a city of glass—fragile, liable to shatter into fragments, and which promises clarity but reflects our own obsessions back to us—it is doomed from the start.

Ghosts

The second part of the trilogy, even more than the first, presents detection stripped down. As Alison Russell persuasively argues, its very title implies that the flesh has been removed from the conventional detective tale.[15] The unadorned prose of the opening lines reinforces this idea: "First of all there is Blue. Later there is White, and then there is Black, and before the beginning there is Brown" (133). Without proper names, it is difficult for the reader even to sympathize with the characters: the emphasis is on generic facts. As if in response to the metaphysical complexities of *City of Glass,* even the case "seems simple enough. White wants Blue to follow a man named Black and to keep an eye on him for as long as necessary. . . . He assumes it's a marriage case and that White is a jealous husband" (133).

If this synopsis promises an untaxing time for the reader, it also suits Blue's personality and worldview. He is a traditional detective, after all, a man disinclined to tricky interpretations, preferring instead to deal with observable truths, to skate "rapidly along the surface of things" (141). When it comes to writing his first report, then, he anticipates no problems: "Blue is an old hand at such compositions and has never had any trouble with them. His method is to stick to outward facts, describing events as though each word tallied exactly with the thing described, and to question the matter no further. Words are transparent for him, great windows that stand between him and the world, and until now they have never impeded his view, have never even seemed to be there" (144).

However, *City of Glass* has already demonstrated that windows are never quite transparent: they seem to offer perspicacity yet also reflect and obscure. And in the quotation above the conjunction "as though" indicates the untenability of Blue's perspective. Just as the view through the window is frequently obscured, so language is not objective; words do not tally exactly with the things described. As Alison Russell says, "Auster's reductionist technique in *Ghosts* is in itself a form of deception—it suggests that the details of the story will be presented in black and white."[16] The crucial fact that Black and White turn out to be the same person (179) reinforces the idea that appearances are always deceptive and that a word never has a straightforward meaning. If Blue learns anything from staring out of his Brooklyn window at Black (and this is debatable), it is that language must be regarded differently from how he has traditionally seen it—not as something objective, but as something shifting and metaphorical. *Ghosts,* it transpires, is about language, reading, and, most important, the edifying potential of literature.

What details there are in the opening pages offer clues to literature's importance in the story. When Blue arrives at the tiny apartment to start his surveillance, the narrator jokes: "The address is unimportant. But let's say Brooklyn Heights, for the sake of argument. Some quiet, rarely traveled street not far from the bridge—Orange Street perhaps" (134–35). He then provides the kind of background information so meticulously denied in the first paragraphs: "Walt Whitman handset the first edition of Leaves of Grass on this street in 1855, and it was here that Henry Ward Beecher railed against slavery from the pulpit of his red-brick church." Then, mock-dismissively, the narrator remarks, "so much for local color" (135).

By including these details, Auster begins the love affair with Brooklyn that continues through to *Smoke* and *The Brooklyn Follies*. He also gives the reader an insight into the borough's character, which is unavailable, at this stage, to Blue. Unbeknownst to the detective, this is a place with a considerable literary, political, and intellectual history. Given that the narrative begins on 3 February 1947—Auster's birth date—it is tempting to see *Ghosts* not simply as a dismantling of Blue's assumptions about the world but an alternative Genesis myth recounting the birth of an artistic awareness. The "Biblical syntax" Alison Russell notes in the opening paragraphs supports this reading.[17] As subsequent events demonstrate, Brooklyn plays an integral part. Unlike Quinn's Manhattan, it is not a place in which to get lost but a place where one might find oneself.

Further evidence for this reading emerges when Blue looks through his binoculars on the first day of the job to see the title of Black's book: "Walden, by Henry David Thoreau. Blue has never heard of it before and writes it down carefully in his notebook" (137). Published in 1854, *Walden* is an account of Thoreau's sojourn in a woodland cabin near Walden Pond, just outside Concord, Massachusetts. Contrary to more caricatured understandings of the book, Thoreau's aim was not a hermit's existence away from human contact. Rather his project was to "live life deliberately, to front only the essential facts of life, and see if I could not learn what it had to teach . . . to live deep and suck out the marrow of life."[18] The catalyst for this reappraisal of life is the kind of contemplative solitude so dear to Auster (not a constant solitude—Thoreau regularly welcomed visitors and walked into Concord on numerous occasions). In fact this solitude is for Thoreau a political as well as a poetic act, a means of reassessing American notions of individuality and one's relationships with others in a democratic, rapidly industrializing nation.

A curious by-product of this solitude is self-doubling, such that the individual splits into experiencer and observer (just as Auster becomes "A." in "The Book of Memory"). In Thoreau's words: "However intense my experience, I am conscious of the presence and criticism of a part of me, which, as it were, is not a part of me, but spectator, sharing no experience, but taking note of it; and that is no more I than it is you. When the play, it may be the tragedy, of life is over, the spectator goes his way. It was a kind of fiction, a work of the imagination only, so far as he was concerned."[19] As this passage suggests, the doubling process presupposes a blurring of the real and the fictional: in looking at oneself, the individual is in effect not looking at the real self, but a representation of it. It is partly for this reason that, as Mark Ford states, "*Walden* avoids identifying itself with any recognizable genre: it glides from spiritual confession to speculative linguistics, from wilderness narrative to jeremiad, from pastiche epic to heroic apologia, from fable to social history. In the process, the literal and metaphorical are insistently confused."[20] It is ironic, then, that intense watchfulness does not inevitably lead to a better understanding of the real self. What it does is make one appreciate the metaphorical aspects of the self and its essential unknowability. This might be especially true of the writer, who, after all, has constantly to deal with the vagaries of language. As Thoreau tantalizingly observes: "You will pardon some obscurities, for there are more secrets in my trade than in most men's, and yet not voluntarily kept, but inseparable from its very nature."[21]

There is also irony in Blue's initial ignorance of *Walden*, because it soon becomes clear that his situation bears uncanny resemblances to Thoreau's. Through spending an extended period on his own, he begins to contemplate matters other than the cold observation of the material world: "with nothing much to see but a vague shadow by the name of Black, he finds himself thinking about things that have never occurred to him before" (141). Suddenly alive to the nuances of his own body and his situation, his observations take on an almost poetical quality: "Life has slowed down so drastically for him that Blue is now able to see things that have previously escaped his attention. The trajectory of the light that passes through the room each day, for example, and the way the sun at certain hours will reflect the snow on the far corner of the ceiling in his room. The beating of his heart, the sound of his breath, the blinking of his eyes." These enigmatic details "persist in his mind like a nonsensical phrase repeated over and over again . . . little by little this phrase seems to be taking on a meaning" (142). In a narrative so interested in language, this simile is appropriate: Blue is slowing down and learning to *read* the world differently, just as Thoreau did.

Integral to this education is the split described by Thoreau in *Walden*. Blue realizes that "in spying out at Black across the street, it is as though Blue were looking into a mirror, and instead of merely watching another, he finds that he is also watching himself" (142). This is an important lesson for the detective: glass reflects, and one's view of the world will always be filtered through one's perceptions. And if one's view on the world cannot be objective, Blue realizes, neither can the language to describe it: "It's as though his words, instead of drawing out the facts and making them sit palpably in the world, have induced them to disappear." At this point Blue understands that "he can no longer depend on the old procedures. Clues, legwork, investigative routine—none of this is going to matter anymore" (144). He is left with, in the absence of concrete facts about Black, "a multitude of stories," "excursions into the make-believe" to fill his notebook (144, 145). Blue, it seems, is being transformed into a fiction writer.

Yet he resists. Such speculative narratives are "a perverse temptation," but Blue is not prepared to accept that his life might be intimately bound up in the lives of others and that the story in which he is involved is a kind of parable of this fact. He admonishes himself for wandering away from facts and into invented stories: "This isn't the story of my life, after all, he says. I'm supposed to be writing about him, not myself." Returning to the "aggravating precision" of his report, "he is forced to admit," after many hours of labor, "that everything seems accurate. But then why does he feel so dissatisfied, so troubled by what he has written?" (145). The source of his anxiety is a creeping awareness that all supposed knowledge of others is an invented fiction and that everything we claim to know about someone is really as much about ourselves. This *is* the story of Blue's life.

That Blue's dissatisfaction turns to "ambivalence and conflict" is due in part to the incompatibility of his detective worldview with his embryonic relationship with Black. He is torn between the spectatorial distance required for recording the facts and the sympathetic feelings arising from this unique case. The narrator explains: "There are moments when he feels so completely in harmony with Black, so naturally at one with the other man, that to anticipate what Black is going to do . . . he need merely look into himself." In painful contrast, there are times "when he feels totally removed from Black, cut off from him in a way that is so stark and absolute that he begins to lose the sense of who he is. Loneliness envelops him"; at such times "he begins to long for some companionship" (153–54).

His initial attempts to find companionship prove, for various reasons, unsuccessful. Writing to his former boss, Brown, is a waste of time because, far from addressing "Blue's torments and anxieties" (154), the old detective stays true to his trade and offers Blue only a bland report about his retirement, carefully withholding any emotion. Then his long-overdue call to "the future Mrs. Blue" goes unanswered (155): having neglected her for such a long period during his self-imposed isolation, he should not be surprised when, upon meeting her by chance in the street with another man, she reacts with such anger. At this point "he realizes that he has thrown away his life" by severing his one meaningful attachment (162). Finally, the sexual solace Blue derives from a "blowsy tart named Violet" in a local bar has, he admits, "nothing to do with love." When "she begins to cry," he wonders "if it's worth the trouble" (157), thus betraying the selfishness of his intentions. Rather than a reciprocal relationship, Blue craves only the fulfillment of his physical needs.

Blue derives temporary solace from his visit to Ebbetts Field. This is partly because "the geometric simplicity" of the baseball diamond, combined with "the sharp clarity of the colors" (156), provides relief from the feeling that he is losing his identity and merging with Black. But the main attraction is the sense of community inspired by supporting the Dodgers, focused primarily on the inspiring figure of Jackie Robinson, the first black Major League player. Brooklyn's pride in its inclusiveness and democratic ethos is channeled through Robinson. So often in Auster's work—for example, in *Squeeze Play*—baseball functions as "social memory,"[22] as a model of togetherness, and as a symbolic representation of how rules and chance operate together. In *Ghosts* it offers Blue an escape from his isolation.

Thoreau's *Walden,* which Blue purchases while tailing Black (150), offers him another chance to escape. Blue turns to the book only after being unsettled by the Robert Mitchum film noir *Out of the Past* (158). To Blue, this is a movie about being "marked by the past" and about entrapment in old habits: "Something happens, Blue thinks, and then it goes on happening forever. It can never be changed." Given that the movie mirrors his own situation, it is understandable that Blue is "haunted by this thought" and "sees it as a kind of warning" (159). His decision to read *Walden,* then, is deliberately made to sound momentous, like a stab at a new life altogether: "The time has come, he says to himself, and if he doesn't make an effort now, he knows that he never will" (159).

Unfortunately Blue initially dismisses the text as "an endless harangue about nothing at all." Despite finding one sentence "that finally says something to him—Books must be read as deliberately and reservedly as they were written," Blue still finds the effort to read slowly and carefully "painful" rather than edifying. He ends up "throwing the book aside in disgust." The narrator here interjects, leaving the reader in little doubt as to the significance of Blue's failure: "What he does not know is that were he to find the patience to read the book in the spirit in which it asks to be read, his entire life would begin to change, and little by little he would come to a full understanding of his situation" (160). As it is, his rejection signals "the beginning of the end" (161). Immediately afterward there is the incident with the ex-future Mrs. Blue, and his life starts to unravel. This unraveling is a direct consequence of his reluctance to immerse himself in Thoreau's book, to learn one of its valuable lessons—that one need not be alone when one is alone. One can "get out of the room that is the book" (167) by staying in the room and reaching out sympathetically to the voices in the text. This is what "The Book of Memory" and now *Ghosts* clearly show, but Blue is not ready.

He does get out, and indeed starts chatting with Black, but not as himself. Instead he resorts to detective convention by donning disguises. It is appropriate that the first of these, "a wise fool, a saint of penury living in the margins of society" called Jimmy Rose (168), shares his name with a character in an 1855 Herman Melville short story and resembles Walt Whitman (169), for Blue's first conversation with Black is all about local literary history. Black tells him about Whitman's abortive brain autopsy (170) and about Thoreau's and Bronson Alcott's visit to Whitman's Myrtle Street home (171–72). Finally, he tells him the story that the critic Richard Swope regards as an important precursor of antidetective fiction, with its protagonist's seemingly motiveless disappearance and its open ending—Hawthorne's "Wakefield" (172–73).[23] Although Black says that "writing is a solitary business" and "a writer has no life of his own. Even when he's there, he's not really there" (172), the overall effect of his anecdotes is to give the impression of a literary community of individuals linked by their working solitude but also by their shared love of ideas. Writers may be, as Blue acknowledges, ghosts (172), but the ghostly dimension to which they find themselves exiled lies between their hearts and minds and the hearts and minds of those they reach out to through their work. It can therefore be a positive state. Black comes across as someone finely attuned to the emotional and educational benefits of literature. As he says, "it helps me to understand things" (172).

Blue on the other hand still does not get it, despite having a dim belief that "even though the talk had nothing to do with the case, . . . Black was actually referring to it all along" (174). He refuses to see that Blue and Black "are two aspects of the same entity" and "reflect the situation of the author as creator of fictions."[24] He is the observer of the world who also observes himself as he writes. When the two men subsequently meet in a restaurant and Black tells Blue that he is a private detective whose job is merely "to watch someone . . . and send in a report about him every week" (177), the truth of the situation finally begins to dawn on Blue. By this time there is no need for his adopted false name; both men know who they are talking to and what they are talking about. Black's description of his case is of course an exact mirror of Blue's (177), but the key statement comes at the end. When Blue asks whether Black's subject knows he is being watched, Black replies: "Of course he knows. . . . He needs my eyes looking at him. He needs me to prove he's alive" (178). For the detective, for the writer, for the reader, for all of us, this is the fundamental truth Blue has ignored: we cannot accept or even know ourselves without reference to others. All identity is exchange, and even if we cannot ever penetrate the core of someone else's identity, their existence helps define us. Black stands for that part of the self that is everybody else.

Blue cannot handle this. He is stuck in the detective mode—isolated, seeking easy answers, picturing his escape from the situation as "a pioneer" and "hero" (183), yet knowing that no escape is possible. His overwhelming emotion is fear: fear of the truth Black and Thoreau have revealed, fear of ambiguity, and fear of the destruction of his old assurance that the world is explicable. Desperately Blue breaks into Black's apartment and steals Black's reports, which, unsurprisingly, turn out to be his own (185). Finally, he confronts Black in his apartment where, to his surprise, Black pulls a gun on him (188). This climactic scene is played out like a bitter parody of the traditional showdown between detective and villain. The difference here is that Black and Blue are essentially the same person and share the exhaustion of their failure to connect. As Black puts it: "I'm in my mind, too much in my mind. It's used me up, and now there's nothing left. But you know that, Blue, you know that better than anyone" (189). *Ghosts* has proved to be an allegory of the individual's need to reach out from his or her own mind to the mind of another, the difficulty of doing so, and the help literature can offer. Still resistant, Blue ends up beating Black to a pulp and leaving him for dead (191).

Finally, Blue becomes a ghost in his own text, walking through the door and disappearing forever. With knowing irony the narrator suggests that he might have gone "out West to start a new life" (192), again mocking the notion of the lone American pioneer hero. Or maybe he has gone to China. While there is the suggestion of hope here, one cannot disregard the closing line: "And from this moment on, we know nothing" (192). This is the truth against which Blue has fought: in essence, we know nothing about anyone, but we must at least *try* to acknowledge their importance.

The Locked Room

Part three of the trilogy is a detective mystery only in the abstract sense that *The Invention of Solitude* is. Both texts are "about the question of biography" (AH 307) and depict a biographical quest that bleeds into a quest for self-definition and threatens the stability of the writer's identity.

The title of part three relates to this difficulty on a number of levels. First, the locked room is the space in which the writer sits, trying to compose but all the while running the risk of missing out on the life experiences about which he is writing. In this sense it is evident that the locked room is, as in *The Invention of Solitude,* a metaphor for the writer's consciousness. As the narrator says, the room is "inside my skull" (286). This is an idea carried through Auster's work right up to *Man in the Dark.* Second, the choice of title suggests a parodic twist on a common subgenre of the detective tale. So-called locked-room mysteries, various permutations of which are outlined in John Dickson Carr's "The Locked-Room Lecture" (1935),[25] posit a crime committed in a room with no conceivable means of ingress or egress. A famous example is Edgar Allan Poe's "The Murders in the Rue Morgue" (1841), in which only the superhuman strength of the killer, an orangutan, allows entry into the locked apartment. Auster's twist is to make the door of 9 Columbus Square, Boston, (where the climactic scene takes place) remain firmly locked. Despite his by now fanatical desire to find his childhood friend, the narrator finds no way of gaining entry to the room where Fanshawe lives in self-imposed exile. So the locked room is not only the writer's head; it also stands for the "secret core" of Fanshawe, and by extension the "mysterious center of hiddenness" in every person (206). Where *The Locked Room* goes farther even than *The Invention of Solitude* and *Ghosts* is in suggesting that the very desire to gain access to the locked room of another person's being can become a form of violation and violence. The narrator's quest to find the disappeared writer Fanshawe is frequently confused with the need "to track him down and kill him" (261) and, as Stephen Bernstein states, with "sexual desire."[26] What is revealed is a wish to take over and *become* Fanshawe.

Not surprisingly, then, *The Locked Room* continues the pattern of doubling seen in the relationship between Blue and Black. It asks again whether an individual identity is even possible without the other, and whether observer and observed can be separated. And once again Auster divests himself of absolute authority by participating in his own literary-historical doubling, reminding the reader that his work would be impossible without the help of literary antecedents. As well as sharing with *Ghosts* a distinct resemblance to "Wakefield," *The Locked Room* makes direct reference to Hawthorne's first novel, *Fanshawe*. As Auster explains: "He wrote it when he was very young, and not long after it was published, he turned against it in revulsion and tried to destroy every copy he could get his hands on. Fortunately, a few of them survived" (AH 281). *Fanshawe* deals in part with the romantic rivalry between two young intellectuals, a theme explicitly borrowed by Auster's story, but part of the attraction for Auster, in a tale of disappearance, is the near disappearance of Hawthorne's text.

The narrator's childhood doubling with Fanshawe is every bit as deliberate as Auster's. "Early on, his influence was already quite pronounced," he says: "If Fanshawe wore his belt buckle on the side of his pants, then I would move my belt into the same position." Among his group of friends, the narrator was "the most devoted, the one who gave in most willingly to the power he held over us" (205). Fanshawe's power is heightened by his detachment and aloofness, the fact that "he was there for you, and yet at the same time he was inaccessible" (206). Even when he demonstrates tremendous generosity, such as in his spontaneous decision to give Dennis Walden his birthday present (207), there is the sense that he is separate from his own actions—all of which only increases the young narrator's desire "to measure up to him" (208) and to solve the mystery of his personality. As the narrator reveals, "to imitate him was somehow to participate in that mystery, but it was also to understand that you could never really know him" (206).

The narrator declares that "the way he lived inside himself could never correspond to the way I needed to live. I wanted too much of things, I had too many desires, I lived too fully in the grip of the immediate ever to attain such indifference" (208). However, the ensuing action seems to support Carsten Springer's view that *The Locked Room* is about the dangers of imitation and the failure to develop "an independent personality." Not only does the narrator remain nameless, suggesting that he "is defined as Fanshawe's friend and imitator,"[27] but as he shares stories from their adolescence, the imitation and infatuation take on more disturbing connotations. For example, the two teenagers, as part of Fanshawe's ongoing project "to take risks, to haunt the edges of things" (210), visit a prostitute in New York. As the narrator waits for his turn, he admits: "I could only think about one thing: that my dick was about to go into the same place that Fanshawe's was now" (211). During the act the narrator becomes distracted, oddly, by Fanshawe's shoes. His overall dissatisfaction with the experience suggests a failed attempt to step into these very shoes. In this anxious sexual union the woman is merely a vehicle.

Time and again this imperfect imitation recurs. After Fanshawe's sudden disappearance, the narrator acts as literary executor, with Fanshawe's wife, Sophie, for Fanshawe's work. His feeling of "dread" has partly to do with "old rivalries" (unsurprisingly, the narrator is also a writer, though his brand of criticism he dismisses as "little short of hack work" compared to Fanshawe's writing [203]) and partly to do with the knowledge that he will become "Fanshawe's spokesman" and be forced to "go on speaking for him" (218). Fanshawe's writing is brilliant, however, and inevitably the narrator does go on speaking for him by getting the work published and, in addition, writing a biographical article to whet the public's appetite (226). Things move quickly, and "a small industry" develops around the absent Fanshawe. "Hindsight tells me that I was looking for trouble," the narrator admits, but "it was probably necessary for me to equate Fanshawe's success with my own." Given what eventually transpires, to say that his behavior at this time is "a little mad" sounds like an understatement (227).

Potentially the most destructive consequence of his madness is the narrator's relationship with Sophie. Her motivations are laudable: she does not want to be "forced to live in the past" by focusing solely on her husband's literary legacy, and sees in the narrator an opportunity for a new beginning. Moreover she is "too young to live through someone else, too intelligent not to want a life that was completely her own" (221). For his part, desire for Sophie makes the narrator feel "more human" and more connected to the world. "By belonging to Sophie," he says, "I began to feel as though I belonged to everyone else as well. My true place in the world, it turned out, was somewhere beyond myself, and if that place was inside me, it was also unlocatable. This was the tiny hole between self and not-self" (228). This is a familiar and necessary realization for an Auster character. Self is not everything, and it is necessary to understand that other people help define who you are. Essentially, that is the nature of love.

Yet Sophie's and the narrator's sentiments ignore the ironies of their getting together in the first place, ironies that almost come to destroy everything they have. For of course she enters into a relationship with a man who is indeed living through someone else. And in living this way, the narrator does not inhabit "the tiny hole between self and not-self," as he believes, but attempts fully to inhabit another individual. There is always a subtle but important distinction to be made in Auster's work between living *with* others and living vicariously *through* others. The first means accepting that everyone is different and at heart unknowable, and at the same time accepting that others help define who we are. The second involves trying too hard to penetrate the core of other people, to the extent that individuality and difference are lost in the bid to consume and *become* someone else. The first requires sympathy plus an acceptance of the limitations of knowledge, the second an obsessive desire to know and subsequent loss of identity.

It soon becomes clear that the narrator is bent on the second course. He is "possessed" (238) but also cripplingly possessive—of Sophie and perhaps of the professional success he has achieved in Fanshawe's shoes. When a letter from Fanshawe arrives, the narrator's decision not to tell Sophie her husband is alive, quickly followed by a sudden marriage proposal, is born out of "panic and fear" (235). "I did what Fanshawe had asked me to do," he admits, "not for him, but for myself. I locked up the secret inside me and learned to hold my tongue" (235). This gives, then, another meaning to the title—the locked room is also the destructive secret.

If this silence represents the narrator's "greatest failure" (235), the decision to write Fanshawe's biography proves almost as disastrous. From the start the book is a deception: "There was never any question of telling the truth. Fanshawe had to be dead, or else the book made no sense" (242). For this reason the narrator finds himself in a doubly paradoxical situation. First, he is embarking on a detective quest to uncover the "real" Fanshawe while accepting that the entire project is founded on a fiction. Second, he becomes, like Blue in *Ghosts,* both observer and observed because he is aiming to objectify Fanshawe, with a view to writing about him, at the same time he is supplanting him by publishing his work and marrying Sophie. With hindsight, he recognizes how untenable this is: "We imagine the real story inside the words, and to do this we substitute ourselves for the person in the story, pretending that we can understand him because we understand ourselves. This is a deception. . . . No one can cross the boundary into another—for the simple reason that no one can gain access to himself" (243).

In what could stand as an antidetective motto, the narrator declares that "lives make no sense" (246), but he soldiers on, poring over Fanshawe's notebooks (249), looking through childhood photos and school reports (252), and interviewing people who might have known him (273) to uncover the truth about his disappearance. The following bold proclamation—"I was a detective, after all, and my job was to hunt for clues" (276)—the reader knows to treat with skepticism, having read "Portrait of an Invisible Man." In truth, the biographical investigation is partly an act of self-justification for the narrator's supplanting of Fanshawe and also, more disturbingly, an act of vengeance. This is especially evident when the narrator visits Fanshawe's mother for a second time. She remarks that the two men look "almost like twins" (256), setting the stage for an uncanny drama of revenge and frustration. The narrator and Mrs. Fanshawe end up drunkenly, violently, having sex, fully aware that she is fantasizing about "fucking her own son" and the narrator about killing Fanshawe (261). With this act he enters the "darkness" (261) and begins to unravel.

He reaches his nadir when he travels to Paris to investigate Fanshawe's life there. Before leaving, he argues with Sophie about the disposal of Fanshawe's possessions. His refusal to throw out the books prompts Sophie to exclaim: "You're bringing him back to life.... If the two of us are going to last, he's got to be dead. Don't you understand that? Even if he's alive, he's got to be dead" (279). Showing awareness of the patterns of repetition and imitation at work, she tells him, "You're going to vanish, and I'll never see you again" (280). He does not vanish, but he almost loses his mind, his increasingly feverish searches throwing up only the realization that "I was no longer alone, that I could never be alone in that place. Fanshawe was there, and no matter how hard I tried not to think about him, I couldn't escape." His pretense at a biographical, theoretical distance has failed, and their identities have almost completely merged: "Fanshawe was exactly where I was, and he had been there since the beginning" (286). As if attempting, despite this realization, to re-create some distance, he latches on to a stranger in a bar, insists on following him and calling him "Fanshawe," and ends up severely beaten, lying in the street (293).

Yet this is no random stranger. His name is Peter Stillman. If Stillman's appearance is disturbing, it is because it reminds us that we are reading a constructed fiction and that the three parts of the trilogy are more closely connected than anticipated. Even more intriguing is the narrator's admission that he is also the writer of *City of Glass* and *Ghosts* (288). Although this appears to answer a nagging question in the trilogy, it also raises others. Is the narrator actually Auster? Is *The Locked Room* the most intimate exploration of his anxieties as a writer? Does this explain the choice, for the first time in the trilogy, of first-person narration? And what exactly has he been "struggling to say goodbye to" (288)? The point is that these questions cannot be answered satisfactorily. To assume that Auster is the narrator confuses the final paragraphs of *City of Glass,* just as the introduction of Stillman confuses the chronology of the three stories. But of course Paul Auster *is* the writer of all three parts, which destabilizes identities even further. A paragraph that appears to offer explanations only takes the reader farther away from the truth. Thus the first-person narration, promising greater confessional intimacy, is a kind of trick designed to keep us locked out. Our experience as readers resembles that of the narrator in his quest to find answers to the Fanshawe puzzle.

The last scene of the story suggests that remaining locked out might be the best thing. Sophie and the narrator, having split up for a year after his Paris trip, get back together and make a "silent pact" never to speak of Fanshawe (294). Soon afterward, a final letter arrives, asking the narrator to come to Boston. By this time, having "tasted death" in Paris (295), the narrator understands a lot more than he did. Fanshawe, like Sam Auster, has come to stand for the power of chance, and hence the meaninglessness and precariousness of life. "For when anything can happen—that is the precise moment when words begin to fail," the narrator explains, adding that Fanshawe functions "as a trope of death" inside him. The narrator has achieved a kind of tolerance: "I learned to live with him in the same way I lived with the thought of my own death" (295). In other words, the narrator may be in a position to move on now that he accepts that some things are simply inexplicable. Fanshawe, speaking from behind the locked door of 9 Columbus Square, says as much: "You can't possibly know what's true or not true. You'll never know" (306). In this climactic near-meeting, much talking is done, and we find out a little about Fanshawe's movements over the years, but his underlying motivations remain opaque. Whether or not Fanshawe goes on to commit suicide (306), he understands that the best thing he can do for the narrator is keep the door locked and let him continue with his life. For them to meet face-to-face would solve or explain nothing. The notebook Fanshawe leaves for the narrator—to which we as readers never gain access—also explains nothing: "Each sentence erased the sentence before it, each paragraph made the next paragraph impossible. It is odd, then, that the feeling that survives from this notebook is one of great lucidity" (307). If this text represents Fanshawe's life, as its author insists it does, it serves to emphasize only that an individual somehow hangs together despite being a mass of irresolvable contradictions. This is all anyone can know about anyone.

It is tempting to see the ending, when the narrator symbolically destroys the notebook and returns to Sophie in New York, as optimistic (308). As Aliki Varvogli says, "it is true that *The Locked Room* does not solve any of the problems the three books deal with, but its narrator is clearer in articulating these problems, while the author's position in relation to them also becomes clearer."[28]

And as Auster argues, the narrator "finally comes to accept his own life . . . to tolerate the presence of ambiguities within himself" (AH 285). Yet this "within himself" provokes a final, haunting thought: What if Fanshawe has never existed? What if he has been entirely within the narrator's head all along? After all, the first line declares, ambiguously, "it *seems to me* now that Fanshawe was always there" (195, emphasis added). Seen in this way, it is a story of madness, with no guarantee of peace or sanity to come.

CHAPTER FOUR

Last Chances
In the Country of Last Things
and *The Music of Chance*

In the Country of Last Things was published by Viking Penguin New York in 1987 and the year after in the United Kingdom by Faber and Faber. Yet the author points out that it "is a novel I started writing back in the days when I was a college student. The idea of an unknowable place . . . it got under my skin and I couldn't let go of it. . . . I must have started the book thirty times" (AH 284). So the novel was evolving at the same time Auster was writing his poetry, and the idea of an "unknowable place," a fragmentary landscape both familiar and yet abstract, is something it shares with the verse.

The "unknowable place" is an unnamed, fast-decomposing city to which Anna Blume, the narrator, has traveled across the ocean in search of her missing brother, William. Her narrative takes the form of a diary or extended letter, describing in at times harrowing detail her struggles to survive in a hellish city. The vast majority of people here are reduced to scavenging, and acts of random violence are common. Not unlike the New York of the trilogy, this is a place of disappearances: "Close your eyes for a moment, turn around to look at something else, and the thing that was before you is suddenly gone. Nothing lasts, you see, not even the thoughts inside you."[1] Yet as the title suggests, it is also a place of persistence, of things that last. At the end of the novel there is a good chance Anna survives. Moreover her letter reaches its destination. The reader knows this from the occasional interjections, such as that found in the very first line: "These are the last things, she wrote" (1). The addressee remains anonymous, but it is clear that it is also intended to be the novel's reader. Thus, despite Anna's observation that "words tend to last a bit longer than things, but eventually they fade too" (89), the book stands as testimony to language's and art's enduring power to create and to move. In engaging with Anna's text, the reader enters into a reciprocal relationship. And, as Auster says, the very act of writing the letter represents Anna's bid "to keep her humanity intact." Writing is an ethical process, and for this reason Auster describes *In the Country of Last Things* as "the most hopeful book I've ever written. Anna Blume survives, at least to the extent that her words survive. Even in the midst of the most brutal realities, the most terrible social conditions, she struggles to remain a human being" (AH 321). And just as the story describes Anna's attempts to connect with other characters—notably Isabel, Samuel, and Victoria—so the reader's reception is a type of human connection.

While the city portrayed is distinctly dystopian and apocalyptic in its appalling social conditions, Auster is keen to emphasize that the novel is not, in one critic's words, "a vision of the future" and should not be classified as science fiction.[2] In fact its working title was "Anna Blume Walks through the Twentieth Century," and an early draft has Anna declare, with heavy irony: "This, I imagine, is what is called the city of the future. The future that has fled, leaving us with nothing more than what we have right here and now."[3] Auster conceives of it as "a book about our own moment . . . and many of the incidents are things that have actually happened." Among other events, the novel refers to the Warsaw Ghetto, the siege of Leningrad in World War II, even "the present-day garbage system in Cairo" (AH 285). Science fiction, while frequently satirizing current events, relies on a chronological distance from the present allied to a fascination with advanced or alternative technologies. Auster's point in denying the generic label is that once again he is merely attempting to represent contemporary realities that are outlandish and shocking. There is no safe distance from such things, because they impact on all of us. Neither are they where we might end up: they are where we have been and where we are.

Padgett Powell, the most insightful of the reviewers, confirms this view. In his *New York Times* review he says that the ruined city is not prophetic, because "there is entirely too much in these pages about the world as we know it." Part of the novel's ambition is to offer, he suggests, a vision of late-capitalist "collapse" and "an industrialist's true nightmare." Powell's analysis is borne out by some of the book's most potent images of homeless individuals picking through consumer waste, pushing shopping trolleys. Far from being "a didactic, finger-wagging account of how we ruined ourselves," however, Powell believes that the novel succeeds because of its "daring touches," such as the unlikely coincidences and allegorical character names like Ferdinand and Isabel.[4] In other words, it is too novelistic to be a simple polemic. Ultimately Powell agrees that it is a novel about the consolations of art and language. For Anna Blume, "if in the beginning there was only the Word, she wants to say that in the end It will still be."[5] Austin MacCurtain, writing in the *Times,* says that, appropriately enough, for a novel so concerned with language, it is "the overall quality of his writing and its imaginative and emotional force" that compels.[6]

What sets this writing apart is the use of the female narrator. *In the Country of Last Things* is the only one of Auster's novels to feature a female protagonist and is also the only one not to center on a literal or metaphorical father-son relationship. (An example of the literal would be Marco and Solomon in *Moon Palace* and of the metaphorical, the narrator's relationship with Fanshawe in *The Locked Room*.) Auster has said that throughout history, "from Cassandra to Anne Frank," the best witnesses to historical events have been women, because "they're usually in a situation of marginality, so their testimonies are more accurate."[7] Moreover the search for William represents a desire to reinstate a fraternal relationship rather than a filial one. Whether or not the brother can ever be found (and the reader knows that he remains lost [39]), the suggestion is that solace is sought in equal, one might say horizontal, relationships of friendship and togetherness, rather than in vertical relationships of paternal authority. Such paternal relationships in Auster's books frequently allegorize people's relationship with a God who may or may not exist. By employing Anna Blume on this rather different mission, the emphasis in this novel seems more humanistic and more focused on the possibility of community.

The diary/epistolary form is also notable. As Aliki Varvogli says, the name of the protagonist and the oppressive situation in which she finds herself inevitably put one in mind of Anne Frank.[8] Frank's diary, published posthumously in 1947, was not only a chronicle of the girl's innermost private thoughts but also became in itself a means of survival, a means of holding on to an inner, emotional life even as external forces promised imminent destruction. Ultimately it became a valuable educational tool for providing insights into the reality of suffering under the

Nazis, partly because of the diary form's immediacy and apparent authenticity. Anna Blume's motivations are strikingly similar. She shares with Frank the desperate need to communicate inner thoughts and experiences: "suddenly, after all this time, I feel there is something to say, and if I don't quickly write it down, my head will burst." Likewise she has the desire to inform: "I am writing to you because you know nothing. Because you are far away and you know nothing" (3). And, finally, Blume shares with Frank an abstract awareness that to keep writing is to keep moving, even if one is effectively incarcerated. In her words, "I put one foot in front of the other, and then the other foot in front of the first, and then hope I can do it again" (2).

In the Country of Last Things shares this idea of writing as movement with Auster's poetry and *City of Glass*. It is explicitly expressed in the prose poem *White Spaces* (1980), where Auster speculates: "To think of motion not merely as a function of the body but as an extension of the mind. In the same way, to think of speech not as an extension of the mind but as a function of the body." Thus to string units of language together into sentences and paragraphs is a physical act of traversing space: "I remain in the room in which I am writing this. I put one foot in front of the other. I put one word in front of the other, and for each step I take I add another word, as if for each word to be spoken there were another space to be crossed."[9] If one accepts this metaphor, then the page itself becomes a kind of landscape.

What *In the Country of Last Things* manages so affectingly is to make Anna's quest for survival in this shattered urban landscape simultaneously physical, ethical, linguistic, and artistic. Like Stillman's New York, this is a place of fragmentation, a place of "rubble" and "sudden clusters of rocks" (5) where "things fall apart and vanish, and nothing new is made" (7).

Such is the degree of breakdown that the essential nature of things is altered, and "nothing is really itself anymore. There are pieces of this and pieces of that, but none of it fits together" (35). When Anna takes up "object hunting" (34), scavenging for things that can be sold to the "Resurrection Agents" for recycling, she realizes that her chief task is to create "archipelagoes of matter" from the fragments of waste around her (36). Not only is this material, in that her day-to-day survival depends on it, but it is also ethical, in that it symbolizes the need to form connections in a city where "instances of shared understanding diminish" (89), where people become islands, and where individual is pitted against individual in a battle simply to exist.

Remembering that the page is a landscape, Anna's task is also a linguistic one. As objects fragment and disappear, so do the words associated with them. They disintegrate into mere "sounds, a random collection of glottals and fricatives, a storm of whirling phonemes," until "finally the whole thing just collapses into gibberish" (89). It is apparent, then, that Anna's object hunting, her task of finding "little islands of intactness" among the waste before they fall apart (36), is symbolic of the need to maintain linguistic as well as material cohesion. As is so often the case in Auster's work, notably in *The Music of Chance,* the stones and rocks littered around the landscape are words on the page, waiting to be formed into meaningful communication. Indeed Anna's letter is explicit about this connection when it describes one character's verbal idiosyncrasies: "Mr. Frick had an odd, ungrammatical way of speaking. . . . It was simply that words gave him trouble . . . he would sometimes stumble over them as though they were physical objects, literal stones cluttering his mouth" (133). This is a particularly striking image for one of Auster's most urgent questions: how can one ever say what one means when words constantly vacillate, get in the way, and deceive?

The answer for Anna, as it is for A. in *The Invention of Solitude,* is to recognize and accept language's elusiveness and be endlessly creative with it. Her gathering of fragments into "archipelagoes of matter" in this symbolic urban landscape is, then, an imaginative, artistic act. When things disappear so rapidly, it is necessary to look at them afresh, to think creatively in order to see new potentials. Anna explains: "The essential thing is not to become inured. For habits are deadly. Even if it is for the hundredth time, you must encounter each thing as if you have never known it before. No matter how many times, it must always be the first time" (7). Elisabeth Wesseling evocatively dubs this "the horror of continual novelty";[10] it is certainly unsettling and horrific, yet it is also the only hope for survival. It takes a particular form of imagination constantly to renew a moribund world where people are preoccupied with the brute realities of existence. As Anna wryly observes, "if anything is in short supply in the city, it's imagination" (61).

Auster's protagonists tend to be self-conscious about their texts, to give the impression that they *know* they are in a book. Anna's musings on imagination, and her deliberate deployment of metaphors such as the "literal stones," suggest that she is aware of the symbolic nature of the city landscape and is prepared to confront it on its own terms. Despite her proclamation that she has become "all common sense and hard calculation" (10), Anna understands the irony of her situation—that the most commonsensical tactic is to bring her creativity to bear on her suffering—hence her need for an audience, her need to engage in literary activity in the form of her epistle.

Anna's gift for imagination finds an unlikely parallel in the figure of Boris Stepanovich (one of Auster's larger-than-life and not always entirely convincing "characters," another example of which is Walt in *Mr. Vertigo*). Boris is the supplier for Woburn House, a hostel for homeless people, where Anna finds herself toward the end. For him, language ceases to be inhibitingly stonelike and is transformed into "an instrument of locomotion —constantly on the move, darting and feinting." His fondness for elaborate storytelling and "conflicting accounts of his life" (146) makes him at best an unreliable narrator, at worst a liar, but these stories are part of "an almost conscious plan to concoct a more pleasant world for himself—a world that could shift according to his whims, that was not subject to the same laws and bleak necessities that dragged down all the rest of us" (147). Yet Anna recognizes that while Boris is no "realist in the strict sense of the word, he [is] not one to delude himself either." Behind the bluff there is "a sense of some deeper understanding" (147). Central to this, once again, is imagination—not fantasy, but an ethical imagination alive to the reality of suffering in social relationships but at the same time negotiating it anew, embellishing it, and making it livable. "It was as though he had imagined every possibility in advance, and therefore he was never surprised by what happened," Anna reflects. By means, paradoxically, of "a pessimism so deep, so devastating, so fully in tune with the facts," Boris is able to construct a "cheerful" imaginative life (147).

While Anna and Boris insist on imaginative renewal of their surroundings, other citizens adopt alternative strategies, invariably with fatal consequences. Much of the early part of the novel is dedicated to descriptions of these strategies. What connects them is first their ritualistic quality, and second their dependence on consoling fantasy. As Anna observes, "when hope disappears, when you find that you have given up hoping even for the possibility of hope, you tend to fill the empty spaces with dreams, little childlike thoughts and stories to keep you going" (9). As well as "the Runners," "a sect of people" who undergo "arduous preparations" for a final suicidal run (11, 12), and "the Leapers," individuals who perform public jumps to their death from high buildings (13), there are those who reach death through pure fantasy and nostalgia. For example, by "describing a meal in meticulous detail," some citizens believe that "you will be able to forget your present hunger" (9, 10). Belief in the restorative power of words alone underlies these conversations; Anna rejects such a belief in "the language of ghosts" because it has "no meaning and no reality." Its absurd, yet to the contemporary reader perfectly familiar, outcome is "the belief that however bad things were yesterday, they were better than things are today. . . . The farther you go back, the more beautiful and desirable the world becomes" (10). Leading to the delusion that "the present day is simply an apparition," this quasi-religious mythology results in undignified demise: the believer typically possesses "a strange smile," a "slight flush to the cheeks," and "a foul smell from the lower body" prior to death. Most tellingly, Anna describes the "weird glow of otherness" with which these people are suffused (11). They have employed their imaginations, in a sense, but only to retreat nostalgically into a fantastical, nonexistent past. Their "otherness" signals that they have also retreated into their own minds, away from the potential solace of the community. It is possible to understand Auster's portrayals of these sects as a satire on the contemporary obsession with nostalgia and the recycling of the past.

Anna recognizes both the attractions and dangers of the lure of the past, and constantly seeks to build a better present and future through meaningful relationships with others. For example, of her relationship with Victoria, she says: "Being with Victoria gave me pleasure, but it also gave me the courage to live in the present again" (157). The key relationships in the novel are formed in three locations: Isabel and Ferdinand's apartment, the city library where Anna meets Samuel Farr, and Woburn House. To employ once again the novel's most powerful metaphor, these sanctuaries can be viewed as "archipelagoes of matter": they are more or less solid, intact structures within a fragmenting landscape that present the possibility of real human contact.

Isabel is an aging and increasingly ineffectual object hunter whom Anna saves from probable death as Isabel stands, dazed, in the path of a group of Runners (45). Having saved her life, Anna returns home with Isabel, recognizing that her "true life in the city" has begun at the moment their special bond of "responsibility" is forged (45, 46). For her part, Isabel regards Anna as a manifestation of divine intervention: "From now on, there will be a roof over your head and food to eat. That's how I'm going to thank God for what he has done. He has answered my prayers, and now you are my dear, sweet, little child, my darling Anna who came to me from God" (49). Regardless of the reader's inevitable sympathies with Isabel, her belief in divine dispensation is shown to be just as much a comforting delusion as the manic cheerfulness embraced by "the Smilers" (26). Anna and Isabel's meeting is not engineered by a benign deity: it is just another example of pure coincidence in a city where "the sky is ruled by chance" (27–28). As Anna declares in one of her many allegorical pronouncements, there is no virtue in "looking for signs in the air" (25). Circumstances cannot be controlled; one can only make the best of the opportunities chance provides.

Ferdinand, whom Anna meets upon arriving at the apartment, has allowed circumstances to beat him into submission, to the extent that he has seceded from all meaningful relationships. He spends all day in the apartment, "rarely saying anything and taking no interest in their survival." His one passion is "making miniature ships and putting them into bottles" (47). This, coupled with his disheveled appearance, leads Anna to observe that he plays "the role of a man marooned on a desert island" (52), a neat image of his isolation. Ferdinand obsesses on the construction of ever smaller ships, which, though "ingeniously designed" (52), symbolize the increasing futility of his existence.

His cruelty is seen in the pleasure he feels at capturing, roasting, and eating the apartment mice (53–54), in his increasingly abusive attitude toward Anna, and in his lack of sympathy for Isabel when she falls ill (58). Things reach a head when Anna throws a mirror at him (60): from this point, tormenting Anna becomes "his only avenue of escape from Isabel" (61). When he overhears Anna masturbating, he releases "a barrage of insinuations and ugly cracks" (63) and then attempts to sexually assault her (64). In one of the novel's pivotal episodes, when Anna begins to strangle him and feels nothing but "a surging, uncontrollable sense of rapture" (65), she experiences a terrible realization. To kill him would be to succumb to the brutality of the environment, to be utterly dehumanized. Feeling "disgust" at Ferdinand and at herself, she releases her grip (66). The next morning the women find him dead anyway (69). Isabel tends to his body, and then they push him from the roof "to make him look like a Leaper" (72). Such is the dehumanization of the city that his body is removed and all his possessions taken by the next morning (76).

After her near-murderous episode with Ferdinand, Anna's compassion for Isabel as she tends to her during the final weeks of Isabel's illness forms a striking contrast and hints at one source of hope in the city—care for others. In a novel so keen to stress the links between language, identity, and the possibility of salvation, it is notable that Anna's descriptions of Isabel's "sclerosis" (77) linger on the deterioration of her speech. "A disintegrating body is one thing," she says, "but when the voice goes too, it feels as if the person is no longer there" (78). One's whole identity, in other words, is bound up in one's unique way of speaking. In a characteristic Auster move, Anna buys a blank notebook so that Isabel can write down messages (79). In addition to their material pleasures, notebooks have a transforming, almost magical quality in Auster's fiction. This one is no exception. After Isabel's death, Anna is inspired to write the letter we are reading in the notebook: "If not for Isabel, there would be nothing now. I never would have begun" (79). So once again death (but also the close friendship the women shared) inspires the literary act. Isabel loses her voice, but Anna gains hers.

It is appropriate, then, that after a series of misfortunes—including the loss of her trolley (82), the invasion of Isabel's apartment by housebreakers (84), and a food riot (92)—Anna should end up at the National Library (93). In this space full of texts, the underlying Jewish sensibility of the novel is revealed. Upon entering the library, Anna unexpectedly comes across a group of orthodox Jews. To her startled statement "I thought all the Jews were dead," the Rabbi responds, "it's not so easy to get rid of us, you know" (95). On another occasion he tells her:

"Every Jew . . . believes that he belongs to the last generation of Jews. We are always at the end, always standing at the brink of the last moment" (112). The Jews embody the paradoxical idea, so productive to Auster and so important in this novel as well as at the end of *City of Glass,* of an "art of hunger."[11] Theirs is a final catastrophe that never quite arrives. Always suspecting that they are the *last* things, they nonetheless *last,* but the desire to record and create is strongest in the belief in imminent total disappearance. For Anna, who reveals that she is also Jewish (95), the constant threat of the end, of starvation, keeps her active in seeking human connection and in writing her account. Surviving with as little food, and as little time, as possible becomes an ethical and artistic act, but the end must always remain theoretical, not actual. In Anna's words, "The closer you come to the end, the more there is to say. The end is only imaginary" (183). The explicit introduction of these Jewish ideas inevitably colors one's reading of the entire novel. It is noteworthy, however, that the Rabbi shows a practical honesty about the situation, which it would be easy to forget if one concentrated only on the importance of the word. "There are more important things than books," he says, "food comes before prayers" (96). To consider words as having their own nutritional value, he reminds Anna, is to drift into dangerous fantasy.

When Anna meets Samuel Farr in the library (99), the Rabbi's words prove apt. Having put most of his money into the mammoth history of the city he is writing, Sam is now "eating only every other day" (104). Though he regards the book as sustenance and hope for the future—"the only thing that keeps me going" (104)—Anna recognizes not only that nobody is likely to read it but also that it is going to kill him. Their "wild leap into intimacy" (106) stems from Anna's offer to live with him and share her money, holding out the possibility that they could both eat and write through the imminent "Terrible Winter" (107). Inevitably, mutual convenience becomes love, and Anna declares her time in the library with Sam to be "the best days of my life" (107), characterized by plans for escape (108), "extreme tenderness" (109), and a strong mutual bond brought about by shared hardship. The fact that they are both exiles and do not "belong" in the city is also significant (106). Full of marginalized religious groups, "scholars and writers" (110), the library is a haven for thoughtful outsiders seeking to transcend the miseries of city life.

Inevitably, however, disaster strikes. When Anna becomes pregnant (117), Sam takes on the role of "demented nurse" (118), abandoning the book to care for her when she contracts a cold. To this end he decides she needs new shoes (119). Promising her a new pair, a man called Dujardin tricks Anna into visiting a human slaughterhouse. In a city where the authorities are primarily concerned with waste and the disposal of bodies, this represents a new low: the human body as commodity. Anna escapes only by leaping from a high window (125).

Anna is picked up by Mr. Frick and Willie, employees at Woburn House. Her first few months there, as she recovers from her physical injuries as well as the emotional trauma of losing her baby, she describes as "darker than any period I have ever known" (130). At first even what she calls "the do-gooder philosophy of the place . . . the idea of helping strangers" she finds "too earnest, too altruistic," and hence no consolation. Yet as Victoria Woburn points out, "broken hearts are sometimes mended by work" (137). This proves to be true: in this socialist environment, where staff and residents are expected to cooperate (139), Anna finds solace. Woburn House is an oasis of communality in a wilderness of individualism, and it is no surprise that some of the residents cannot handle it. As Anna observes: "You grow accustomed to looking out for yourself, to thinking only of your own welfare, and then someone tells you that you have to cooperate with a bunch of strangers" (140).

But this type of cooperation is the key to understanding the place. In practical terms Woburn House is a failure and is built, in Boris's words, "on a foundation of clouds" (154). People stay only a few days, and are then returned to deprivation. Some even mutilate or kill themselves to avoid going back. To work there, Anna says, is to accept "the utter futility of the job" (142), because there are always too many people for too few spaces. But in ethical terms Woburn House provides the main hope for civilization, because it demonstrates that it is still possible for people to pay attention to the wider community. Even if it offers only temporary respite, there is hope for humanity in the simple fact that society still exists within the walls of Woburn House. Anna begins a relationship with Victoria (158) and is then reunited with Sam (160), but the diverse collection of individuals working together is the main focus of this section of the novel. Here Anna fulfills her ambition to become part of significant "archipelagoes of matter."

Unfortunately Woburn House is doomed. The money runs out (169), Mr. Frick dies (172), an illegal burial is performed (173), and the police come to investigate (174). After a mass betrayal by the desperate residents, the police are bribed and leave (177), but when Frick's grandson Willie goes on the rampage with a gun (180), there is no choice but to close. Despite this series of disasters, Anna's letter ends on a note of optimism. She, Sam, Victoria, and Boris remain together, making plans for their escape from the city. In an ironic reworking of American myth, they are likely to head west for their new beginning (185). Throughout these preparations, Anna continues to write in the dwindling pages of her notebook, knowing that she will never really reach the end: "You might have to stop, but that is only because you have run out of time" (183). There will always be something more to say, and this is the beauty and the tragedy of literature. Anna's last words hint at words that last: "Once we get to where we are going, I will try to write to you again, I promise" (188). This is all the writer can hope for—the chance to write again.

To date *The Music of Chance* has had two incarnations. The novel, one of Auster's strangest yet most popular with critics and scholars, was published in 1990 in the United States by Viking and in the United Kingdom by Faber and Faber in 1991. Three years after the book's American release, Philip Haas directed a movie adaptation, starring Mandy Patinkin and James Spader. One of the movie's curious aspects is that the majority of the action is taken from the second half of the novel, which is, ostensibly, far less amenable to cinematic treatment, taking place as it does almost exclusively in a Pennsylvania meadow. On the surface *The Music of Chance* appears to be divided into two distinct narratives, one of freedom and one of confinement. Yet one of the strengths of the novel is the way in which it forces the reader to reconsider these apparently polar opposites to the extent that the opposition eventually collapses. Physical confinement, it suggests, does not mean imaginative confinement, just as a writer locked in a room has the freedom to create worlds. And conversely, when one considers Auster's Jewish heritage, it is clear that the wanderings of exile can represent a rootlessness that is not freedom, but entrapment in vexed questions of identity.

Just as *The New York Trilogy* acknowledges and subverts the conventions of detective fiction, so *The Music of Chance* begins as a kind of road narrative that merges the typically American imaginings of the open road with the existential musings on exile and space typical of Jewish writers. Jim Nashe embarks on a life of aimless driving after his wife leaves him and his father dies. He simply drives for the sake of it, seeing in his car freedom from the anxieties of his former life and the possibility of total disengagement in "a realm of weightlessness."[12] With his money fast disappearing, he meets Jack Pozzi, a feckless gambler who offers him the chance to make some easy cash by taking on a couple of eccentric millionaires, called Flower and Stone, in a high-stakes poker game. Things do not go according to plan, and the second half of the novel becomes a twisted prison narrative. Having lost the poker game and found themselves heavily in debt, Nashe and Pozzi have to honor their debts by constructing a monumental wall on Flower and Stone's land from ten thousand stones. Thus the novel can be understood, in Auster's words, as "a political parable about power" and "a book about walls and slavery and freedom."[13]

Formally, *The Music of Chance* differs from the majority of Auster's novels in its employment of free indirect discourse. This is a form of third-person narration that appears at key moments to enter the consciousness of the characters, which allows for ambiguity in the interaction between internal and external viewpoints. Many of the passages focusing on Nashe use this technique; for example: "how was he supposed to take care of a two-year-old child when his work kept him out of the house at all hours of the day and night?" (2). Given this "pseudo first-person" approach,[14] it is perhaps surprising that several contemporary reviewers bemoaned the lack of characterization. Robert

Nye, in the *Guardian,* writes that "as with other Auster heroes the fellow is more or less a cipher, a compendium of floating symbols, a sum of all the books that he (and his author) has read." Pozzi, the first of Auster's attempts at a more vernacular voice, engages in monologues described by Madison Smartt Bell in the *New York Times* as "shakily, inconsistently written."[15]

Octavio Roca, writing in the *Washington Times,* is more complimentary, lauding the novel's "crystalline wit" and prose that manages to remain "fast and enjoyable . . . despite or because of his philosophical and literary intentions." Matthew Gilbert in the *Boston Globe* says that it "suffers slightly from the anarchic aimlessness that is one of its themes." Yet he concludes that Auster is "a writer unafraid of intensity, eager to enlarge his clever novels with universal questions."[16]

What are these "universal questions"? As the title would suggest, one of the most important is the relationship between order and chance. One traditionally thinks of music as emerging, for all its beauty, from more or less strict scales and harmonic possibilities. Even improvised music tends to adhere to certain patterns. So to combine "music" and "chance"—that which is unbound by structure—is obviously paradoxical, a kind of "ordered disorderedness," according to Tim Woods.[17] Yet the novel explores the idea that chance almost seems to attain a sort of logic all its own simply by being so dominant.

From the very first page this tension between structure and chance is evident. Nashe's encounter with Jack Pozzi is "one of those random, accidental encounters that seem to materialize out of thin air" (1). Having said this, however, the narrator then tells us: "It all came down to a question of sequence, the order of events. If it had not taken the lawyer six months to find him, he never would have been on the road the day he met Jack Pozzi, and therefore none of the things that followed from that meeting would have happened" (1–2). Nashe recognizes the role of chance, but then proceeds to establish a causal chain of events, so that the chance meeting ends up feeling inevitable or fated. This is partly, perhaps, an effect of hindsight: it is always possible, or even desirable, to tidy up one's experience after the event. But it nonetheless reveals a tension that assumes far greater importance as the narrative progresses, and is to some extent played out in the contrasting attitudes of Nashe and Pozzi to their incarceration. Whereas Pozzi tends to view the universe as structured, musical, ruled by a "fundamental law" of harmony (138), Nashe at least tries to acknowledge the power of randomness. For him, talk of "God or luck or harmony" as something systematic is simply "a way of avoiding the facts" (139). This view, valid though it is, is constantly put under pressure by the strange events of the narrative.

Just as it did for Auster himself, chance intrudes on Nashe's life in the form of a surprise inheritance. Shortly after his wife, Thérèse, walks out on him and he sends his daughter Juliette to live with her aunt in Minnesota, he discovers that his father has died and left him "a colossal sum—close to two hundred thousand dollars" (2). In fact the money is "so extraordinary to him, so monumental in its consequences," that it brings about an equally unexpected reaction (3). Nashe pays off his debts, buys a gleaming Saab 900, and impulsively leaves Boston for Minnesota, hoping to reignite the relationship with his daughter. Typically for the Auster protagonist, however, he soon finds himself in less-than-splendid isolation: Juliette has "forgotten who he was," and he has become one of Auster's living ghosts, merely "a vaporous collection of sounds" on the end of a telephone (4).

With all immediate familial ties effectively broken, Nashe then succumbs to the lure of chance and does "something crazy" (5). He gets into his car, intending to return to Massachusetts, but misses the ramp to the freeway. Instead of getting "back on course," he "impulsively [goes] up the next ramp, knowing full well that he [has] just committed himself to the wrong road." It is "a sudden, unpremeditated decision," but in the end, Nashe decides, there is "no difference" (6). Rather than being fatalistic, he accepts the cards chance deals, and with such an attitude it is true that nothing really matters. There is an almost Zen-like philosophy at work here, similar to Ray Smith's epiphany in Jack Kerouac's *The Dharma Bums:* "It's all the same thing."[18]

At this point *The Music of Chance,* as Bernd Herzogenrath makes clear, becomes a road narrative in the tradition of Kerouac's *On the Road* (1957). Herzogenrath is also right to observe that Nashe's days of aimless driving embody "the uncanny relation between the dream of freedom and the nightmare of oppression."[19] Taking the wrong ramp and driving for "seven straight hours," Nashe considers it "a dizzying prospect—to imagine all that freedom, to understand how little it mattered what choice he made" (6). The very next day, however, as he continues his road trip, he feels "no longer in control" and in the grip "of some baffling, overpowering force" (6–7). Once again paradox asserts itself: the very freedom he pursues has become a means of control and compulsion. Yet he is powerless to resist: in fact he has no desire to. Upon returning to Boston he decides to resign from his job with the fire department, "the only job that had ever meant anything to him," to "throw it away on the strength of an impulse" (8). Moreover he continues the process of removing himself from significant relationships by conducting a "mass burial" of Thérèse's possessions (10). Feeling strangely enriched, "as if the farther he took himself away from the person he had been, the better off he would be in the future" (10), he finishes his purge by selling his piano, representative of music and therefore order. He is now ready for the visceral thrill of his random journeys: "He just walked out, climbed into his car, and was gone" (11).

Without "any definite plan," Nashe is far less concerned with destinations than with movement in and of itself (11). Movement represents for Nashe willful abandonment and solipsistic withdrawal from the external world: "Nothing around him lasted for more than a moment, and as one moment followed another, it was as though he alone continued to exist. He was a fixed point in a whirl of changes, a body poised in utter stillness as the world rushed through him and disappeared" (11–12). He craves the ultimate escape from himself and from his troubling memories (12). (At key moments in the narrative, such as his arrival at Flower and Stone's mansion, Nashe experiences this "almost imperceptible feeling of dizziness" [65], the feeling that he has abdicated responsibility for all actions.) To settle anywhere other than in the virtual reality of his car would require him, as he sees it, to engage in the complicated network of human interactions and would thus impinge on his newfound freedom. What he does not realize at this stage is that he is not truly free to be himself without these relations. He is in fact in a state of self-imposed entrapment and exile.

This state is emphasized when he bumps into, again "purely by chance" (14), his old friend Fiona Wells in a Berkeley bookshop. Their "fluke encounter [calls] for an extravagant response, a spirit of anarchy and celebration" (15), and the explosive romantic relationship that follows seems destined to allow Nashe a meaningful return to the world. He is even tempted to ask

Fiona to marry him. Yet his inexplicable insistence on punctuating their relationship with extended periods of driving destroys everything. Using the language of business and finance (one of many hints at an increasingly important aspect of the novel), she declares, "I can't count on you, Jim," before returning to her ex-boyfriend (18).

Resigned to "a dull, indeterminate sadness" (18), Nashe finds himself driving merely for want of anything better to do. He also finds himself in the grip of another paradox: "The money was responsible for his freedom, but each time he used it to buy another portion of that freedom, he was denying himself an equal portion of it as well. The money kept him going, but it was also an engine of loss, inexorably leading him back to the place where he had begun" (17). Several critics, notably Eyal Dotan, have remarked on the novel's underlying critique of capitalism,[20] and in Nashe's paradox one sees a vivid illustration. Money promises freedom—the freedom to consume, and also the freedom to follow the unexpected opportunities chance throws up—but forces the user to play by its rules, creating specific consumerist desires and provoking a kind of enslavement. Having money only necessitates the getting of more money. The logical endpoint is the collapse into scavenging witnessed in Anna Blume's city.

Given that gambling is a "symptom of late capitalism,"[21] an allegory of financial market speculation, and an activity in which rules and chance combine, it is no surprise that Nashe turns to gambling in order to arrest his slide into poverty. Having blown thousands of dollars on the horses (19), he meets, by chance (or is it fate?), the battered figure of self-proclaimed hotshot poker player Jack Pozzi (20). Just to make the link between gambling and the markets more explicit, Pozzi tells Nashe that he received his beating after a poker game with "the rich boys from New York who play for a little weekend excitement. Lawyers, stockbrokers, corporate hot shots. . . . Solid Republicans, with their Wall Street jokes and goddam dry martinis" (25). Nashe's decision to stump up ten thousand dollars for Pozzi's next big poker game at the home of two eccentric millionaires is really just another gamble disguised as a "business partnership" (33). And Pozzi, with typically raw insight, recognizes this, calling his companion both "a venture capitalist" (33) and "a regular soldier of fortune" (62). He is both of these things, and also a surrogate father figure, a temporary replacement for Pozzi's own errant father, who spent time in jail for "selling stocks in a dummy corporation" (43–44). Nashe's sudden injection of cash into Pozzi's life echoes Nashe's own inheritance. What connects *all* the characters in *The Music of Chance,* at least initially, is a series of financial speculations and cash deals. It is no accident that Nashe and Pozzi's relationship only truly becomes a friendship when they are penniless and working together in the meadow. The implication is that money only alienates.

Flower and Stone, the reclusive millionaires, are no exception to this rule. Their fabulous wealth derives from the ultimate game of chance—the lottery. Yet in keeping with the novel's underlying tension between chance and fate, they are reluctant to attribute their winnings entirely to luck. Flower explains to Nashe and Pozzi that "seven years ago this October fourth, Willie and I punched out the holes a little more deliberately than usual. I can't say why that was, but for some reason we actually discussed the numbers we were going to pick." Their deliberation is based on the idea that "each number has a personality of its own. . . . Numbers have souls, and you can't help but get involved with them in a personal way" (73). In choosing prime numbers, "numbers that refuse to cooperate, that don't change or divide, numbers that remain themselves" (73–74), Flower and Stone act out a fantasy of control or agency. They believe that by carefully considering their choices, and by choosing numbers with supposedly strong, independent identities, they can influence chance itself. Their subsequent financial success with commodities, bonds, and real estate convinces them that they have power over the universe (75). Just as the winning numbers acted as "the key to the gates of heaven" (74), so the rapid increase in their wealth makes them feel "as though God has singled us out from other men." Flower even declares, "I feel that we've become immortal" (75). Rather than the workings of chance, then, Flower and Stone credit divine design for their success, a divine design that has in turn made them divine.

As soon as the reader enters the Pennsylvania mansion there is a palpable change of atmosphere. Although order and chance are still the dominant ideas, the emphasis shifts. From the ostensible freedom of the road, we have now entered a claustrophobic realm of surveillance, containment, and control in which Flower and Stone's megalomaniac musings on their lottery win are only the beginning of a nightmare fantasy of power. What is played out in the ensuing action is essentially a theological debate between predestination and free will, and nowhere is this better symbolized than in the City of the World model.

This "miniature scale-model rendering of a city," dotted with "microscopic human figures" (79), is Stone's pet project, and he and Flower proudly lecture Nashe and Pozzi on it during their tour of the house. Despite Flower's assertion that it is "an artistic vision of mankind" (79), the City of the World, for all its skillful construction, is less about artistry than about the politics of power. It is one man's attempt to play God, to take control of time and space and to eradicate chance and individual free will altogether through meticulous construction. As Stone puts it: "It's the way I'd like the world to look. Everything in it happens at once" (79): thus everything that happens to the inhabitants is predestined from the start. Mark Brown correctly observes that Stone's city resembles Anna Blume's in being a "negative utopia."[22] However, the difference is that Anna's city is characterized by fragmentation, whereas Stone's relies on enforced cohesion. Stone uses "the Hall of Justice, the Library, the Bank, and the Prison" as means of policing society and denying agency or free choice. These "Four Realms of Togetherness" maintain "the harmony of the city" (80) at the expense of meaningful social interaction. Each miniature figure is destined to stand alone, arrested in time, unable to develop or reach out to others, and always under the gaze of the ultimate authority figure, Stone himself. Considering Auster's evident interest in capital and enslavement, it is notable that the bank and the prison sit side by side. Upon closer observation, Nashe sees in the figures of smiling, grateful prisoners something sinister and, perhaps, a premonition of his situation after the disastrous poker game: "A threat of punishment seemed to hang in the air—as if this were a city at war with itself, struggling to mend its ways before the prophets came to announce the arrival of a murderous, avenging God" (96).

Stone's desire to build "a separate model of this room" (80) reveals another allegorical aspect of his project. To make this miniature room would require "a second city to fit inside the room within the room" or, as Nashe says, "a model of the model" (80–81). Auster is wryly mimicking his own aesthetic practice, which is, frequently, to embed stories within stories—for of course Stone would theoretically have to build an infinite number of ever smaller models-within-models, just as the process of narrative embedding is theoretically endless. And there is another, more serious point to be made about the connection between Stone's city and the novel. Although Auster wants his fiction to convey the importance of chance, and even if he plays with authority by occasionally including himself as a character, he is also aware that writing a novel is a creative act every bit as megalomaniacal as Stone's city. An author can create and destroy whole lives, just as Stone has done, and oversees his or her created world like a divine authority. Throughout his fiction, particularly *The Music of Chance, Leviathan,* and *Oracle Night,* Auster signals his awareness of this potential danger. The hope for the writer is always that "the reader and the writer make the book together,"[23] that the different interpretations readers bring to the text make the process of producing meaning more collective and less author-centered.

If Stone's model embodies some of the novel's big ideas about power, freedom, and free will, then Flower's collection of "historical memorabilia" (82), the next stage of Nashe and Pozzi's house tour, signals another of the big issues: the United States' ambiguous relationship with the past. Flower considers himself "an antiquarian" who likes to surround himself "with tangible remnants of the past" (82). With characteristic use of cliché, he believes that in contrast with "our cousins on the other side of the pond," Americans "are always tearing down what we build, destroying the past in order to start over again, rushing headlong into the future" (84). In a nation founded on myths of regeneration and new beginnings, there is some truth in this: Auster himself has said: "we're in a country without a long past, a place in which most people have obliterated their connection to the past" (AH 337).

The real problem, Nashe recognizes, lies in Flower's idiosyncratic response. His collection of objects, which includes "a pearl earring worn by Sir Walter Raleigh" and "General McClellan's field glasses," is merely "a monument to trivia" (83). Most important, it does not have the effect Flower intends—the reclamation and celebration of the past. Nashe's thoughts on this are eloquent: "Flower's museum was a graveyard of shadows, a demented shrine to the spirit of nothingness. If those objects continued to call out to him, Nashe decided, it was because they were impenetrable, because they refused to divulge anything about themselves. It had nothing to do with history, nothing to do with the men who had once owned them. The fascination was simply for the objects as material things, and the way they had been wrenched out of any possible context" (84). In the end, these disembodied objects, the authenticity of which is impossible to verify, have about as much true connection to the past as does the Eiffel Tower in Las Vegas or the rebuilding of the London Bridge in Lake Havasu, Arizona, in 1971. In imagining Flower's collection, Auster is satirizing the tawdry appropriation of past culture for tourists symbolized by such landmarks.

All the novel's big issues come together in the image of the wall, which dominates the second half of the novel. The ten thousand stones that are to make up the wall used to belong to "a fifteenth-century castle" in Ireland, which Flower and Stone, after haggling with the owner, bought and had transported to Pennsylvania (85). In this respect they represent another example of the crude appropriation of the European past. Where they differ from the London Bridge in Lake Havasu is in the fact that the millionaires do not want faithfully to reassemble the castle, but instead to build a wall that will serve, in the words of Flower, as "some enormous barrier against time" and "a memorial to itself" (86). The key word here is "barrier." From Auster's earliest poetry, through the one-act plays that were the direct precursors of *The Music of Chance*,[24] and into the novels, walls (and in Anna Blume's city, barricades made of trash) have figured as powerful symbols of isolation and separation—the separation of one person from another, the individual from an objective understanding of the world, and the individual from language. Stones carry many meanings, therefore. They are meaning itself; they are the impenetrable heart of human identity; they are words; and in this case, given that the ten thousand stones equal the ten thousand dollars lost in the poker game, they reinforce how money isolates and enslaves. Indeed earlier in the novel Pozzi explains how the gambler needs "to build a wall" around himself "and not let anyone in" (63).

However, just as the freedom of the road becomes an ironic imprisonment for Nashe, so he cannot bring himself, initially at least, to view his new situation wholly as punishment. For Pozzi, the payment of their gambling debt through construction of the wall "sounds like a goddam chain gang," but to Nashe it is "a cure, a one-way journey back to earth" (110); he even senses that "he [has] already won back a measure of his freedom" (116). His life now has a goal, a purpose, and the monotony of his labor actually has a kind of dignity to it. Even Nashe's and Pozzi's bovine supervisor, Calvin Murks, waxes lyrical on the job's virtues, in words that recall Anna Blume's "I put one foot in front of the other" comments: "You put down a stone, and something happens. You put down another stone, and something more happens. There's no big mystery to it. You can see the wall going up, and after a while it starts to give you a good feeling" (148). Seen in this way, and for all its negative associations, the building of the wall offers the same satisfactions as the writing of a narrative. This may be one of the reasons Nashe warms to his task: his driving was aimless, whereas here a story is unfolding, stone by stone, with a conclusion in sight.

But Murks is wrong to assert that there's no mystery. In fact he is "a being as insubstantial as a shadow" (209), the embodiment of the mysterious air of threat hanging over the meadow and of the power relations at work. He has "the smugness of someone content with his place in the hierarchy, and as with most of the sergeants and crew chiefs of this world, his loyalties [are] firmly on the side of the people who [tell] him what to do" (129). In this case those people are Flower and Stone, the men who won the poker game and drew up the contracts for the wall job. But from the moment Murks greets Nashe and Pozzi on the first morning, we never see the millionaires again. The foreman's name provides clues to what is happening. "Calvin" connotes a punitive, Puritan deity, one whose decisions are arbitrary and whose authority cannot be challenged.[25] "Murks" reminds readers that the operations of this unseen God—who has people's lives mapped out from birth and hence is always one step ahead of them—will forever remain inscrutable.

This is precisely the bind in which Nashe and Pozzi find themselves. Working through their emissary Murks, the absent millionaires do indeed seem to be one step ahead at every critical juncture. Every decision the workers make is anticipated beforehand. For example, when Nashe and Pozzi, having cleared the original debt, decide to work on for a few more days to earn some proper money, Murks appears with a contract already drawn up. Whether or not "the trailer has been bugged," the eerie atmosphere of surveillance and predestination is only heightened by Flower's and Stone's apparent telepathy (151). More sinister still,

Pozzi's escape attempt is foiled almost immediately: he leaves under cover of darkness one night, only for his "pulverised" body to appear in the meadow the next morning, as if somebody knew he was intending to escape (171). Nashe never finds out who attacked Pozzi, and once Murks has taken Pozzi to the hospital, Nashe never sees his friend again.

Such events appear to support Pozzi's belief in "a fundamental law" of existence (138). Indeed Pozzi attributes their misfortune to Nashe's decision to take a walk while the poker game was in full swing, during which he snatched the figures of Flower and Stone from the City of the World model on yet another random impulse (97). In Pozzi's words: "We'd come to the point where everything was turning into music for us, and then you have to go upstairs and smash all the instruments. You tampered with the universe, my friend, and once a man does that, he's got to pay the price" (138). What the wall-building narrative really demonstrates, however, is not some delicate universal harmony, but the exercises and abuses of brute power. Whether or not, as Nashe comes to believe, Murks and his grandson Floyd are responsible for Pozzi's hospitalization (176), the fact that Murks has started wearing a gun to work after Pozzi attacked him proves something definitive: "Murks felt he had a right to carry it—and that he had felt that right from the very beginning. Freedom, therefore, had never been an issue. Contracts, handshakes, goodwill—none of that had meant a thing. All along, Nashe and Pozzi had been working under the threat of violence" (144). It is true that Nashe is being paid, but the allegorical implications are clearer than ever. This is tantamount to a labor camp, and the wall itself begins to resemble not so much the Western Wall in Jerusalem, but more the oppressive symbolism of the Berlin Wall, or Kafka's "Great Wall of China," whose function is purely to divide, to create a milieu of fear and suspicion, and to keep those in authority mysterious and unassailable.[26]

Realizing the truth, Nashe finds himself in another bind. From a personal point of view, he has regarded the work as redemptive, as a way of atoning for his past sins and making himself free (147). He even recognizes the narrative qualities of the construction: his record of the stones added each day becomes "a journal, a logbook in which the numbers stood for his most intimate thoughts" (203). Yet what made the work redemptive was the burgeoning friendship with Pozzi, which jolted Nashe from his isolation. With Pozzi gone (and Nashe admits to himself how much he misses "the kid" [205]) he can gain no consolation from the work because there is no free will involved. What appears to make him free—the labor—is the very thing that maintains the hierarchy, keeping the rich in power and the poor subservient.

The novel ends highly ambiguously. On his birthday Nashe brings himself "back to zero" and, technically, "wins back his freedom." His intention is to stay on, however, and "earn some traveling money" (204). It is significant that the reader never sees the conclusion of the work. With the little surprises Flower and Stone keep springing, such as the sudden revelation that food and entertainments are not gratis (163), there is no guarantee that Nashe will ever be free. Craving a change of scene, he agrees to go out for a drink with Murks and Floyd (206). After thrashing Floyd at pool and, symbolically, refusing to take his winnings (213), Nashe asks if he can drive them all home in Murks's car (which is in fact Nashe's old Saab, given to Murks by Flower and Stone after the poker game). Feeling strangely "happier than he had been in a long time" (214), he drives through the snow, imagining it covering the land in "an avalanche of whiteness" symbolic of new beginnings (215). Yet this is the end. Nashe, lost in private reverie, keeps accelerating until, in the novel's climactic scene, he hurtles toward the headlights of another vehicle and certain death (216).

What has happened here? The headlights might symbolize the light of heaven, but if the previous action has demonstrated anything, it is that, as Aliki Varvogli notes, abstract ideas such as free will, God, and fate are inextricably bound up in material concerns.[27] In other words, money is the only god of any real importance. Nashe at this point has nothing and, despite his dreams of new beginnings, is doomed to return to the meadow and resume his place in the capitalist order. Perhaps that is why death is the better option.

A postscript—in an interview Auster says, "The very day I finished writing *The Music of Chance* . . . the Berlin wall came down. There's no conclusion to be drawn from this, but every time I think of it, I start to shake" (AH 294). The only conclusion that might be drawn is that chance still rules, and that is something that no ideological system—capitalist, religious, or otherwise—can control.

CHAPTER FIVE

Auster's Frontier Novels
Moon Palace and *Mr. Vertigo*

If *In the Country of Last Things* and *The Music of Chance* deal with symbolic frontiers—between past and present, between self and other—*Moon Palace* (1989) and *Mr. Vertigo* (1994) concern themselves much more with the frontier as a specifically American mythological and ideological idea. Since Frederick Jackson Turner delivered his lecture "The Significance of the Frontier in American History" in 1893, it has been, for both the critics and artists who have embraced Turner's assertions and those who have rejected them, central to discussions of an evolving U.S. identity.

The Frontier and the West

From James Fenimore Cooper's novels to the Coen brothers' 2006 movie adaptation of Cormac McCarthy's *No Country for Old Men,* the frontier has endured as an abundant source of iconic images: wild landscapes; rugged Wild West heroes; encounters with Native Americans; ramshackle, improvised settlements. Whether or not these images bear any relation to historical reality has been consistently open to debate, and Paul Auster's "frontier" novels expressly deal with the tension between history and mythology, reality and representation.

Turner's thesis is at heart straightforward and is summed up in an often-quoted statement: "The existence of an area of free land, its continuous recession, and the advance of American settlement westward, explain American development."[1] In other words, people became progressively more "American" as they moved westward from the Atlantic coast, dubbed by Turner "the frontier of Europe," and into the wilderness expanses of the continent.[2] The harshness of the wilderness promotes a rugged individualism. Ironically, this individualism is conducive to a form of democracy resistant "to any direct control,"[3] such as local government, and is instrumental in character formation. Turner continues: "The wilderness masters the colonist. It finds him a European in dress, industries, tools, modes of travel, and thought. It takes him from the railroad car and puts him in the birch canoe. It strips off the garments of civilization and arrays him in the hunting shirt and the moccasin. It puts him in the log cabin of the Cherokee and Iroquois and runs an Indian palisade around him. Before long he has gone to planting Indian corn and plowing with a sharp stick; he shouts the war cry and takes the scalp in orthodox Indian fashion."[4]

Such a romantic conception provides clues to the problems with Turner's thesis, which in the last few decades have attracted much critical attention. In celebrating the "exceptional" character engendered by the wilderness—coarse yet acute, inventive, family-oriented—Turner borrows the iconography of the Native Americans while coyly hiding their supplanting from land that may never in fact have been "free" in the first place. The frontier is very deliberately described as "the meeting point between savagery and civilization" to set up a strict opposition between the white (male) settler and the "savage."[5] In so doing, a linear and triumphalist conception of American history emerges, with white settlement systematically replacing the Native American past, even as it romanticizes that past for its own purposes.

In recent years new Western historians such as Patricia Nelson Limerick and Brian W. Dippie have sought to reappraise frontier mythology and promote "a more balanced view of the western past."[6] Proceeding from the assumption that each generation interprets history in new ways, these historians revisualize and indeed remap the frontier to include "failure as well as success; defeat as well as victory . . . ; women as well as men; varied ethnic groups and their differing perspectives as well as white Anglo-Saxon Protestants; an environment that is limiting, interactive, and sometimes ruined as well as mastered and made to bloom . . . ; and, finally, a regional identity as well as a frontier ethic."[7] "The West," envisaged in this way, becomes a series of diverse regions, races, and cultures interacting in complex ways.

Auster has long had an interest in addressing and redressing stereotypical conceptions of the West, of settlers and "savages." In an early unpublished piece called "The Surveyor's Letter," he describes the meeting between the surveyor narrator and a Native American tribe who have until this meeting remained completely undiscovered by whites. A parody of the Indian captivity narratives that were popular in the late seventeenth and early eighteenth centuries, it aims, through the character of the tribal chief, to overturn preconceptions. This chief is no savage: he studied at Columbia and Harvard, passing himself off as "an Indian of the Asiatic variety."[8] He has the air "of a sophisticated, slightly bored English nobleman, perhaps a baronet," who takes "a dilettantish, fugitive interest in the finer questions of art and literature."[9] What is more, he recognizes that whites need the image of the savage to bolster their own fragile sense of power, declaring to the surveyor: "we have lived in your heart, unseen, since the beginning of time!"[10] Finally, he proposes—and this is an idea reprised in *Moon Palace*—that the persecution of Native

Americans stems from Christopher Columbus's original mistake. The term "Indian," he remarks, is "entirely without basis in fact," and subsequent tragedies sprang from Columbus's "failure to name things as he saw them."[11] In other words, Columbus was an American Adam gone wrong,[12] and his misnaming was a version of the fall of man. "The Surveyor's Letter" is rather heavy-handed, but it touches on ideas developed in later novels.

Moon Palace and *Mr. Vertigo,* while evidently fascinated with the more traditional elements of frontier mythology, also participate in their reappraisal by focusing on, among other things, Native American subjugation, the romanticization of the West in art, and the political need constantly to be conquering new frontiers. In *Moon Palace* the new frontiers are space and Vietnam. In *Mr. Vertigo,* more fantastically, a boy who can fly breaches the frontier between land and sky.

Moon Palace

Readers of *Moon Palace,* published in 1989 by Viking in the United States and by Faber and Faber in the United Kingdom, would already have been familiar with Auster's penchant for outlandish incidents and outrageous coincidences. Starting with the chance meetings described in "The Book of Memory," such unlikely occurrences frequently propel the narrative forward, while reminding the reader of chance's centrality. *Moon Palace* goes farther: with its tales of incredible adventures in the Wild West and freakish chance rediscoveries of long-lost fathers and grandfathers, it is a novel that, in the words of one reviewer, "courts disaster in its dedication to the unconventional and extreme."[13] Though critics such as Joyce Reiser Kornblatt in the *New York Times* argue that the exuberance and "heartfelt" emotion of the characters redeem the novel's "unbelievable" plot, "its obvious architecture, [and] its shameless borrowings," others are less forgiving. To Gary Indiana, writing in the *Village Voice, Moon Palace* feels "fake, overly contrived, etiolated, and borrowed."[14]

One way of understanding and justifying the apparent contrivance is to see it as *deliberately* over-the-top, to the point where it becomes "a kind of metafictional, postmodern counterpractice."[15] In other words, it becomes fiction about making fiction and draws the reader's attention to the self-consciousness of the process. This view makes particular sense in light of Auster's treatment of the frontier and the Wild West. As the protagonist, Marco Stanley Fogg, travels west to Utah, into a landscape "too massive to be painted or drawn" (157), and follows in the footsteps of his grandfather Thomas Effing, the novel consistently implies the same questions. Can the United States' foundational mythologies actually be believed? Is Turner's frontier thesis not simply a kind of tall tale? And when confronted with the vastness of the American landscape, something beyond easy representation, how can the artist fail to exaggerate? *Moon Palace* can therefore be understood as participating in a long tradition of tall tales, the prime exponent of which is the nineteenth-century writer and satirist Mark Twain. His 1872 work *Roughing It* narrates a series of adventures out West: in fact the farther west the protagonist travels, the more outlandish the stories become. Twain's book, like *Moon Palace,* implies that the frontier and the West refer both to geographical spaces and to romantic conceptions of heroism, struggle, and progress. One should not be surprised, then, that one of the few recognizable coordinates in the Utah desert where Marco Stanley Fogg and his father, Solomon Barber, begin their search for Thomas Effing's cave is a town called Bluff (287). The name of this town encapsulates the underlying tension between fact and fantasy in all frontier accounts.

The many tall tales achieve unity within the novel's overarching genre. *Moon Palace* can be called a coming-of-age story or bildungsroman, a novel charting the development of an individual within a defined social order. Famous examples of the bildungsroman include Charles Dickens's *David Copperfield* (to which Auster has explicitly compared his novel [AH 285]), *The Adventures of Augie March* by Saul Bellow, and J. K. Rowling's *Harry Potter* series. Such novels chart the growth of a young protagonist who has to overcome trials and hardship on the way to maturity. Whether the journey undertaken is real, spiritual, or a combination of both, the genre typically presents an argument between individuality and conformity, such that the protagonist has to find both his or her identity and a place in society. Frontier environments are particularly amenable to the bildungsroman, first because there is the same tension between individualism and the need to forge a surviving community. Second, they are very often characterized by the physical and mental struggle necessary for a protagonist's development. And finally, they work allegorically. Turner saw American identity forged at the frontier, and a text like *Moon Palace* is therefore not just about Marco Stanley Fogg's coming-of-age, it is also about America's coming-of-age during a pivotal historical period starting in the late 1960s. Marco looks for himself and for his country, and, as Aliki Varvogli says, "the two quests are often hard to tell apart."[16]

This is made very clear by the first line: "It was the summer that men first walked on the moon" (1). Marco's voyages of discovery coincide with America's, but there is a darker side to the nation's crossing of frontiers. The triumphalism of the Apollo mission is balanced with the war in Vietnam and political protest: "By the spring of 1968, every day seemed to retch forth a new cataclysm. If it wasn't Prague, it was Berlin; if it wasn't Paris, it was New York. There were half a million soldiers in Vietnam" (25). Against the backdrop of these historical events, the first part of the novel reads like a traditional bildungsroman, describing the teenage orphan's early hardships and calling on many familiar Auster ideas. We hear of the mysteriously absent father about whom Marco's mother would never speak (4); the death of his mother, after which, in a little joke at the expense of Auster's influences, he cries "like some pathetic orphan hero in a nineteenth-century novel" (5). The multiple possibilities of his name are explained—"Stanley" and Livingstone, Phileas Fogg, and "M. S." for "manuscript," signifying the writing of one's life (6–7).

Mostly we learn about Marco's eccentric uncle Victor, a musician and dreamer who is part father figure and part friend (6). Just before Marco leaves for university in New York, Victor heads out on the road with his band, The Moon Men. His description of the coming adventure provides a taste of things to come: "We'll be setting a westerly course, plunging into the wilderness. . . . A bunch of city slickers in the land of cowboys and Indians. . . . Who knows if some new truth will not be revealed to me out there?" (12). His self-conscious mythologizing sets a pattern for the novel, as all the main characters eventually travel west in a bid to find truth or wisdom. However, Victor's experiences also expose the grim economic realities behind the myth. The band splits up; he sells his clarinet and ends up broke. Marco tries to contact him, but hears nothing more until news of Victor's death comes through. "I imagined all the things that can happen to a man between Boise and New

York," Marco says, "and suddenly the American continent was transformed into a vast danger zone, a perilous nightmare of traps and mazes" (18). These two versions of the West—the grand mythological West where dreams are made versus the harsh landscape where dreams are shattered—compete throughout *Moon Palace*.

Posing as an "intellectual" while wearing his uncle's tweed suit "for sentimental reasons" (15, 16), Marco goes through college in a haze of pretentiousness and grief. His increasing isolation and irrationality are revealed when he moves into a studio apartment in Manhattan during the vacation (16). Through a gap between two buildings, he spies "a neon sign, a vivid torch of pink and blue letters that [spell] out the words MOON PALACE." In reality, it is just a Chinese restaurant sign (though one that assumes greater significance as the story progresses), but Marco regards it as "magic" and "a message from the sky itself." He thinks of Uncle Victor, and "in that first, irrational moment" feels better. "A bare and grubby room had been transformed into a site of inwardness," he says, "an intersection point of strange omens and mysterious, arbitrary events. . . . I understood that I had come to the right place" (17). Marco's room clearly reflects his state of mind, and he has made a mistake common to many Auster characters: he has started to believe in fate and look for signs in the air.

Withdrawal followed by oblivion is the fate he envisages. Through a combination of excessive drinking and Victor's funeral expenses, he finds himself, like Daniel Quinn and Jim Nashe, having to eke out an existence with his money fast disappearing. It is symptomatic of his "despair" that rather than doing anything about the situation, he opts for "a militant refusal to take any action at all," an approach he regards as "nihilism raised to the level of an aesthetic proposition" (20–21). Like many Auster characters—for example, Maria Turner in *Leviathan* and Hector Mann in *The Book of Illusions*—Marco attempts to turn his life into art. His error, however, is to make this attempt away from the eyes of others, in total isolation. One's life cannot truly be art without an audience. This is why the aesthetic is intrinsically ethical in Auster's world, because it always involves sympathies and interactions between people.

Reading should be an ethical act, as "The Book of Memory" demonstrates. When Marco begins working his way through the boxes of books left by Uncle Victor, redemption, or at least escape from "inevitable" demise, seems likely (21). However, Marco chooses to view these books as part of his fated oblivion rather than as a way out of isolation. He has been using the boxes as furniture, and now, as he opens each box, he can watch his room empty out and himself "disappear." Reading contributes only to the "gathering zero" of his life (24). Moreover he refuses to make the necessary aesthetic judgments about these texts (21), preferring to regard them as a "debt" to be paid off to his uncle. Each time he finishes a box, then, he takes the contents to Chandler's Bookstore and "converts the books into cash" (23). So, even if Marco correctly equates reading with exploration, "following the route of an explorer from long ago, duplicating his steps as he thrashed out into virgin territory, moving westward with the sun" (22), his reading marathon turns out to be an economic project rather than an aesthetic or ethical one.

Marco's physical deprivations become more intense and his isolation more pronounced. On the day of the moon landing, he sells the last books. This is a symbolic moment in several ways. First, the connection between the myth of the American Adam and space exploration is again made explicit when Marco declares, "since the day he was expelled from Paradise, Adam had never been this far from home" (31). Second, the final emptying out of his room suggests that Marco himself has crossed a symbolic frontier into a new psychological realm akin to insanity. His delirious ruminations on the "Moon Palace" sign suggest that his private madness can be equated with the madness of American history and myth. Sparking "clusters of wild associations," the sign leads him to think about "Uncle Victor and China, rocket ships and music, Marco Polo and the American West . . . the parallels between Columbus and the astronauts. The discovery of America as a failure to reach China" (32). Although, momentarily, Marco senses in "these secret correspondences . . . some fundamental truth about the world" (33), they really reveal how mixed up it all is. America was discovered by mistake, and Auster implies that no matter how powerful and inspiring they might be, the myths underpinning U.S. identity are based on misconceptions, falsehoods, and arbitrary connections between random ideas.

One could argue that the somewhat confused imagery Auster occasionally employs in the novel is there to reinforce this view. For example, when Marco first meets Kitty Wu at David Zimmer's old apartment, she is described as "a small Chinese girl of nineteen or twenty with silver bracelets on both wrists and a beaded Navaho band around her head" (36). This description brings together the Far East and the West, Asian and Native American, in one catchall exotic figure. Similarly, when Zimmer and Kitty rescue Marco from his period of vagabondism and sleeping rough in Central Park—a "sanctuary" from the dangerous streets, a parodic contemporary version of Eden, perhaps (56)—he has just had a heavily romanticized "dream of Indians" in Manhattan. Upon seeing Kitty in her headband, he calls her "Pocahontas" (70). Despite the mixed associations, this rescue by his friends is a key moment. After the customary period of exile and homelessness, when the protagonist has metaphorically "jumped off the edge" of the world, something catches him "in midair" (50). Marco calls this love, and it is the spiritual home Auster protagonists seek but do not always find.

During his convalescence, Marco successfully flunks the Vietnam draft (81), takes on some translation work for Zimmer (90), and gets together with Kitty. Connected by their common orphanhood (87), their relationship represents for Marco "some dramatic crumbling of inner walls, an earthquake in the heart of my solitude" (94). And yet there is also the suggestion that her perceived exoticism is part of the attraction: "This beautiful Chinese girl had dropped down in front of me, descending like an angel from another world. It would have been impossible not to fall in love with her" (94–95). There are warning signs here. Given that the imagery surrounding Kitty consistently mixes Oriental with Native American, Marco's desire for her otherworldliness points ahead to the novel's many examples of America's romanticized representations of both its "Indian" and its frontier past.

Marco's job as "live-in companion" (97), reader, and surrogate pair of eyes for old Thomas Effing (122–23) heralds the arrival of the novel's tallest tales and most outrageous coincidences (for instance, Effing turns out to be Marco's grandfather) and, not coincidentally, the most vivid depictions of the Wild West and the frontier. The first of these depictions is Ralph Blakelock's painting *Moonlight,* which Steven Weisenburger calls the "ideological center" of the novel.[17] Soon after announcing his intention to write his obituary (128), Effing orders Marco to visit the Brooklyn Museum to study *Moonlight* and "enter the mind of the artist" (135). What Marco does not appreciate at this point is that his assignment will specifically prepare him for an obituary taken up, to a large extent, by visions of the American West. After his initial disappointment, Marco begins to notice idiosyncratic details in the painting. To him, the sky above the Indian figures, illuminated by the moon, seems "too visible." What is more, it has "a largely greenish cast" that matches the color of the lake too exactly (138). The human figures are vaguely realized "illegible shadows" and are "dwarfed by the bigness of the scene." Yet they exist "comfortably in their surroundings, at peace with themselves and the world." Marco's conclusion is that Blakelock "hadn't been trying to represent an actual landscape," but rather the Native Americans' spiritual "connection between heaven and earth." The deliberately nonnaturalistic approach suits the depiction of "an American idyll, the world the Indians had inhabited before the white men came to destroy it." Ultimately Marco decides it is "a death song for a vanished world" (139).

Moonlight can be regarded as the ideological center because it exemplifies in visual form one of the novel's most important aphorisms: "you cannot live without establishing an equilibrium between the inner and outer" (58). In choosing to portray his subjects in the abstract, Blakelock aims to reconcile their inner states with the majesty of the landscape they inhabit. The landscape, it is suggested, is not simply a mirror of one's psyche, but must be accepted as something distinct from oneself and, in the end, unrepresentable in any objective way. To represent it "as it is" is merely to impose one's own viewpoint on it and is therefore an exercise in power and dominance rather than an expression of an emotional truth. This is why Effing dismisses the

Romantic naturalism of painters such as Thomas Moran. He sees it as an ideologically driven way of capturing an idealized West for capitalist ends: "The first painting of the Great Salt Desert, the first paintings of the canyon country in southern Utah—they were all done by Moran. Manifest Destiny! They mapped it out, they made pictures of it, they digested it into the great American profit machine" (149).[18] One could argue that *Moonlight* is equally romanticizing, but at least it attempts a different aesthetic, one not about dominance, and one that recognizes that the individual's view of nature is partly based on the individual's view of himself or herself.

This is something Effing comes to accept during his Wild West adventure, to which a considerable chunk of the novel is devoted (152–91). Living in a cave after the death of his companion, Byrne (161), Effing—or, to use his real name, Julian Barber—learns that "the true purpose of art [is] not to create beautiful objects." It is "a method of understanding, a way of penetrating the world and finding one's place in it." The landscape becomes for Effing "an equal partner" and the resultant works "raw . . . filled with violent colors and strange, unpremeditated surges of energy" (170). He stops trying to represent the unrepresentable, to show this vast landscape "as it is," and instead shows it as it feels to him. His art becomes an ethical engagement with its subject that recognizes its own limitations.

Effing's story-within-the-story, culminating in the shoot-out in the cave (180), is, as Aliki Varvogli points out, unverifiable (and is in fact dismissed as a hoax by the editors to whom Marco eventually sends it [231]). It is a tall tale of "how a man reinvented himself" in "an already much-mythologised land, the Wild West."[19] This is why the first part is narrated in Effing's own words, as if to suggest that Marco cannot quite bring himself to believe what he hears. The second part shifts to the third person, hinting at Marco's increasing willingness to be seduced by the extravagant absurdity. There is a serious point to this. History is no more "how it was" than a painting is "how it is." Though they have come to be accepted as integral to U.S. identity, national stories involving the frontier and the Wild West reflect personal anxieties and obsessions, and develop from self-mythologizing and self-aggrandizing impulses.

As if to reinforce this point, the last part of the novel turns into a straightforward filial drama set against a background of the traditional westward journey. After the completion of Effing's autobiography, Effing's plan to give away his money to strangers (204), the rainstorm (213), and Effing's death on exactly the day he predicted (220), Marco makes contact with Solomon Barber, Effing's son. Solomon is the living embodiment of the tall tale, "titanic in his obesity" with "a legendary quality about him" (235). His life story (237–71) contains references to his work that further reinforce the view of history as personal preoccupation. *Kepler's Blood,* "written in the sensational style of thirties pulp novels" (253), is a far-fetched tale about a white man's integration with Native Americans and his relationship with his son. With its "bare-breasted maidens" and "lascivious sexual fantasies," it is easy for Marco to dismiss it (conveniently forgetting his comments on *Moonlight*) as "pure make-believe," a picture of "prelapsarian innocence" and "noble savages" (258–59). In the end, Marco judges, it is "a complex dance of guilt and desire" about Solomon's own missing father (263). Moreover Barber's later scholarship on Native American civilizations covers similar territory. Though "scrupulous and professional," it reveals "a personal motive" and "a secret conviction that he was somehow digging into the mysteries of his own life" (263).

One of the potential problems with *Moon Palace* is that despite Auster's obvious understanding that history tends to equal personal preoccupation, it is never clear whether he regards this as a negative thing or envisages a preferable way of understanding history. All the key elements that remind us of the arbitrariness of U.S. mythology are abandoned, and the reader is left with the white boy and his father playing out their own "dance of guilt and desire." Kitty, most disappointingly, exits the narrative after she and Marco fail to agree over an abortion (282). Soon after, during their journey out West to find Effing's cave, Marco discovers that Solomon is his father (292), only for the father to reach an absurd end when he falls into Emily Fogg's grave and breaks his back (293). This anticlimax is rapidly followed by another. Marco travels to Bluff, only to find that Effing's cave is no longer there, the plain having been flooded two years earlier (304). Then his car and his money are stolen, and he starts a long, lonely walk to the West Coast (305).

This use of bathos is important, as it deflates the self-aggrandizing associated with western legends. It also reveals a curious ambiguity about the frontier and the Wild West. As Edwin Fussell observes, these notions suffer from "double vision." In Turner's thesis, they represent the transition from "Old World to New, reality to beatitude," and hence the future.[20] Yet to travel out West is also to revisit the past. America, as the novel shows, consistently breaches new frontiers such as outer space, but in so doing retreads the same mythological ground, so that it is unclear whether such expeditions are progressive or regressive. Marco, too, ends up walking the westward trail so many have walked before, in the footsteps of his grandfather. When he arrives at the Pacific and the moon rises (307), it symbolizes new beginnings, but cannot hide the fact that *Moon Palace* has returned to a familiar father-son drama at the expense of its other historical concerns (such as Vietnam). Perhaps this is unavoidable when one writes about the frontier. It is certainly a criticism that could also be leveled at Auster's next frontier novel, *Mr. Vertigo*.

Mr. Vertigo

Moon Palace challenges foundational mythologies through its employment of tall tales; *Mr. Vertigo* goes much farther, crossing the frontier of credulity and entering the realm of fairy tales. Published by Viking and Faber and Faber in 1994, it resembles *Moon Palace* in being a bildungsroman. Like its predecessor, *Mr. Vertigo* starts out with the protagonist as an orphan living with his uncle. Once again he undergoes a series of trials in the desert. And once again the book is concerned with fathers and sons. The key differences here are that the father figure—a top-hatted Hungarian Svengali called Master Yehudi—is even more fantastical, and the orphan—Walter Rawley, aka Walt the Wonder Boy—is a scruffy urchin who learns, under Yehudi's tutelage, to fly. The novel is Walt's first-person account of his weird and wonderful life, starting with his chance encounter with the Master on the streets of St. Louis and progressing through the move out west, his arduous three-year apprenticeship, the success of the levitation show, the years of drifting, crime and revenge plots following the Master's tragic death, and the eventual decision to write these memoirs at the age of seventy-seven.

As the novel's most powerful image, levitation can be read in several ways. Auster regards it as symbolic of "a resistance to heaviness, to a certain weightiness of the previous novel [*Leviathan*]."[21] Certainly there is some validity to this assessment. Both *Mr. Vertigo* and its successor, *Timbuktu*, have a playfulness, a vernacular prose style, and a seeming reluctance explicitly to explore the darker, metaphysical ideas of previous texts like *The New York Trilogy.* None of the narrators before Walt would say something like, "I was a boogie-toed prankster, a midget scatman with a quick tongue and a hundred angles."[22] Yet the apparent levity fails to disguise the historical and political allegories at work, for this is a "rise-and-fall" story set against a specific historical background of economic expansion and growth, Prohibition, and the 1920s stock market crash. It is no coincidence that the blinding headaches and vomiting that finally put pay to Walt's levitational career coincide not only with the onset of puberty—that is, Walt's emerging adulthood—but also with the period of Yehudi's and Walt's greatest financial success, when the act is beginning to "rake in millions" (191). This tall tale about a flying boy, then, comments on another aspect of U.S. mythology: the American Dream. Economic aspiration, the desire for individual success, can bring dizzying rewards but can also bring about a tragic fall. The transgression of the frontier between earth and sky, somewhat idealized in *Moon Palace,* here connotes that between success and failure, national self-image and insalubrious reality.

Joan Smith and Danny Calegari, writing in the *Financial Times* and the *Sunday Age,* respectively, recognized the novel's allegorical aims. "Walt's story is also that of his century," Smith states, "of turning away from confused ideals of white America's European roots to an obsession with making money." Calegari calls Walt's flight "a symbol of American optimism in the '20s, the belief that the bubble of speculation and youthful exuberance would never burst." While enjoying Walt's "no-nonsense" narrative voice, Smith ultimately believes that the novel is let down by the sense of "deliberate disengagement which holds the reader at arm's length." In contrast, Calegari acknowledges that there is a danger of a readerly deflation to mirror Walt's adult anticlimaxes, but the characters themselves "are well-rounded and lovable."[23]

The tendency of critics to measure and judge all Auster's work against earlier successes, particularly *The New York Trilogy,* was reflected in several reviewers' comments. Phil Edwards, writing in the *New Statesman,* bemoaned the lack of cerebral reflexivity seen in earlier works. "Shorn of the intense self-consciousness of the typical Auster narrator, the book's symbolism seems laboured and arbitrary," he insists. And the more vernacular narrative voice is to him nothing more than "a constant outpouring of bad puns and smart answers, just the kind of linguistic jangle Auster has previously banished from his writing."[24] Although Jay Cantor describes the language as "brilliantly filigreed demotic, making it, of course, highfalutin in its own way," his review is ultimately more generous because he appears to treat *Mr. Vertigo* on its own terms. "It has a fairy tale's compulsion to it," he says, "and one can hardly wish other perspectives or thicker textures on Mr. Auster if they might loosen the compulsion and ground the dreamer."[25]

Literary scholars have not shown much interest in Auster's fairy tale. This is mainly because of the continuing academic preoccupation with *The New York Trilogy,* a work that has set up critical parameters within which *Mr. Vertigo* does not sit comfortably. Those who have written on *Mr. Vertigo* at length have adopted varying approaches. Brendan Martin argues that "Auster addresses the blurring of fact and fiction and the role of the author" and sees Walt's coming-of-age as encouraging a mix of "skepticism and incredulity" in the same way as Auster's autobiographical work.[26] Just as *Moon Palace* places its extravagant fictions against a historical background, *Mr. Vertigo,* Martin suggests, is characterized by fictional and factual meetings, such as the one between Walt and the real-life baseball legend Dizzy Dean (255). Mark Brown's interpretation of the novel is consistent with his overarching interest in the spatial aspects of Auster's work. In his view the novel "describes the five major and discernible stages of [Walt's] life, and plots each onto a map of the urban centres of St. Louis, Chicago and Wichita, as well as the plains of Kansas and the backwoods towns of the midwest."[27] Without explicitly using the terms, Brown offers a new Western istorian's regionalist reading of the novel. This is a particularly fruitful approach to a text so keen to tell forgotten stories about American identity and history.

The opening paragraphs are a distillation of the novel's main themes and ideas. Its dazzlingly understated first sentence—"I was twelve years old the first time I walked on water"—puts the reader immediately in mind of Jesus (3). When one considers in addition that Master Yehudi derives his name from the Hebrew word "Yehuda," meaning "praise God," it is evident that the familiar father-son relationship at the heart of this novel can be understood in religious terms. (This is made very explicit later on, when Walt reflects that Yehudi has made him "in his own image" [57] to be "the holy of holies" [74].) Moreover in this rags-to-riches tale the American Dream is presented as a combination of spiritual striving and cold, hard materialism. When Yehudi, the God figure, first rescues Walt, Walt is "an orphan boy begging nickels on the streets of Saint Louis." After three years of training, Walt goes public with his flying ability, only to plunge to earth in 1929, "a few days before the October crash" (3). The message is clear from the start: if the American Dream proposes that "the smallest, the dirtiest, the most abject" can make it big (3), the danger is that concentrating on material wealth at the expense of spiritual betterment can lead to a humiliating fall.

Once Yehudi has persuaded Walt that his "mean and ugly" uncle Slim and "dough-fleshed sow" aunt Peg won't miss their nephew (5), the new companions take the archetypal American journey west, through Missouri into Kansas City, then on to the small town of Cibola, Kansas, and Yehudi's farm in the open countryside beyond. There is nothing mythic or exciting about this location. As Yehudi deadpans, with direct reference to *The Wizard of Oz,* "we're not in Missouri anymore, my little friend. We're in Kansas. And a flatter, more desolate place you've never seen in your life.... There's nothing to tell you where you are. No mountains, no trees, no bumps in the road. It's as flat as death out here, and once you've been around for a while, you'll understand there's nowhere to go but up—that the sky is the only friend you have" (11). In a literary effect common in frontier novels such as James Fenimore Cooper's *The Prairie* (1827), the psychological disorientation of the protagonist is mirrored in the wilderness. Yehudi recognizes that such desolate surroundings are perfect for what he has in mind for Walt. From his lonely farmhouse in the middle of nowhere—"a shit hole, the world capital of boredom" (15)—the only way is up.

Although the midwestern plains provide the backdrop for some extraordinary events, there is throughout *Mr. Vertigo* a concerted effort to highlight the gap between the glorious, notorious Wild West past and prosaic reality. Upon arriving for the first time in Wichita, Kansas, Walt complains: "The place was Podunk City, a pimple of yawns on a bare white butt. Where were the saloons and the gunslingers and the professional card sharks? Where was Wyatt Earp? Whatever Wichita had been in the past, its present incarnation was a sober, joyless muddle of shops and houses" (29). And again, much later, he remarks: "I hate to debunk popular legends, but there wasn't a hell of a lot that roared in Wichita" (109). Not only are there no Wichita cowboys in 1925, but the complete absence of traditional heroes suggests that, contrary to popular imaginings, the West might never have been as heroic as it has been painted.

Another way to challenge both Turner's thesis and the legends that have arisen from it is to tell the story from, as it were, the other side. Yehudi's home, Walt discovers, houses a community of America's dispossessed and enslaved, all those written out of dominant narratives of westward expansion and manifest destiny. As well as Yehudi, a Jewish immigrant from Eastern Europe, and Walt himself, "a representative of the white urban underclass,"[28] there are Aesop and Mother Sue (or Sioux). At first Walt dismisses Aesop as "a full-fledged Ethiopian, a pickaninny from the jungles of darkest Africa," and says, "I ain't shaking hands with no nigger" (13), but Yehudi responds with "all men are brothers, and in this family everyone gets treated with respect" (14). His plan is to educate Aesop and send him to a prestigious college so that he can be "a shining example to all the downtrodden black folks of this violent, hypocritical country" (19). Despite Walt's initial prejudices, he does accept that Aesop is the only person who shows him "any genuine kindness" (20). And when Aesop later sticks up for Walt in the face of Yehudi's anger, the first part of Walt's sentimental education is complete. Aesop becomes "the first real friend I'd ever had . . . my comrade, my anchor in a sea of undifferentiated sky" (39). (In fact there is a strong suggestion that Aesop inspires Walt to write his autobiography [89].) Walt's choice of the "anchor" metaphor is telling: in Auster's world only friendship, connection with others, can provide coordinates for the individual and anchor them as they wander in the desert. This ethical imperative is given a political slant in *Mr. Vertigo* by the interracial friendships Walt enjoys. The Master's house represents an ideal of American democracy; it is a place where unity in diversity becomes a working reality, not a forgotten ideal.

Compassion and friendship are in fact the difference between life and death in *Mr. Vertigo*. After getting caught in a Wichita blizzard, Walt contracts a terrible fever, which Yehudi dubs "the Ache of Being," a necessary part of his training (34). According to Walt, the tender ministrations of Mother Sue, including her "chanted prayers to the Great Spirit" (34), are the "first step" to his recovery from the fever (35). Awaking for the first time from his torpor, Walt feels Mother Sue kiss him, and he remarks, "It was the first kiss anyone had given me since my mother died, and it brought on such a warm and welcoming glow, I realized that I didn't care where it had come from. If that chubby Indian squaw wanted to nuzzle with me like that, then by God let her" (35). The message is sentimental, but nonetheless important: love is love, and it transcends racial differences. When Walt suggests that "it's possible that her magic was what did the trick" (34), he acknowledges not only the legitimacy of Native American culture but also the fact that love itself is a type of magic.

Before teaming up with Yehudi, Mother Sue took part in Buffalo Bill Cody's "Wild West" shows, which began in Nebraska in 1883 (78). These entertainments are mentioned in *Mr. Vertigo* because they illustrate very clearly the problematic relationship between history and popular culture, history and fiction. Even though Buffalo Bill Cody was a campaigner for Native American rights, his shows invariably included blood-and-thunder tales of the West with the Indians cast as the marauding bad guys. What is more, these images of whooping, scalping savages attacking wagon trains have passed into national folklore and have been reproduced in countless westerns and rodeo shows. Cody's overdramatic portrayals of frontier life did, however, include many real-life figures, notably Sitting Bull, and it is history's tendency to merge with cultural representation that particularly interests Auster. His characterization of Mother Sue can be seen as an attempt to dig behind the popular myths to retrieve some of the inglorious truths of frontier race relations. This includes the disturbing connection between African American slavery and the treatment of Native Americans. Toward the end of Mother Sue's narrative, Walt reveals how Aesop told him that "there wouldn't have been no black slaves from Africa if the white folks had been given a free hand with the Indians. He said they wanted to turn the redskins into slaves, but the Catholic boss man in the old country put the nix on it. So the pirates went to Africa instead and rounded up a lot of darkies and hauled them off in chains" (79). Simplistic though this analysis might be, it reinforces the idea that the oppression of others underpins myths of the frontier and that historical narratives are interconnected.

It is only when Walt has laid his prejudices to rest and been fully integrated into the community of the downtrodden that the serious part of his training can begin. Whereas the first twelve stages of Yehudi's thirty-three-point plan have mostly involved domestic chores, stage thirteen heralds the beginning of a series of brutal trials. Walt experiences, among other degradations, being buried alive (44), "flogged with a bullwhip," "thrown from a galloping horse," and "dunked repeatedly for six straight hours in a tubfull of vinegar." In a highly symbolic act, he also "cuts off the upper joint of [his] left pinky" (45). As Walt remarks of his temporary burial, "everything that happens to you on the surface is connected to those hours you spent underground . . . even though you've won the struggle to survive, nearly everything else has been lost. Death lives inside you, eating away at your innocence and your hope" (44). The message, though much more literal here, is familiar from Auster's earlier works: in order to create something beautiful—in this case, flight—the artist must first have been at absolute rock bottom, to have virtually died, to have lost a significant part of himself or herself. What is especially interesting here is that Auster quite deliberately brings together his Jewish heritage and his fascination with American myths. Walt's deprivations in the Kansas wilderness echo the Jews' trials in the wilderness narrated in Deuteronomy 8. Thus the American Dream narrative symbolized by Walt's desire to fly is connected to the Jewish experience of exile so important to Auster as an artist.[29]

These "gruesome" physical trials over, what follow are "the stages of mental struggle, the showdown between myself and myself," the inner battles necessary to become an artist (52). Yehudi no longer unleashes "skull-denting cruelty" on Walt and has "turned into a gentle, munificent guide" as he persuades Walt to undergo "a vow of silence," teaches him "to laugh and cry at the same time," and blindfolds him for a week (52–53). Their relationship has altered such that the Master's newfound gentleness lets Walt access "places of such inwardness that I no longer remembered who I was" (52). Paradoxically, they become closer because Yehudi allows Walt his solitude.

Walt's first successful levitation is a direct result of his newfound affection for Yehudi. Coming downstairs early one morning, Walt cannot find the Master anywhere and concludes that "he's upped and skedaddled." Spinning from "sorrow to anger, from belligerence to laughter, from snarling grief to vile self-mockery," Walt collapses into tears (61). At his lowest ebb, with "no more feelings in [his] heart," he experiences "a placid wave of nothingness, utterly detached and indifferent" to the world (62). At this moment he takes off, and the invisible frontier between earth and sky is breached for the first time. What is happening in this episode is a rehearsal of the filial drama of *The Invention of Solitude*. Perceived loss of the father figure, though premature here, inspires a flowering of creativity. When Walt levitates for his surrogate family as a Christmas present, the drama is taken even farther, the phallic exchange of Walt's left pinky signifying his coming-of-age, the point at which the father gives the son his manhood (71).

For some critics, the increasing emphasis on the father-son relationship in *Mr. Vertigo* is a weakness. Carsten Springer, for example, believes that despite the presence of Mother Sue and Aesop, "the only crucial relationship in the novel is that of Yehudi and Walt."[30] Such a view is borne out by the narrative action. Soon after Walt and Yehudi start honing Walt's technique by working intensively on "loft and locomotion" (73), Aesop gains a scholarship for Yale. The whole group is "looking ahead to the future . . . beyond the boundaries of the farm" (86), until history intrudes on the magic and tragedy strikes. At the end of a particularly successful day's training, the Ku Klux Klan set fire to the farm and hang Aesop and Mother Sue in front of Walt and Yehudi (95–96). Walt's sense of horror and sadness is genuine. "I felt as if I had just witnessed the end of the world," he says (96).

It may feel like the end of the world, but in many ways it is the beginning of Walt's and Yehudi's main adventures. With Aesop and Mother Sue gone (although they continue to haunt the edges of the story as "angels" [133]), the stage is now set for a less political narrative, which is part rags-to-riches tale, part road narrative, and, later on, part revenge tragedy. When Yehudi finishes his mourning with a cathartic smashing up of the house (112), he is ready to take Walt the Wonder Boy on the road. The community of outsiders makes way for the father-son drama, and, despite the increasingly amazing aerial acrobatics, the story is much more conventional and arguably less original as a result. Even Yehudi's partner, Mrs. Witherspoon, is ejected from the narrative during this formative period. Yehudi passes up "the opportunity of a lifetime" (125) when he fails to insist on her tagging along with them. Now it is just Yehudi, Walt, and the road to glory.

The first show, "at the Pawnee County Fair in Larned, Kansas" (115), is a disaster. Walt gets hit in the head by a bottle, and the performance descends into "angry, wordless howls" and accusations of charlatanism from the crowd (117). In Walt's opinion, the "nancy-boy angel" costume is to blame, as it separates performer from audience and suggests arrogance and superiority. Yehudi's extravagant approach is "more suited to the corny prewar style he'd grown up with than to the jump and jangle of the new age" (121). In Walt's desire for something "sleek and savvy and direct" (121), it is possible once again to find reference to Auster's own literary practice. *Mr. Vertigo* represents an attempt at something new, something with a conventional narrative drive more reminiscent of children's stories than the multilayered puzzles of Auster's earlier works. Like Walt, Auster is seeking a more direct connection with the reader.

There is further evidence for this reading. As the act improves with the introduction of Walt's "Huck Finn costume" (126) and the audiences respond more and more rapturously, it becomes clear that the audiences are part of the creative process. Walt experiments with new locomotive stunts and admits: "without the eyes of the crowd to spur me on, I doubt that I would have mustered the courage to try half the things I did" (135). Just as Auster believes that writer and reader make the book together, so Walt learns that allowing audiences "to share in the mystery" (137) is the key to "evolving into an artist" (136).

Brute economics are never far from the surface, however, despite Yehudi's romantic belief that the performances can "bring spiritual uplift to thousands of suffering souls" during the Depression (129). The next section of the novel begins when Uncle Slim walks in on Yehudi and Walt in a Gibson City diner. Claiming that Yehudi made "a deal" with him back in St. Louis, he demands 25 percent of the profits (140). The Master is contemptuous, but Walt fears the worst. Making the most of the novel's biblical and frontier imagery, he muses: "My uncle had been wandering in the desert for forty years, and all he had to show for it was a history of stumbles and wrong turns, an endless string of failures. . . . I understood that he had a purpose now, that the fucker had finally found a mission in life" (141). Indeed he has—revenge on "that lousy Jew" and a fifty thousand dollar ransom (147). Walt undergoes another trial in the wilderness when he is kidnapped by Slim and locked up in "an abandoned prospector's house" in South Dakota, which looks (with obvious reference to *Moon Palace*) "more like the moon than the earth" (147). What we have now is a familial drama, a variation on *Hamlet* with the malevolent uncle and the good father. Walt manages to escape, of course, and there is a tearful reunion with Yehudi in Rapid City (160).

These place names—Gibson City, Rapid City—are chosen very carefully. In a novel set at a time of rapid urbanization and industrialization, it is significant that the story constantly switches between cities and wilderness. With Walt's growing reputation, Yehudi books the act into theaters in "real cities . . . Providence and Newark; New Haven and Baltimore; Philadelphia, Boston, New York" (170). Walt's career seems to follow an archetypal American path from desert to small town, to riches in the big city.

Even the latest levitation routine looks like an allegory of the American Dream: from humble, stumbling beginnings (173), to the climbing of a symbolic ladder into the sky (174), to the joys of walking on air (175), and culminating in the patriotic bombast of "America the Beautiful" (176). Yet the narrative keeps returning Walt to the desert, back to his (and America's) symbolic beginnings. For example, when the headaches arrive just before the big New York gig and Yehudi cancels the act (200), the two companions embark on their journey to Hollywood, which necessitates a road trip through the "barren landscape of rocks and cacti" in Arizona and New Mexico (210).

In the middle of the Mojave Desert, they are attacked by Uncle Slim and his cronies. Yehudi is shot, the car crashes, and Slim makes off with their savings (212). Badly wounded from the shooting and, he reveals, riddled with cancer (220), Yehudi urges Walt to save his own life by shooting him. Walt refuses, and in a tragic, sentimental scene that will reverberate through the final part of the novel, the Master takes his own life (221). So the father-son relationship is forged in the Wild West, and the father also meets his end there.

If the remainder of the novel "seems to go Awol [*sic*],"[31] it is partly because Walt's adult life is itself aimless, but also because narrative progress is held up by the need to keep going back to the father figure's death. Walt could not kill Yehudi, but he can stage substitute scenes in an attempt to assuage his guilt. So three years later he tracks down Uncle Slim, now a bootlegger, in Illinois and forces him to drink strychnine (231). In taking his own life, Slim is made to suffer in the way Yehudi did. Later, as the co-owner of a Chicago club appropriately named "Mr. Vertigo's" (253), Walt gets acquainted with the washed-up baseball legend and incipient alcoholic Dizzy Dean. Bizarrely, Walt offers to shoot Dean, partly to give him back his "dignity" (269) but chiefly, in Walt's words, to "go back to the desert and do the job that was never done" (270). He thinks that by finally pulling the trigger on one of his heroes, he can put the past to rest.

The subsequent episodes of the novel reveal both a journey toward old age and a return to the past. With the help of the club's co-owner, Bingo, Walt avoids jail but has to leave Chicago (272). In Newark, he gets together with Molly—"the first woman I'd ever loved" (280)—and spends twenty-three happy years with her. After her death from cancer, Walt hits rock bottom, slipping into "an alcoholic stupor" (281). What saves him from oblivion are his dreams about Master Yehudi, dreams in which he is "walking on water again, strutting my stuff before gigantic, overflowing crowds" (281). Returning to his boyhood in his dreams means that he is "no longer ashamed to look at the past" (282). Rather than using this newfound acceptance to move on, however, he ends up back in the old Wild West, in Wichita, looking for Mrs. Witherspoon in a symbolic return to the past. They start living together "like husband and wife" (288), suggesting that Walt has replaced the Master rather than genuinely accepting the loss of his father figure. When Mrs. Witherspoon dies, Walt begins the memoir we are reading (289).

Mr. Vertigo, in the early stages, promises a lot. It promises a rewriting of frontier and Wild West myths, as well as a satire on the American Dream and the brute realities of capitalism.

Ultimately it does not quite deliver either. It could be argued that in this novel, as in history, minority groups get pushed to the margins so that the main business—the father and son drama, or the symbolic relationship between whites and their God—can hog the foreground. Yet the text remains haunted by the ghostly figure of Aesop, in particular, right to the end. Walt's cleaning woman has a "rude and incorrigible" son called Yusef, who not only acts like the young Walt but has a face that "resembles Aesop's to an almost appalling degree" (291). Perhaps Walt's desire to train Yusef to be "the next Wonder Boy" (292) indicates guilt at his own survival, or even hints at the need to put marginalized people back in the center, to give them equal opportunities to make it big. Unfortunately the novel closes with a rather simplistic declaration of the American Dream: "We all have it in us—every man, woman, and child—and with enough hard work and concentration, every human being is capable of duplicating the feats I accomplished as Walt the Wonder Boy" (293). If you try hard enough, it seems, anything is possible. The problem is that previous events suggest this simply is not true, and so for all its optimism, the ending strikes the reader as rather insincere.

CHAPTER SIX

The Book of Illusions

In Paul Auster's interview with Jonathan Lethem, the two Brooklynite novelists discuss the virtues of "ekphrasis." Lethem's definition of this term is "the novel's capacity for extensive descriptions of other art forms." Auster calls it "a rhetorical term meaning the description of imaginary works of art."[1] Examples from his earlier work would include the description of Blakelock's painting *Moonlight* in *Moon Palace* and Mr. Bones's "symphony of smells" in *Timbuktu* (44). *The Book of Illusions* (2002) shows more awareness than most books that the ability to "swallow a song, a poem or a film" is "one of the novel's defining strengths."[2] Narrated in the first person by David Zimmer, who, in a characteristic piece of intertextual play, is Marco's friend in *Moon Palace,* it follows Zimmer's relationship with the cinematic works of Hector Mann, a former silent movie actor unseen since his disappearance at the age of twenty-nine. The novel culminates in Zimmer's meeting with the reclusive Mann at his New Mexico ranch, lending weight to Mark Brown's argument that *The Book of Illusions* follows *Moon Palace* and *Mr. Vertigo* in describing a "westward journey" of "revelation and discovery."[3] A considerable proportion of the text is given over to highly detailed and evocative descriptions of the movies: first, the silent movies in which Mann starred in his twenties, and finally the more expressionistic works written and directed at Blue Stone Ranch. One of these, *The Inner Life of Martin Frost,* has recently been seen in a new incarnation as a movie by Auster himself, starring David Thewlis, Irène Jacob, and Sophie Auster.

It is tempting to attribute the presence of the movies in this novel to the author's experiences working on *Smoke, Blue in the Face,* and *Lulu on the Bridge,* yet Auster disputes this. He says, "The fact is that Hector was born inside me long before I got involved with the movies myself. He came to me one day in the late eighties or very early nineties, full-blown in his white suit with his black moustache."[4]

Ultimately the movie descriptions are best regarded as a variation on the story-within-a-story structure familiar from other novels: they are yet another series of frames through which "reality" recedes, yet which have some bearing on "real" events. The irony, perhaps, is that despite dealing with a visual medium, their most profound effect is to celebrate the power of words to conjure up images. As Auster notes: "After I published *The Book of Illusions,* I sent a copy to my friend Hal Hartley, the filmmaker. And he said to me, 'You know, I think maybe written films are better than real films. You can see them in your head and yet everything is exactly as you want it to be.'"[5] It is watching one of Mann's silent movies that rescues Zimmer from despair after the death of his wife and children: in a novel concerned with the redeeming power of art and the imagination, the reader has an important part to play. Zimmer's aphorism about silent movies applies equally well to the reading of Auster's imaginary movies: "The third dimension was in our head."[6]

Most reviewers emphasized the filmic aspects of the novel, as well as acknowledging that after the relative levity of *Mr. Vertigo* and *Timbuktu, The Book of Illusions* returned to darker, more philosophical territory. This was not to everybody's liking. D. T.

Max, writing in the *New York Times,* concludes that "there was great pleasure in watching the gifted Auster testing the walls of his cell, looking for his way out. Seen thus, *The Book of Illusions* for all its pleasures seems an acknowledgment of the cage."[7] While admiring its Gothic excesses, John Crowley in the *Washington Post* ultimately thinks that the novel is "strangely without warmth" and that the silent movie synopses are partly responsible. "The gentle and human art of the silent comedy," he observes, "reaches the heart directly and simply. The whole of this novel feels as though it were underlaid with a longing, impossible to fulfill, for that simplicity, at once evanescent and immortal."[8]

Janet Maslin, on the other hand, finds this same affectionate longing to be a strength. It is "carefully alert to the fundamental illusions of cinema," she states. The character of Hector Mann, at once vividly realized and elusive, inspires "eloquence and affecting admiration" in both David Zimmer and his author, Paul Auster. And, Maslin contends, "readers will respond to Hector as fully as Zimmer does, for he is an inspired creation. The most transporting parts of *The Book of Illusions* are those that simply consider Hector's life and work. And it is in fathoming Hector's nature that the book finds its own voice most successfully."[9] In other words, the meticulously detailed descriptions of Mann's cinematic creations are further examples in Auster's work of art's vital role in trying to enter into sympathetic relations with another individual. Ironically, as Maslin's review intimates, articulacy and beauty result from the impossibility of expressing another person. Thus it is not too fanciful to read "Mann" as "Man"; the following analysis of his cinematic alter ego could easily sum up Auster's attitude to all human identity: "Unpredictable in his behavior, full of contradictory impulses and desires, Hector's character is too complexly delineated for us to feel altogether comfortable in his presence. He is not a type or familiar stock figure, and for every one of his actions that makes sense to us there is another one that confounds us and throws us off balance" (35).

A clue to this central concern is provided by the novel's epigraph: "*Man has not one and the same life. He has many lives, placed end to end, and that is the cause of his misery.*" The writer of these rather bleak words, the French Romantic François-René de Chateaubriand, is one of two significant literary presences in the novel, the other being Nathaniel Hawthorne. Chateaubriand attributes the existential anguish of man (Mann) to his plurality. A coherent identity is difficult to establish when we apparently have so many varying lives. There are echoes of "Portrait of an Invisible Man" here, but *The Book of Illusions* pushes the issue even farther. Janet Maslin's review has the title "A Novel's Actor More Real Than Many Made of Flesh," and the questions posed most arrestingly by the book are these: Given the plurality of the self and therefore the impossibility of knowing another person, do the versions of others created in texts such as novels and movies end up becoming as, or even more, real than the "real" ones? Are lives simply a series of performances, and is character simply, in F. Scott Fitzgerald's memorable phrase, "an unbroken series of successful gestures?"[10]

By alluding to Chateaubriand's *Memoirs of a Dead Man* Auster makes an important point about allusion as an aesthetic practice in itself. In a novel so concerned with deaths-within-life, which opens with the words "everyone thought he was dead" (1) and has Hector Mann undergo multiple resurrections, the presence of the *Memoirs* suggests that *The Book of Illusions* might be understood as a kind of Gothic fiction. It is full, like traditional Gothic romances such as Horace Walpole's *The Castle of Otranto* (1764), of mysterious and treacherous documents, including Hector's films, Hawthorne's "Birth-Mark," and the *Memoirs* itself. It is the last of these that best illustrates the Gothic sensibility through its funereal imagery. Forced to mortgage his memoirs "to finance his old age" (63), Chateaubriand nonetheless stresses in his introduction that he would like to have published the complete work posthumously: "*I have been urged to allow some portions of these* Memoirs *to appear in my lifetime, but I prefer to speak from the depths of my tomb. My narrative will thus be accompanied by those voices which have something sacred about them because they come from the sepulchre*" (67). Zimmer has also had his book published posthumously. He assures the "dear reader" at the close of *The Book of Illusions* that "the man who wrote it is long dead" (318).

Zimmer and Chateaubriand merely make explicit—just as Auster does in "The Book of Memory"—something that is intuitively true of all allusive acts, and all reading acts. As T. J. Lustig notes, "All writing evokes, revives or resurrects what is not present. In this sense . . . the history of literature is bound up with the ghostly."[11] Hector writes in his notebook of his own reading: "*I talk only to the dead now. They are the only ones I trust*" (147–48). So to quote from other writers is to summon revenants, and to read allusive texts such as *The Book of Illusions* is to participate in this ghostly commune, this "poetics of absence." The literary voices heard in these pages are in-between, exiled to a dimension of both absence and presence, past and present. Likewise, when Chateaubriand muses on "*mysterious unity*" (67), he is referring not only to his own plurality, and hence his unknowability, but also to the way in which his past affects his present and his present his past: "*My cradle recalls something of my tomb, my tomb something of my cradle*" (67). In *The Book of Illusions* each individual is a "mysterious unity," an entity that somehow hangs together despite appearing to be fragmentary. Moreover every book is like this: presents and ghostly pasts combine to produce an artifact real and tangible, yet simultaneously illusory and elusive. Likewise in true Gothic fashion the book becomes a product of both the rational mind and mysterious, perhaps supernatural, influences.

David Zimmer begins his narration, like Daniel Quinn before him, as virtually a dead man, in a state of isolation induced by despair. Random death yet again shatters the delicate equilibrium of life and heralds the beginning of his story. On 7 June 1985 his wife, Helen, and their two sons, Todd and Marco, are killed in a plane crash. Zimmer, at this time a professor of comparative literature, retreats into "a blur of alcoholic grief and self-pity, rarely stirring from the house." Eschewing the company of others, he decides "it was better to be left alone . . . better to gut out the days in the darkness of my own head" (7). "Zimmer" means "room" in German: the locked room is commensurate with the writer's head in Auster's work, and it is here Zimmer intends to stay.[12]

What saves him from total disappearance is something spontaneous and human—a laugh. Watching a clip from one of Mann's silent comedies, *The Teller's Tale,* Zimmer laughs, and with that "unexpected spasm," that moment of connection with another, he realizes that he hasn't "hit bottom yet" (9). The episode is life-affirming and life-changing: "on the strength of two minutes of film and one short laugh, I chose to wander around the world looking at silent comedies" (13)—specifically, the Mann comedies anonymously sent to film archives in the United States, London, and Paris. Although Zimmer insists that "I wasn't attracted to mysteries or enigmas" (13), it is clear that the strange reappearance of these shorts, coupled with Mann's sudden disappearance and presumed death in 1929, is part of the attraction. Given that Zimmer regards himself as "just someone who pretended to be alive" (102), a man who has done his best to disappear from society, it is also true that he sees in Mann's story a mirror of his own. Zimmer's decision to write "a study of his films" (3) becomes "an odd form of medicine" (5)—a way to deal with estrangement by focusing on the work of another estranged individual. "It was the life of a monomaniac," Zimmer admits, "but it was the only way I could live now without crumbling to pieces" (27).

Moreover silent cinema itself has a Gothic quality because it lives on beyond the grave. It is "a dead art, a wholly defunct genre that would never be practised again," yet it can still be seen. Another aspect of its attraction for Zimmer and Auster is its freedom from "the burden of representation." Precisely because silent movie actors use "a syntax of the eye, a grammar of pure kinesis" that makes no pretense at representing "the real world," they can communicate to a contemporary audience across the "great chasm of forgetfulness" and create a separate world of screen and image unencumbered by language (15). This world is timeless because it is removed from reality. When the talkies took over, Zimmer observes, a paradox came into play: "the closer movies came to simulating reality, the worse they failed at representing the world" (14). Silent cinema possesses an honesty and purity that talking pictures lack. Typically, this paradox is reproduced in Auster's own art. Language may distance us from reality, but it is necessary in order to conjure up the nonlinguistic form the author so reveres, and in so doing demonstrates its own great power, the power of ekphrasis.

The brilliantly, meticulously detailed readings of Hector's movies and his idiosyncratic "syntax of the eye" are not there just to show off Auster's verbal dexterity, however, but serve several important functions. First, one can assume that they are extracts from Zimmer's book, *The Silent World of Hector Mann,* in which case they add yet another narrative layer or frame. As one engages with Hector's unique world, one reads Auster's novel, which frames Zimmer's narration, which frames his critical analysis of the movie, which in turn frames the movie itself. One could argue, following the critic Eve Kosofsky Sedgwick, that there is a Gothic quality to this narrative technique. Just as "live burial"[13] is a convention of Gothic texts such as Poe's "The Cask of Amontillado" (1846), so each layer of story is, as it were, buried alive within another. Embedded narratives are reminiscent of, and in Auster's work frequently linked to, secret chambers or rooms as well as to psychological secrets.

Every story or text in *The Book of Illusions* is multiply framed in this manner, such that the reader is forced to accept a particular worldview—that "reality" or "truth" is unavailable other than through textual representations, a multitude of shifting signs. Such a view is familiar from *The New York Trilogy,* but again Auster goes farther here by having Zimmer declare that "the world was an illusion that had to be reinvented every day" (57). The texts-within-texts are necessary reinventions of a world that remains elusive. Although that elusiveness is disconcerting, it also provides an opportunity for the individual endlessly to be creative, to live his or her life deliberately *as* illusion or as art.

This is the approach Hector adopts,[14] and a second reason for these protracted movie descriptions is to show not only that the actor's life comes to resemble his art (and vice-versa) in unsettling ways but also that there is no qualitative difference between the "real" Hector and the roles he plays as a silent actor. They merge into each other and have equal weight. And his status as a representative, everyman figure, at least in Zimmer's eyes, reflects the fact that we are *all* creatures of illusion and continual reinvention. To illustrate this point, Zimmer spends a lot of time in his early analyses describing the trademark, close-up "antic gyrations" of Hector's mustache. As the mustache twitches, "the face is essentially still, and in that stillness one sees oneself as in a mirror, for it is during those moments that Hector is most fully and convincingly human, a reflection of what we all are when we're alone inside ourselves" (30). So this fundamentally unrealistic acting mode nonetheless reflects an emotional reality.

Hector may be a point of identification or empathy as he struggles to avoid messing up his white suit (31) and attempts to retain dignity in the face of "bad luck" and "bizarre physical occurrences" (33), but he is a complex one. If we see ourselves in Hector, we also see our own unpredictability and variety: "Hector has the same personality in every film, but there is no fixed hierarchy to his preferences," Zimmer says. "He is both a populist and an aristocrat, a sensualist and a closet romantic, a man of precise, even punctilious manners who never hesitates to make the grand gesture." The task of pinning him down is made more difficult by his "sense of detachment, as if he were somehow mocking himself and congratulating himself at the same time." Like every artist in Auster's universe, including Auster himself, he is "at once engaged in the world and observing it from a great distance" (35). All of this contributes to another of the novel's insoluble paradoxes: through these vivid commentaries on his work, the reader feels closest to the character of

Mann, but that close identification derives from the appreciation that one can never get close to the real Mann. His illusory nature is what makes us believe in his reality.

Zimmer's readings of Hector's movies nonetheless emphasize supposed biographical links to his life. For example, Zimmer comments that Hector's movie character displays "all the striving ambitiousness of a hardworking immigrant, a man bent on overcoming the odds and winning a place for himself in the American jungle," and yet "one glimpse of a beautiful woman is enough to knock him off course" (35). This touches on aspects of Hector's life that assume greater importance later on. As the "four profiles written between August 1927 and October 1928" reveal (79), Mann was indeed a European immigrant and a serial womanizer whose brief appearances in the newspapers were "usually in the company of a woman" (87). The trouble is that all four profiles contradict one another: they amount to nothing more than "bits of movie reportage rife with hyperbole, erroneous suppositions, and out-and-out falsehoods" (79). In the *Photoplay* interview Hector arrives in the United States from Germany via Argentina and still speaks heavily accented English (80–81). In *Picturegoer* his accent is flawless (81). In *Picture Play* he originates from Stanislav and has Polish as his native language (82). With such disparities, Hector "is reduced to a pile of fragments, a jigsaw puzzle whose pieces no longer connect" (83).

And it seems that this is exactly how he wants it. "Every time he is asked a question," Zimmer says, "he gives a different answer. Words pour out of him, but he is determined never to say the same thing twice" (83). Far from becoming frustrated with Hector's deliberate obfuscation, the journalists "can't resist him," "stop pressing him about the facts and give in to the power of the performance" (84). Even Zimmer's convincingly argued reading of events—that Hector is Jewish and escaped from Galicia to South America at the time of the Russian pogroms (85)—is inevitably just another subjective interpretation.[15] As well as the unreliability of supposed documentary sources, an idea with which the Auster reader will already be familiar, there are two interconnected implications. First, it is apparent that Hector plays himself rather than being himself: his identity is, to use the gender critic Judith Butler's term, "performative," in that it is performed or acted rather than innate or essential.[16] He is an accumulation of texts or versions.

Even the supposedly definitive story of Hector's life, told by Auster via Zimmer via Alma Grund (126–98), only serves to emphasize Hector's performativity. It takes the form of a series of metaphorical deaths and resurrections. After the tragic death of his lover, Brigid O'Fallon, at the hands of his fiancée, Dolores, Hector disappears and changes his appearance "by removing his most identifiable feature, transforming his face into another face through a simple act of subtraction" (143). As he loses the mustache, he finds a hat with the name "Herman Loesser" written inside it: "Some would pronounce it *Lesser,* and others would read it as *Loser.* Either way, Hector figured that he had found the name he deserved" (144). And so he becomes Herman, which, he observes, echoes "Herr Mann" and thus allows him to retain part of his old identity for himself. This last point is important. As Hector continues his wandering, the penance he regards as "a continual work in progress" (146), he assumes various identities. These include the autodidactic, obsessive reader (147); the acting manager (in both senses of the adjective) of the sports shop owned by Brigid's father (168); the masked performer in private sex shows (183); and finally the reborn Hector Mann who saves the life of Frieda Spelling (and almost loses his own) during a bank raid in Sandusky, Ohio (195). Yet none of these roles obliterates the ones that came before. Each one is laid on top of the other while retaining a trace of its predecessor, so that identity becomes a palimpsest. There is an ethical aspect to this: Hector cannot work through his guilt if he does not remember his past. Memory, though frequently painful, is the catalyst for future improvement and reconnection with the world.

The old man Zimmer eventually meets is a "mysterious unity" composed of all his former roles. Tellingly, Zimmer has trouble believing in him as "an authentic person" rather than "an imaginary being" (222), and can barely recognize him except through reference to his old movie persona: "It had been sixty years since he'd worn the mustache and the white suit, but he hadn't altogether vanished. He'd grown old, he'd grown infinitely old, but a part of him was still there" (223). This older, wiser Hector—Hector Spelling after getting married to Frieda (203)—is still a role, and, were he to live on, there would undoubtedly be others. To repeat Zimmer's phrase, identity itself is a "work in progress"; it is never complete.

The second implication of the abundance of texts and versions in the novel is this: the more conflicting texts Auster/Zimmer includes, the more the reader becomes aware that just like Hector, *The Book of Illusions* itself is a work in progress, a series of evolving performances rather than a single, strictly cohesive object. Therefore one of the ways to deal with its complexity is to focus on the key performances. In addition to the extracts from Zimmer's translation of Chateaubriand, the key performances are Hector's silent comedy *Mr. Nobody* (39–54); Alma's interpretation of Nathaniel Hawthorne's short story "The Birth-Mark" (120–23); and Hector's later work, *The Inner Life of Martin Frost* (242–69). *The Book of Illusions* may appear to be "a book of fragments" (316), but focusing on these texts can facilitate a "mysterious unity" by forcing the reader to examine the different points each of them makes about identity, reading, and the creation of art. It then becomes possible for one to work out a relationship with the book—to work out, as it were, how to read Auster's novel as one is reading it.

Mr. Nobody was the last of Hector's complete movies for Kaleidoscope Studios. Zimmer's analysis makes clear from the outset that the film is allegorical, "a response to [the] mounting frustration" the actor felt about the coming of talkies and the disastrous financial dealings of studio executive Seymour Hunt. The deals on which Hunt reneged resulted in the refusal of the theaters to show the movies: as Zimmer points out, Hector effectively became invisible when audiences could no longer watch him (39). In *Mr. Nobody* this metaphorical invisibility is made the main motif when the evil vice president of the Fizzy Pop Beverage Corporation, C. Lester Chase ("Chase" equals "Hunt"), attempts to take control of the company and destroy Hector by giving him a magic invisibility potion (40). In this movie Hector starts off as president, and it is noteworthy that this is "the first and only time that Hector presents himself as a rich man. In *Mr. Nobody*, he has everything a person could possibly want: a beautiful wife, two young children, and an enormous house with a full staff of servants" (40). His "hardworking immigrant" character has reached the top of the pile, and although his subsequent misfortune could be attributed solely to the machinations of his unscrupulous vice president, it is tempting to read the movie as a salutary tale about the soul-destroying properties of capital in general. As in *The Music of Chance,* once the individual is defined through wealth, his identity is effectively erased.

So the achievement of the immigrant dream is simultaneously its death.

After drinking the potion, the president becomes "a specter made of flesh and blood, a man who is no longer a man" (40). The fact that this is precisely what has happened to Zimmer, and presages what will happen to Hector, suggests a complex interrelation between art and life. As Nicci Gerrard observes, "the lost films show stories that the characters then enact, as if they have made their fates into art before experiencing them in life."[17] It is a conventional notion, but for Auster a vital one: art does not simply imitate life, but can influence it. As an ethical space in which the individual interacts with others, the artwork allows the working through, consciously or unconsciously, of emotional or intellectual concerns, which are then translated into real life action. One might accuse Auster of being simplistic, but he has a sincere belief that the roles adopted in the creation and consumption of art have a direct bearing on the roles we play in life, to the extent that there is very little in the end to distinguish between them.

As viewers and readers, we are in a privileged position with regard to the erased Hector. We can see him, although nobody else can, and he has no reflection (43). Hector experiments with his new status: he strips down to his underwear on a street corner (44), "knocks off the hat of a passerby," then "picks up the hem of a woman's dress and studies her legs" (45). Part of the comedy derives from the viewer/reader's privileged glimpse of his expressions as he performs these tricks. But the situation can also be understood as an allegory of reading itself. One reads or even listens to a book privately, and "sees" the characters as unique mental images to which nobody else has access. So in a sense the characters are like Hector—invisible to others, visible only to the reader. Moreover Auster is making a highly suggestive point about the reader's location in relation to his or her two worlds—the real world in which he or she sits while reading, and the world of the book in which he or she is temporarily involved. In effect, the reader becomes a specter just like Hector, exiled to a dimension between the two worlds. To use a cliché, a reader "loses himself or herself" in the story while remaining in the real world.

Needless to say, Hector triumphs in the end. He frames Chase for a jewelry heist he himself has committed under the cloak of invisibility. His victory is a hollow one, however, because for now "he is still invisible" (49). And in fact the details of his revenge matter much less than the transformational scene that closes the movie. Still invisible, Hector falls asleep next to his wife: "The screen fades to black. When the picture returns, it is morning, and daylight is flooding through the curtains" (51). This dawn is also a symbolic one, for it soon becomes apparent that Hector has become visible again. After kissing his wife, he checks that he has regained his reflection. There is a moment of "chilling blankness" in Hector's expression, and then he slowly smiles. To Zimmer, "the smile suggests something more than a simple rediscovery of himself. He is no longer looking at the old Hector. He is someone else now" (52). A circle closes around the enigmatic smile, and slowly the image is engulfed in blackness.

Clearly this transformation is a kind of farewell and prefaces the series of real-life changes Hector is soon to undergo. And equally clearly this is a movie about "the anguish of selfhood" (53). Yet given the self-referencing nature of the story, it is possible to read it another way. If Hector's experience as a specter is shared by the reader of the book, then the final reappearance and transformation are also shared by the reader as he or she finishes the story. Emerging from the space between the real world and the world of the book, the reader is somehow altered by the experience and undergoes a rebirth influenced by the narrative within which he or she has been lost. It may sound grandiose, but Auster intends *Mr. Nobody* not simply as a meditation on the easy loss of one's identity, but as a parable of the transforming power of art, its ability to take life in a new direction.

In David Zimmer and Alma Grund's discussion of Hawthorne's "The Birth-Mark," the next of the novel's key performances, the relationship between art and the individual is further explored. Zimmer first meets Alma when she turns up unexpectedly at his Vermont house one night. She has been sent by Frieda Spelling, Hector's wife, to persuade a drunk and hostile Zimmer to visit Blue Stone Ranch before Hector dies (99). One of the first things he notices is the birthmark on the left side of her face: "It was a purple stain about the size of a man's fist, long enough and broad enough to resemble the map of some imaginary country: a solid mass of discoloration that covered more than half her cheek." She holds her head "at an awkward tilt" so that her hair covers most of the mark, a tic Zimmer attributes to "a lifetime of self-consciousness" (100).

Her self-consciousness is matched by the narrative, which quickly makes it clear that her face functions as a text to be *read*. What is striking is how, at first, Zimmer sees ghosts of his past there: "When she turned around and faced me again, I could see only her right side. She looked different from that angle, and I saw that she had a delicate, roundish face, with very smooth skin. . . . Her eyes were dark blue, and there was a quick, nervous intelligence in them that reminded me a little of Helen" (101). Still haunted by his memories, Zimmer is unable to see Alma for who she is, and insists on a decidedly Gothic reading by commenting on her "strange double face" (108). One half of her face has the birthmark, the other represents his dead wife.

Alma can, as her name suggests, be regarded as the soul and the ethical grounding of the novel ("alma" means "soul" in Spanish, and "grund" means "earth" or "foundation" in German). During their dramatic encounter, Zimmer reaches his nadir and comes out the other side to begin the next stage of his rehabilitation. When Alma draws a gun in desperation, Zimmer experiences a "sublimely exhilarating" moment, a feeling akin to being, as he puts it, "an inch or two beyond the confines of my own body" (108). Feeling "perfectly calm and perfectly insane" (109), he urges her to shoot. It is a kind of negative epiphany in which he feels absolute indifference to life or death. Driven by this indifference, he ends up snatching the loaded gun, putting it to his head, and pulling the trigger (111). Only the fact that Alma has accidentally left the safety catch on saves him from death. It appears that chance has once again intervened, but Alma's error is key. It is she who functions as the agent of chance, and thus she can be seen as instrumental in what Zimmer regards as his resurrection: "A series of accidents had stolen my life from me and then given it back, and in the interval, in the tiny gap between those two moments, my life had become a different life" (112). Their resulting intimacy stems partly from shared loneliness, and partly from a characteristic Auster irony: the sense that this chance encounter is somehow fated.

Zimmer decides to visit Hector's ranch, and they set off the next morning (117). During their conversation on the journey, the full significance of Alma's birthmark becomes apparent. After the shattering incident with the gun, Zimmer's reading of Alma's face has altered. No longer does he see resemblances to his wife. Instead he tells Alma: "It makes you different, someone who doesn't look like anyone else. You're the only person I've ever met who looks only like herself" (119). This perceptual change is important for two reasons. First, it suggests that Zimmer is finally emerging from his melancholia. No longer trapped inside his own head and entirely in the past, he is able to recognize, appreciate, and connect with Alma's uniqueness. Second, the fact that Zimmer's readings of the mark tell us at least as much about his state of mind as they do about Alma emphasizes the point that the mark operates, as does *Mr. Nobody,* as an allegory of reading processes and, specifically, the mutually affecting relationship between text and reader.

Precise physical details offer clues to this allegorical reading. In Nathaniel Hawthorne's 1843 tale Georgina's birthmark "looks like a human hand" (120), and in Auster's novel it is "about the size of a man's fist" (100). This is the hand of God made corporeal or, in self-conscious literary terms, the mark of authorship, a sign that both Georgina and Alma have been deliberately created by male writers. It is, as Alma says, "simply what we think of as human" (120), but it is also a sign that draws attention to the fictionality of the work. Additionally, for Georgina's husband, Aylmer, it "destroys her physical beauty. It's a sign of some physical corruption, a stain on Georgina's soul, a mark of sin and death and decay" (120). Therefore one could also read the hand-shaped birthmark in Hawthorne's tale as representative of male oppression—specifically, the way men restrictively read women by imposed standards of beauty and moral perfection.

The birthmark is for Auster another variation on the idea of framing. It is a permanent site of representation that emphasizes the fact that any individual is marked, in the sense of being constantly read and interpreted by others. For Georgina, this is a burden that leads to her attempt to remove the stain and ultimately to her tragic death. As Zimmer observes, "The birthmark is who she is. Make it vanish, and she vanishes along with it" (121). But Alma reads Hawthorne's text willfully in order to regain the process of reading and interpreting for herself. While accepting that she "would always be defined by that purple blotch on [her] face," she also realizes that she can read others through their responses to the mark: "I knew what people were thinking. All I had to do was look at them, study their reactions when they saw the left side of my face, and I could tell whether they could be trusted or not. The birthmark was the test of their humanity" (121). If Alma's birthmark is a kind of text, then Auster is suggesting that as one reads a text—a book, a movie, or indeed a person—it effectively *reads back*. In other words, to engage with and interpret a text is to have profound questions asked about one's own attitudes, about one's fundamental humanity and sense of self. People are composed textually, as an endless series of rewritings by self and others. Elsewhere in *The Book of Illusions* there is a certain bleakness to this notion: the individual is lost in a sea of representations, and no "real" identity is possible. But Alma's story provides a more positive gloss. For her, the reciprocal process of reading and counterreading is an ethical one. It is, like the birthmark itself, what we think of as human. By closely examining the multitude of ways in which we frame or mark each other, we can learn crucial things about prejudices and allegiances. Rather than an exercise in invasion or imposition, then, reading becomes an ethical testing ground, a conduit for the exchange of personal ideas and attitudes.

The last of the key performances, *The Inner Life of Martin Frost,* is the culmination of the novel's internal debates on art and life and distills many of the ideas from *Mr. Nobody* and Alma's birthmark narrative. It is in fact the only one of Hector's later works Zimmer gets to see. Immediately after her husband's death Frieda carries out with maniacal zeal his request to destroy the movies. (This is a harsher injunction than Chateaubriand gave to his wife, who had the choice of whether to publish or suppress his manuscripts [66].) Zimmer reads the request as the final part of Hector's penance, the last attempt "to pay off his debts to a God he refused to believe in." In Zimmer's analysis: "only by sacrificing the one thing that would have given his work meaning—the pleasure of sharing it with others—could he justify his decision to do that work in the first place" (278). The lost films are another set of specters, invisible to others, exiled to a place between existence and nonexistence.

It is not surprising, then, that *Martin Frost* is, like *The Book of Illusions,* concerned with the relationship between the real and the spectral. Despite being filmed on the grounds of Blue Stone Ranch with "deadpan realism, such scrupulous attention to the particulars of everyday life" (242), it takes place, Zimmer soon realizes, on "the inside of a man's head—and the woman who had walked into that head was not a real woman. She was a spirit, a figure born of the man's imagination, an ephemeral being sent to become his muse" (243). The woman in question, Claire Martin, suddenly appears in Martin's bed soon after he begins work on a new short story (247). Her surname hints at the indelible connection between them—albeit a narcissistic one, given that she is Frost's own creation—and they rapidly fall in love. After initial resistance, Frost comes to accept her existence, and they settle into something resembling cozy domesticity as he continues his story and she studies for her philosophy degree. As he approaches the end of the story, however, Claire falls ill (262).

The dramatic final scenes of the movie consist of a series of crosscuts between the two characters, emphasizing that the closer he gets to ending the story, the closer she gets to death (266–67). Finally realizing who Claire is, Martin throws the pages into the fire, sacrificing his art to resurrect Claire as a physical being, not simply a fictional idea (268). Yet her reaction is unexpected: rather than delight, Claire expresses anguish. Now that "Martin has solved the riddle of his enchantment, she seems lost. What are we going to do? She says. Tell me, Martin, what on earth are we going to do?" (268).

Claire's anguish is later echoed in Alma's tragic death. After ordering Zimmer to leave the ranch (274), Frieda proceeds rapidly with the incineration of the movies (275) but then goes much farther, deciding to destroy all traces of Hector's existence. This includes Alma's completed biography, which is burned in the manner of Frost's story (304). Alma foregoes the happy future she was planning with Zimmer in Vermont and commits suicide (309). Unlike Martin Frost, Frieda understands the central message of *The Book of Illusions*—that the separation of life and art is impossible, and in fact undesirable. The individual lives through his or her work and *is* the work, which is why Claire is distressed by Martin's sacrifice and why Alma cannot bear the destruction of her manuscript. Moreover, as Hector's life and the commentaries on *Mr. Nobody* and "The Birth-mark" illustrate, life is a series of reading and writing performances. In short—and *The Book of Illusions* makes this message more boldly than any previous Auster novel—life is art in progress.

Words endure, and if the ending appears bleak, this bleakness is leavened by knowledge that something of the individual survives in the artwork. Throughout the novel, art is connected with death but also with endurance. Mark Brown is wrong to observe that "the connection between 'our' world and the world of the book is broken by the death of the first-person narrator."[18] The connection is actually made stronger by the reader's empathic awareness that all of us will one day—like Hector, Zimmer, and Alma—exist only as ghosts, memories, and texts. That is why Zimmer wants to believe that Hector's films still survive, and why his novel ends with these words: "I live with that hope" (321).

CHAPTER SEVEN

Other Works

The Early Poetry

Between 1974 and 1980 Paul Auster published five poetry collections: *Unearth* (1974), *Wall Writing* (1976), *Effigies (1976), Fragments from Cold* (1977), *Facing the Music* (1980), and the prose poem *White Spaces* (1980). His poems were first anthologized in *Disappearances* (1988), and in 2004 Overlook Press produced his complete *Collected Poems.*

The early collections were published by small, independent houses, with little critical or commercial success, so it is unsurprising that dedicated reviews of Auster's poetry began to appear only with the publication of *Collected Poems,* when he was already an acclaimed novelist. This delay in the recognition of Auster as a serious poet resulted, inevitably, in a search for continuity between the poems and the prose. Critics treated the poems archaeologically, digging for stylistic or thematic precursors of the author's "future" concerns, while neglecting to mention in most cases that Auster was writing "hundreds and hundreds of pages" of prose in the period when the poetry was being published (AH 298). (Even his very earliest efforts, such as "Prolusion: The Clown's Universe" [1966], are essentially surreal prose works.)[1] Gerard Woodward, writing in the *Guardian,* is typical, arguing that the poems take the form of "short jabs of expressionistic imagery" rather than being in any way narrative. Yet in the "concern with language and representation, with identity, absence and perception," one can see the genesis of Auster's novelistic ideas. In a by now familiar observation, Woodward states that the verse is so "tightly controlled" and so "devoid of any specificity" that the move to the "bigger canvas of the novel" was inevitable if Auster were fully to explore wider human relations.[2] Eric McHenry, writing in the *New York Times*, wearies at the poems' "terminal indeterminacy" and prefers the "more involving mysteries of [Auster's] prose."[3]

For Auster, the tension between tightness and indeterminacy is precisely the point, and is what makes the poetry specifically attuned to its subject matter rather than an impoverished ancestor of the novels. "I set very high stakes for myself very young," he has said, "and it was very difficult. I consciously reduced the range of imagery I was going to allow myself to work with."[4] The predominant images are stones, the eye, earth, and walls. Not only does this narrow range evidence an intense authorial self-discipline, it also requires discipline and effort from the reader. If there are a limited number of images, and if any image can carry a multitude of meanings, then the interpretive routes "in" to the poem are restricted at the same time a single meaning is impossible to locate. The archaeological metaphor is appropriate: as the title of Auster's first collection suggests, the reader has to dig deep to unearth an interpretation.

Encountering an Auster poem, then, is hard work. As in the encounter with another human being, there is a need to connect, but language and the ego make connection difficult. Poetry is, for Auster, more locked into one point of view than the novel: it is "that way of using language which forces words to remain *in* the mouth."[5] Or, as he expresses it in the *Unearth* sequence: "You ask / words of me, and I / will speak them—from the moment / I have learned / to give you nothing" (CP 48). The reader can feel removed from the work and the world even as he or she attempts to enter them. But the important thing is the attempt, the journey itself. So it is clear that the poems inhabit a similar ethical territory as novels like *Moon Palace* and *In the Country of Last Things,* while the form and lexis allow the reader to *feel* the difficulty of connection in a more direct manner.

Auster's main poetic influences are the American objectivists and French modernists, particularly Stéphane Mallarmé. Objectivist poetics, emergent in the 1930s in the writing of Louis Zukofsky, Charles Reznikoff, and George Oppen, is characterized by the treatment of the poem itself as an object. It is an object constantly under a human gaze that must strive for sincerity and clarity, and unstinting attention to particular, often everyday words and things. From Mallarmé, Auster takes a fascination with sound relations between words rather than strict poetic meters, as well as unexpected juxtapositions of objects and ideas that engender an almost surreal quality.

The first poem in *Unearth* clearly demonstrates these features:

> Along with your ashes, the barely
> written ones, obliterating
> the ode, the incited roots, the alien
> eye—with imbecilic hands, they dragged you
> into the city, bound you in
> this knot of slang, and gave you
> nothing. Your ink has learned
> the violence of the wall. Banished,
> but always in the heart
> of brothering quiet, you cant the stones
> of unseen earth, and smooth your place

> among the wolves. Each syllable
> is the work of sabotage.
> (CP 37)

Alliteration is a key sound relation and is frequently employed for emphasis, as in "Along with your ashes." Yet, ironically, this phrase also reminds the reader that the poem is being unwritten, in the sense of losing meaning, as it is being written—hence the paradox of "obliterating / the ode." When Norman Finkelstein describes Auster's verse as "a farewell to poetry," he means that it is always about its own limitations. How can a poet actually say what he or she means, or mean what he or she says?[6]

So despite the sincerity of the poet's attention to his or her images, the key to understanding such a poem is in fact *mis*understanding, and thus the process of interpretation has an ironic edge. This can best be seen in the final line: the word "sabotage" implies that just as one reaches an understanding of a poem, or indeed an individual word, its meaning treacherously shifts. The snakelike sibilant sounds of the final sentence imply that language cannot be trusted. Rather than illuminating, it ends up binding its users in a "knot of slang" (language supposedly understood only by the initiated) or worse, committing a kind of violence against them. Equally, *imposing* a meaning on experience is itself a form of violence.

Although it is never made explicit, certain recurring images, many of them to do with actual or implied violence, evoke Auster's Jewish heritage. Not only can the wall, for instance, be regarded as a symbolic barrier to understanding, it also puts one in mind of Jerusalem's Western Wall, or Wailing Wall.[7] Revered for its proximity to the Holy of Holies, the holiest site in Judaism, the Western Wall serves as a site of prayer, of communication with God. Hundreds of tiny slips of paper, written prayers, are deposited daily into the crevices of the wall, and this is an image Auster would find productive, representing as it does a variation on the ancient process of inscription in stone, the earliest known form of writing. So the wall is simultaneously a barrier to comprehension and something that inspires the act of writing.

There is, then, a tension throughout the poems between creation and destruction in writing, often connected to images of stones and walls. This is best illustrated by the poem "Wall Writing." When Auster describes "the whiteness of a word, / scratched / into the wall" (CP 81), he understands that the process of erosion makes the words visible. Something is therefore always destroyed in the production of language, art, and indeed history. Thus the "ashes" in "Unearth" can refer in an abstract way to the destruction of meaning, but also to the incineration of bodies and the attempt to wipe out the Jews during the Holocaust. To memorialize those deaths through art, Auster would recognize, is yet another paradoxical process. It resurrects in aesthetic form while confirming death and emphasizing lost-ness.

The result, for the Jewish American, for all Jews, for the artist, and for the reader, is the state of exile. (It is no coincidence that included in the thrice daily Jewish prayers at the Western Wall are pleas for the return of Jewish exiles to Israel.) Somehow between life and death, between self and other, the reader of Auster's poetry wanders an archetypal landscape where the lack of specificity deliberately forces him or her into an abstract meditation on questions of selfhood and one's connection with others. In this landscape, which could be external or internal—that is, in the reader's consciousness—the "I" and the "you" are un-specified and risk blurring into each other. Thus they are "Banished, / but always in the heart"—shut out from an understanding of each other, of language, of the world, and of tragic history, yet with a yearning to understand that gives the verses their affective power.

Despite deriving from his Jewish American identity, the concerns with banishment and exile allow Auster, in the barren and abstract environments of his poetry, to engage with other civilizations that have faced persecution. "Quarry," from *Fragments of Cold,* offers an example:

> No more than the song of it. As if
> the singing alone
> had led us back to this place.
>
> We have been here, and we have never been here.
> We have been on the way to where we began,
> and we have been lost.
>
> There are no boundaries
> in the light. And the earth
> leaves no word for us
> to sing. For the crumbling of the earth
> underfoot
>
> is a music in itself, and to walk among these stones
> is to hear nothing
> but ourselves.
>
> I sing, therefore, of nothing,
>
> as if it were the place
> I do not return to—
>
> and if I should return, then count out my life
> in these stones: forget

> I was ever here. The world
> that walks inside me
>
> is a world beyond reach.
> (CP 138)

As the first line of the poem indicates, the "we" has been dispossessed, such that the voice and the person have become separated. Viewed in this way, "Quarry" is a melancholic response to the affirmative, joyous pronouncements of Walt Whitman's "Song of Myself" and "I Sing the Body Electric." In these Whitman poems, merely to sing the names of objects and people is to confirm their existence, whereas the aim of Auster's poem is to give voice to those people who have lost a voice. The syntactical ambiguity of "we have been lost" implies that outsiders have actively brought about that loss. Thus "Quarry"—whose very title hints at hunting and extermination as well as mining the past—can be seen as an oblique response to the subjugation practiced upon native people by colonizers. Not only does this take the form of real, physical violence, it is also the violence of redacted history: "We have been here, and we have never been here" testifies to how ancient civilizations are erased through the writing of history by dominant participants. Typically, then, the stones that litter the poem represent both the remains of ancient monuments as well as the fragmented words of the people who built them.

And this is the ultimate irony of Auster's poetry. Stones are indeed words, words that invite interpretation but simultaneously close it out. They litter a landscape that is also, for the writer, symbolic of the page. To put words onto the blank page is itself a form of colonization, therefore, and the poet is caught between his or her responsibility to the past and the danger of imposing violence on the past with his or her language. "A poetics of absence" beautifully describes Auster's work in these verses. Full of elisions, gaps, pauses, and ambiguities, they allow the reader to *experience* those absences more affectively than the novels, which are more inclined to fill the spaces with words in an effort to *describe* absence. It is apt that Auster's last poetic work was entitled "White Spaces." One is left with the impression that the consummate "poetics of absence" would be a series of blank pages where the reader could walk freely with the poet and the voices in their heads.

Timbuktu

In a *New York Times* interview, Paul Auster describes *Timbuktu* as "a book about feeling . . . a pure, unadulterated, unironic form" of storytelling.[8] Certainly, like its predecessor *Mr. Vertigo*, *Timbuktu* has a lightness of tone largely missing from, say, *The New York Trilogy* and *Leviathan*. Praised by one reviewer for being "less self-consciously clever" than these earlier works, it distinguishes itself primarily by having a dog as its hero.[9] Mr. Bones is a scruffy mutt who embarks on an itinerant existence after the death of his owner, Willy G. Christmas. Willy himself is a vagabond, keen to eschew worldly possessions, "to embody the message of Christmas every day of the year, to ask nothing from the world and give it only love in return"—in other words, "to turn himself into a saint" (21). The fact that Willy is inspired to secular sainthood by a vision of Santa Claus talking to him during a television commercial is, along with Mr. Bones's observations on the bourgeois family later in the novel, indicative of the book's ironic nature.

Auster employs, as he does in *The Music of Chance,* free indirect discourse to provide a narrative voice that, in blurring the objective and subjective, the external and internal, allows for ironic comment on Mr. Bones's experiences in human society. Moreover the viewpoint of a trusting and ingenuous dog can perhaps expose the hypocrisies and absurdities of contemporary American society more effectively than the wise-guy first-person reflections of Walt Rawley in *Mr. Vertigo*. And, as Willy makes abundantly clear, a dog is emblematic: "Dog as metaphor, if you catch my drift, dog as emblem of the downtrodden," and "people get treated like dogs, too, my friend" (56, 120).

Nonetheless, critical opinion was divided on Mr. Bones. While one reviewer thought that the author has created a voice "without a trace of the cloying anthropomorphism to which decades of Disney cartons and animated features have accustomed us," others remain less convinced.[10] Jim Shepard, writing in the *New York Times,* wearies at Auster's insistence on dog-as-metaphor, claiming that "such moments seem more committed to providing answers than to fully interrogating questions." He also winces at the sentimentality of the many "archetypal collisions between boy and dog" one encounters in *Timbuktu*.[11] Russell Celyn Jones in the *Times* is more scathing. Denouncing the book as "an imaginative failure," he highlights the "clichés" and "exhausted language" and, crucially, argues that the novel "fails as allegory" of racism and prejudice because its ideas are undeveloped.[12]

Whether or not one agrees with Celyn Jones, it is unarguable that he has identified one of Auster's key aims in *Timbuktu*. The novel is allegorical and at times satirical. Among its targets are the transformation of 1960s hippie radicalism into bourgeois domestic conventionality, the suburbanization and homogenization of the American landscape, and the flawed reality behind the ideals of America's "melting pot" thesis of acculturation and assimilation. Its primary technique is defamiliarization, the making strange of that which is commonly accepted as normal. The "vantage point of a canine mind"[13] is the perfect vehicle for such a project. Not only is Mr. Bones "a hodgepodge of genetic strains" and an "immigrant" (5, 6), therefore reflecting the experience of many Americans, but his childlike view of the nation (something he inherits from Huckleberry Finn) allows him inadvertently to poke fun at it.

"Timbuktu" is used in its more vernacular sense to suggest somewhere distant and virtually inconceivable. Early on in the novel it is made clear that for Willy and Mr. Bones, Timbuktu is equivalent to heaven: "That was where people went after they died. . . . It was called Timbuktu, and from everything Mr. Bones could gather, it was located in the middle of a desert somewhere" (48). Reachable only via "a realm of eternal nothingness" (48), it is far from any American city and, as Mark Brown suggests, is a "mythical and magical" space "beyond the limits of the material or knowable world," which Auster constantly sets against the mundane and frequently harsh realities of American life.[14] In the novel's sentimental climax, Mr. Bones dashes across a busy highway "toward the glare and the roar that were rushing in on him from all directions," aiming to join Willy in Timbuktu (181).

The America Mr. Bones presumably leaves behind is "the America of two-car garages, home-improvement loans, and neo-Renaissance shopping malls" (157–58). It is a place of sprawling suburban developments lacking the community-in-diversity and the sheer adrenalin of the urban spaces about which Auster customarily writes. It is characterized by rampant consumerism and a serial sameness profoundly at odds with the hippie ethics of the 1960s from which Willy G. Christmas, formerly William Gurevitch, child of Eastern European Jewish immigrants, emerged.

When Willy first "set forth on his career of vagabondage," the United States "was crawling with dropouts and runaway children, with long-haired neo-visionaries, dysfunctional anarchists, and doped-up misfits" (26). But before long "the runaways had crawled back home to mom and dad; the potheads had traded in their love beads for paisley ties; the war was over" (27). Willy's refusal to "blend in" (27) or to abandon his itinerant existence and antiauthoritarian stance led inevitably to alienation and persecution.

In an individualistic capitalist society like this, where everyone is pursuing the American Dream, there is a profound lack of solidarity even between immigrants on the margins of society. Soon after Willy's death, Mr. Bones is taken in by an affectionate and lonely Chinese American boy called Henry Chow. The destruction of their blossoming friendship by the boy's father, Mr. Chow, inspires one of the novel's allegorical observations: "what good was a home," the reader is asked, "if you didn't feel safe in it, if you were treated as an outcast in the very spot that was supposed to be your refuge?" (112). In other words, promised lands are seldom what they are cracked up to be.

Escaping from Mr. Chow, Mr. Bones finds himself in the Virginia home of the Jones family, where "the air was filled with the sounds of lawn mowers, sprinklers, and birds," and where, in an omen of the novel's climax, "on an invisible highway to the north, a dull bee-swarm of traffic pulsed under the suburban landscape" (121). The Jones's home is ostensibly paradise: Mr. Bones is taken in, fed, cleaned up, and fussed over by the Jones's sugary-sweet daughter Alice. Even the humiliation of being renamed "Sparky" cannot shatter the idyll (132). Willy's wilderness wandering has been transformed into the bland but comforting stability of the suburban garden. However, when the Jones family go out and leave Mr. Bones alone and tethered to a post, his feelings change: "Had he walked to the ends of the earth and found this blessed haven only to be spat on by the people who had taken him in? They had turned him into a prisoner" (140).

Where *Timbuktu* succeeds is in showing what a life of bourgeois estrangement like the Jones's does to a person. Live long enough in such an environment, it suggests, and the consumer comforts begin to mask the underlying enslavement. Mr. Bones feels himself succumbing: "Now that Mr. Bones was on the inside, he wondered where his old master had gone wrong and why he had worked so hard to spurn the trappings of the good life. It might not have been perfect in this place, but it had a lot to recommend it, and once you got used to the mechanics of the system, it no longer seemed so important that you were tethered to a wire all day" (158). Here the supposed inclusiveness of democracy and the melting pot is jettisoned in favor of divisive notions of "inside" and "outside." White middle-class affluence is considered normal; anything else is deviant and threatening.

Mr. Bones is lucky enough to realize how suffocating this new life is, and eventually escapes. The question that *Timbuktu* does not quite answer is: what kind of escape is actually possible from the system? If Mr. Bones makes it to Timbuktu, in the middle of a desert, it seems he has arrived back at the beginning, in the wilderness where Willy and fellow vagabond pioneers aspired to a less materialistic way of life. Yet the novel implies that most desert wanderers end up in the suburbs anyway. So maybe there is no realistic way out, unless one regards Timbuktu simply as a place of dreams or an "oasis of spirits" (48). In an unashamedly sentimental story, perhaps this is the best way of understanding it: in a world designed to suppress freedom and difference, heaven is in the head.

After 9/11: *Leviathan, Oracle Night, The Brooklyn Follies, Travels in the Scriptorium,* and *Man in the Dark*

In an interview in the *Observer,* Auster identifies in *Oracle Night* a trend that began with *The Book of Illusions:* "Maybe it's my age, but I think I am going through a period of writing about debilitated men," he says. "I've started something new recently, and though it's very early days and things could change, this character, too, is somewhat wobbly. I don't know what it is except maybe this moment of my life, this sudden sense of encroaching mortality."[15] The trend continues in *The Brooklyn Follies* (2005), *Travels in the Scriptorium* (2006), and *Man in the Dark* (2008). When *Oracle Night* was published in New York and London in 2003, Auster was fifty-six years old, and it would be easy to accept his biographical explanation for all these "debilitated men."

There is another potentially more interesting explanation, however. Although the term "post-9/11 novel" has in recent years become hackneyed in the convenient labeling of fiction by writers as diverse as Ian McEwan, Don DeLillo, Jay McInerney, and John Updike, there is evidence in *Oracle Night* that, obliquely at least, Auster was beginning to confront some of the implications of the catastrophe. Put simply, the narrator Sidney Orr's writer's block, coupled with his physical weakness and his temporary sexual impotence, can be viewed as emblematic of the contemporary writer's crisis of confidence after 11 September 2001.

An event like 9/11 raises significant questions. First, is any writer intellectually or emotionally capable of writing about unimaginable catastrophe and suffering? When reality becomes so monstrous, is fiction not robbed of its power? And, to revisit an issue raised in Don DeLillo's novel *Mao II* (1991), does the terrorist now wield more power to alter public perceptions than the artist? Of course, the haunting presence of the Holocaust throughout Auster's work has always cast doubt on art's ability to portray the world in all its horror. Yet the destruction of the World Trade Center forces a reconsideration of these ideas, not least because it happened on U.S. soil and hence constitutes a direct attack on the American ideals of democracy and self-reliance so important to Auster. Second, the impact of the attacks was immediate and intensely visual. Captured live on television, camcorders, and mobile phones, the event elevated the visual image to the point where words suddenly seemed redundant. Moreover, "the safe distance of the TV screen" was no longer applicable.[16] The televisual image brought home political reality in spectacular fashion and, arguably, much more effectively than the written word could have done.

Auster appears partially to acknowledge this in *Man in the Dark*. At the end of the novel there is a vivid description of an Internet execution video. In it, Titus, the boyfriend of August Brill's granddaughter, is decapitated by Iraqi kidnappers. As Brill explains: "We all knew it would go on haunting us for the rest of our lives, and yet somehow we felt we had to be there with Titus, to keep our eyes open to the horror for his sake, to breathe him into us and hold him there."[17] Although, of course, words are needed to describe this horrific event, the decision to make this the climax of the novel suggests that the visual images themselves have the most potency and immediacy.

There are four Auster novels that can be viewed as "post-9/11," all of which adopt slightly different approaches to the problems 9/11 presents the writer: *Oracle Night, The Brooklyn Follies, Travels in the Scriptorium,* and *Man in the Dark. Leviathan* (1992) was published well before 9/11,[18] but takes on added significance in the light of those attacks. The first-person narrator, Peter Aaron, writes the story in order metaphorically to reconstruct the life of his friend, fellow writer and "political revolutionary" Benjamin Sachs, who, the reader is informed in the first line, recently "blew himself up by the side of the road in northern Wisconsin."[19] After a near-fatal fall from a balcony, Sachs decides that "the days of being a shadow are over. I've got to step into the real world now and do something" (137). This decision and his subsequent disappearance into the Vermont woods trigger the bizarre chain of events leading to his rebirth as "the Phantom of Liberty." This "anguished, soft-spoken prophet" (244) travels around the United States blowing up replicas of the Statue of Liberty to highlight the degradation of the political ideals the statue represents and enlighten the public "about the nature of institutional power" (252).

Leviathan contains much that is familiar. It is full of writers; chance events; meditations on the nature of storytelling and truth; fragmented, plural identities; and paranoid believers in fate. Yet it is distinguished by the central, powerful image of the shattered Statues of Liberty. On the one hand this is a novel that celebrates e pluribus unum, "democracy, freedom, equality under the law . . . the best of what America has to offer the world" (242), while recognizing through the figure of the increasingly disillusioned Sachs how debased these ideals have become in the contemporary world. The questions it poses are: Can acts of terror do more than art and literature to alert people to the debasement of these ideals? And which is more powerful—the leviathan of the state or the leviathan formed by the interconnections between all human beings? Finally, whether or not, as Thomas Hobbes believes, the state is the means by which "a multitude of men, are made *one* person,"[20] how can the state possibly pretend to unite individuals who are already, in themselves, fractured, fragmented, and plural? These questions of fragmentation versus unity, division versus integration, are even more pressing given events post-9/11, and they force the reader to appraise the novel afresh.

Oracle Night is in many ways Auster-by-the-numbers. It is about the struggles of its narrator, Sidney Orr, to start writing again after a near-fatal illness, and about the notebook with seemingly magical properties that inspires him again (6). It is characteristically structured like a Russian doll, layer upon layer. At its heart is the image of Nick Bowen, the protagonist of one of the many stories-within-stories, locked in an underground room "with no conceivable means of escape" (106). This is a neat image of the writer's impotence post-9/11, and the feeling is exacerbated by the many true stories and real texts Auster includes. There is the story of the prostitute who gave birth to a stillborn child during sex, dumped it in the garbage, and went straight back to her client (112–15).[21] There is a reproduction of the real Warsaw phone directory from 1937/38, which haunts Sidney because "it occurs to him that nearly every Jewish person listed in the book is long dead" (91). The conclusion is unmistakable: reality is much worse than fiction could ever be. In the end Sidney is reduced to writing paranoid stories about a possible love triangle between him; his wife, Grace; and their mutual writer-friend John Trause (212–19). Despite its formulaic Austerian nature, *Oracle Night*'s power lies in its depiction of the many ways in which trauma, and the resultant flurry of imaginative activity, can affect the domestic, private lives of individuals.

Peter Conrad describes *Oracle Night*'s depiction of Auster's home in morbid terms: "New York is the place where mankind came to an end, where human life, unredeemed by literature, lost its meaning."[22] The novel that succeeded *Oracle Night*, however, constituted a bold attempt to redeem human life, the sympathetic power of literature, and New York itself, or at least part of it. *The Brooklyn Follies* was published in 2005 by Henry Holt in New York and by Faber and Faber in London. "Comic," "happy," and "reader-friendly" are the attributes with which it is most frequently associated. Auster himself, in a conversation with Jonathan Lethem, describes it as "an attempt to write a kind of comedy."[23] Jeff Turrentine, writing in the *Washington Post*, expands on this idea: "the manner in which everyone's miseries converge and nullify one another is what defines *The Brooklyn Follies*, ultimately, as a comedy." It is, he believes, "a big-hearted, life-affirming, tenderly comic yarn."[24]

If *Oracle Night* is a post-9/11 novel in its dissection of violence and human tragedy, it is tempting to regard its successor as self-consciously "life-affirming" in reaction to the mass murder. Indeed the narrative describes the transition from self-absorption and isolation to willing involvement in the lives of others. The narrator, Nathan Glass, starts out as a cantankerous old grudge in remission from cancer who moves to Brooklyn "looking for a quiet place to die" and admits that "there is something nasty about me at times."[25] By the time the complex dance of interwoven tales ends, he has survived a heart scare, found the love of an irascible old widow called Joyce, and decided "to form a company that would publish books about the forgotten ones," that is, biographies about ordinary people for their friends and relatives (303). On the way to this decision, he has become entangled in the dramas of an eclectic Brooklyn cast, including his nephew Tom Wood, a failed academic and one-time taxi driver; the charming gay bookstore owner and art forger Harry Brightman; Rufus, the Jamaican drag artist; and Lucy, Tom's niece, who arrives on his doorstep one morning refusing to speak or give details of her disappeared mother's whereabouts. It is the realization that all these disparate lives are connected that leads to Nathan's redemption, encapsulated in his final declaration (rehearsing the ending of *Oracle Night*): "I was happy, my friends, as happy as any man who had ever lived" (306).

Perhaps the most contentious aspect of the novel for contemporary critics is the fact that his sentimental education culminates on 11 September 2001, when "the smoke of three thousand incinerated bodies would drift over toward Brooklyn and come pouring down on us in a white cloud of ashes and death" (306). Choosing to end the action with the catastrophe is not intended to undermine what has gone before. Rather *The Brooklyn Follies* serves as a retroactive preparation for that tragedy, and as evidence that whatever horrors might be visited upon the citizens of New York and the world, community and friendship will endure, destroying hate and prejudice in the process.

Even more than *Oracle Night,* this is a novel concerned with the small stories of everyday lives. But it is much more enchanted by the humor and the redemptive value of reality than its gloomy predecessor. Its main influences are Auster's editorial work on the collection *I Thought My Father Was God* and the brief vignettes in the movie *Blue in the Face,* which have ordinary Brooklynites sharing statistics about the borough or expounding on quirky topics such as the difference between Belgian waffles in Belgium and the United States. Less concerned with darker existential aspects of storytelling than *The New York Trilogy,* less preoccupied with the struggle to create than *Oracle Night, Brooklyn*

Follies instead suggests that community is composed of a multitude of small stories, some true, some perhaps not. To listen to the mostly ordinary, sometimes extraordinary, frequently laughable anecdotes of the different groups of people around you is to uphold the ideal of unity in diversity fundamental to American identity. For Auster, Brooklyn exemplifies this ideal. This is "New York and yet not New York" (50), a place with a "multilayered chorus of foreign accents" (181), the place where people, according to Nathan, "are less reluctant to talk to strangers than any tribe I had previously encountered" (5). It is very much a community built from narrative, and to echo this, the novel itself takes the form of a series of anecdotes, each chapter given its own idiosyncratic title such as "The Sperm Bank Surprise" (68) or "The Queen of Brooklyn" (81). To read the novel in its entirety is to construct Brooklyn from these unique yet interconnected stories. The very act of reading, then, takes on ethical importance.

"We have never been perfect, but we are real" (xvi). Auster summarizes the *National Story Project* with this, and it could also serve for *The Brooklyn Follies*. It is of course a work of fiction, but one that, unusually in Auster's work, insists on "reality" as a viable idea. There are obvious fakes here, including Harry Brightman's art forgeries (42–48) and "The Hotel Existence," Brightman's imaginary retreat from the world, which Nathan realizes is "just talk" (182). Yet there are also fictions, with a significant shift of emphasis, that are designed to enable people to live more comfortably in the real world. For example, Tom Wood tells Nathan the story of the dying Franz Kafka who, upon seeing a little girl in the park crying over her lost doll, proceeds to invent an elaborate story about the doll's holiday, her decision to move away, and her eventual marriage. This tale he unfolds for the girl in a series of carefully worded and highly literary letters. They constitute "a beautiful and persuasive lie, ... a different reality—a false one, maybe, but something true and believable according to the laws of fiction" (155). Kafka has created what one might call a "true fake," a fiction that possesses a sympathetic and ethical truth transcending its content. Contrary to what Tom himself believes, it is not the case that "reality no longer exists" (156). It is rather that the pains of reality—from the loss of a favorite doll to the horror of a terrorist attack—are best dealt with not by retreat into self-penned narratives, but by immersing oneself in a community of stories, true or otherwise. Brooklyn is such a community, and *The Brooklyn Follies* is Auster's sincere attempt to produce a true fake, something imperfect but real.

Travels in the Scriptorium appeared in Europe barely a year after *The Brooklyn Follies*. Both in terms of form and content, it came as something of a surprise. Where its predecessor had been, in the words of one critic, "entertaining" and "relatively mainstream," *Scriptorium* was dark, introverted, and deliberately frustrating.[26] To borrow one of Auster's favorite metaphors: *Follies* took the reader out of the locked room and back into society, only for *Scriptorium* to place the reader firmly back inside.

The locked room is assuredly the author's head. An elderly writer, known only as Mr. Blank, wakes up in a room with no recollection of how he arrived there. Another debilitated individual, Mr. Blank is of an "advanced age," has considerable difficulty "bending [and] crouching," and "is nothing if not forgetful."[27] He never makes an attempt to leave this room, and it is never made clear whether the door is physically locked at all: the incarceration is mostly psychological. Periodically Mr. Blank is visited by characters from his own work, including

Anna Blume, Daniel Quinn, and Samuel Farr. These are "the phantom beings that clutter his head" while his mind wanders "adrift in the past" (3). Clearly Mr. Blank is Mr. Auster, and equally clearly the reader is being granted for the first time a privileged insight into the writer's thought processes, memories, and anxieties. In fact the reader's perspective might best be described as "voyeuristic." We watch Mr. Blank through a hidden camera "planted in the ceiling directly above him. The shutter clicks silently once every second," and he has no idea he is being observed (1). In keeping with the scientific tone of much of the book, or "report" as the narrator prefers to label it (8), the reader seems to be complicit in some kind of experiment, invited "to study the pictures as attentively as [he or she] can and refrain from drawing any premature conclusions" (1–2). The atmosphere is paranoid and claustrophobic, which in part may represent another oblique reaction to a post-9/11 world of detention and surveillance. Indeed one of the many manuscripts-within-the-story is the confessional prison memoir of Sigmund Graf, who is held captive in the mysterious "Confederation." With its meditations on power and betrayal, the fear of different cultures; its hints at ethnic cleansing (121); and its central image of prolonged imprisonment without trial, it is not hard to make the connection between Graf's predicament and a post-9/11 world where Iraq, Guantanamo Bay, and debates about Islam in modern society are seldom far from the media glare.

If *Scriptorium* has any message, however, it is this: literary characters endure beyond the life of their creator. As the narrator expresses it: "Without him, we are nothing, but the paradox is that we, the figments of another mind, will outlive the mind that made us, for once we are thrown into the world, we continue to exist forever, and our stories go on being told, even after we are dead" (144). It is, according to Angel Gurria-Quintana, an idea borrowed from Luigi Pirandello's play *Six Characters in Search of an Author* (1921).[28] Whether or not one chooses to regard the work as derivative, it is evident this is the Auster text that most self-consciously scratches away at the author's anxieties about his position in the literary marketplace and the scrutiny that accompanies celebrity. For all his success, he might just be an elderly man, locked in his own work like Nick Bowen / Sidney Orr, yet under the scrutinizing gaze of his readership and powerless to change anything in the real world. The fact that the narrative is circular and regressive, ending with Mr. Blank picking up the manuscript of the very same novel we have been reading, testifies to this entrapment. And the fact that the manuscript is written by "N. R. Fanshawe," the disappeared writer in *The Locked Room,* only reinforces the sense that the writer can find no way out from his work (140). For all its hints at a political subtext, *Scriptorium* feels like a retreat into the author's head and a refusal directly to confront contemporary issues.

Man in the Dark, published by Henry Holt and Faber and Faber in 2008, treats contemporary U.S. politics both more and less obliquely than its predecessor. In one respect it pretends that the Twin Towers massacre never happened. It does this by means of a literary mode sometimes called "uchrony"—that is, speculative fiction about alternative histories. A uchrony is an extended "what if," and imagines how things might have turned out if history had unfolded differently after a key event. In the imagination of August Brill, our bed-ridden, insomniac narrator, the 2000 election of George Bush led to the secession of several states from the Union to form "the Independent States of America." 9/11 did not happen, and neither did the Iraq invasion, but as the federalists fight back against the independents, a second civil war erupts (62).

One could argue that Auster is much more daring here than he is in *Scriptorium*. His invented scenario directly expresses anger at the Bush administration, and as Owen Brick, the protagonist of the story-within-the-story, travels through the eerily quiet and "cratered streets" of the city (25), the narrative feels eminently plausible—but only to a point. Brick's mission, we soon learn, is to find a writer called "Blake" or "Black" or even "Bloch" (9)—it turns out of course to be Brill—and assassinate him. The war is a story being written by Brill, and, as Sergeant Serge Tobak deadpans, "we're all part of it" (10). In a typically Austerian move, the two fictional layers or universes, Brick's and Brill's, coalesce once again in the author's head. In fact Brick's uchrony ends very abruptly and rather arbitrarily halfway through the novel, when Brill finally decides he has had enough (118).

Brill then spends his time narrating real stories from World War II and the cold war (119–29). After this, he tells his granddaughter Katya the story of his marriage, separation, and eventual reconciliation with his wife (131–62). Finally, we read Titus's story—his ambitions to be a writer (169), his decision to work in Iraq so he can be "out in the big rotten world and discover what it feels like to be part of history" (173), and finally the execution video (175–76). The stories get progressively closer to home, more harrowing, and more real. The uchrony, though compelling and plausible, cannot compete, indeed should not compete, with the present-day reality of August and his family.

9/11 did happen, and there is a need to confront it. Ultimately *Man in the Dark* resembles *The Brooklyn Follies* more than *Scriptorium*. Its message, to borrow a line from Nathaniel Hawthorne's daughter Rose, is "the weird world rolls on" (180). Life is full of horror, and the night full of stories of suffering, but as the dawn symbolically breaks (177), there is the solidarity and solace of our loved ones to console us and keep us moving forward.

Notes

Chapter One: Understanding Paul Auster

1. Tim Lewis, "An Audience with Paul Auster," *Esquire* (December 2005): 125–30. Auster's Asturias acceptance speech is reprinted in "I Want to Tell You a Story," *Observer,* 5 November 2006, 23.

2. Hugh McDonald asks: "is he [Auster] the first Undisputed Heavyweight Author of the 21st century? . . . he could be a contender." *Glasgow Herald,* 1 January 2005.

3. Paul Auster, *Hand to Mouth* (New York: Henry Holt, 1999) 125.

4. François Fallix, ed., *Lectures d'une úuvre: Moon palace de Paul Auster* (Paris: Editions du Temps, 1996); Catherine Pesso-Miquel, ed., *Toiles Trouées et deserts lunaires dans Moon palace de Paul Auster* (Paris: Presses de la Sorbonne Nouvelle, 1996); Yves-Charles Granjeat, ed., *Moon Palace, collectif* (Paris: Ellipses, 1996); Marc Chénetier, *Paul Auster as the Wizard of Odds: Moon Palace* (Paris: Didier Erudition-CNED, 1996).

5. Auster talks about his filmmaking experiences with Annette Insdorf in *3 Films: Smoke, Blue in the Face, Lulu on the Bridge* (New York: Picador, 2003). All parenthetical citations are from this edition.

6. E. M. Forster, *Howard's End* (1910, rpt., Harmondsworth: Penguin, 1984), 188.

7. *The South Bank Show: Paul Auster,* pres. Melvyn Bragg, ITV Granada (U.K.), 7 July 1996.

8. "Interview with Larry McCaffery and Sinda Gregory," in *The Art of Hunger: Essays, Prefaces, Interviews* (New York: Penguin, 2001), 315. All parenthetical citations are from this edition.

9. Interview with Stephen Capen, *Worldguide,* 21 October 1996, http://worldmind.com/Cannon/Culture/Interviews/auster.html.

10. Paul Auster, *The Invention of Solitude* (New York: Penguin, 1988), 20. All parenthetical citations are from this edition.

11. Christopher Bigsby, *Writers in Conversation: Volume Two* (Norwich: EAP Publishing, 2001), 23. Even as an undergraduate, Auster was concerned with solitude and collectivity. In an essay on the sixteenth-century French essayist Michel de Montaigne, he describes the writer "sitting in solitude, listening to the utterances of his self's many voices" (Berg Collection, New York Public Library, Box 79, Folder 2).

12. Paul Auster, *The New York Trilogy* (New York: Penguin, 2006), 144, 145. All parenthetical citations are from this edition, where appropriate as "CG" (*City of Glass*), "G" (*Ghosts*) and "LR" (*The Locked Room*).

13. Ralph Waldo Emerson, "The Poet," in *Selected Writings* (New York: Signet, 2003), 344.

14. Paul Auster, "Narrative," in *Collected Poems* (Woodstock and New York: Overlook Press, 2004) 143.

15. Paul Auster, *Moon Palace* (New York: Viking, 1989), 122, 123. All parenthetical citations are from this edition.

16. Paul Auster, *I Thought My Father Was God and Other True Tales from NPR's National Story Project* (New York: Henry Holt, 2001), xvi. All parenthetical citations are from this edition.

17. Tom Deveson, "At Cross Purposes," *Sunday Times Books* 1 February 2004, 52.

18. Paul Auster, *Timbuktu* (New York: Picador USA, 1999), 65. All parenthetical citations are from this edition.

19. Janet Maslin, "A Novel's Actor More Real Than Many Made of Flesh," *New York Times,* 9 May 2002.

20. D. T. Max, "The Professor of Despair," *New York Times,* 1 September 2002.

21. Paul Auster, "Why Write?" in *Collected Prose* (New York: Picador, 2003), 269.

22. Angel Gurria-Quintana, "Haven't We Met Before?" *Financial Times,* 7 October 2006, 40.

Chapter Two: *The Invention of Solitude*

1. Bigsby, *Writers in Conversation,* 22.

2. W. S. Merwin, "Invisible Father," *New York Times,* 27 February 1983.

3. Michael Walters, "Life's Punning Plots," *Times Literary Supplement,* 17 February 1989, 158; Jacqueline Austan, "The Invention of Solitude," *American Book Review* 6.1 (November–December 1983): 23.

4. Adam Begley, "Case of the Brooklyn Symbolist," *New York Times,* 30 August 1992.

5. The poet Ann Lauterbach, speaking in Begley, "Case of the Brooklyn Symbolist," 52.

6. Paul Auster and Michel Contat, "The Manuscript in the Book: A Conversation," *Yale French Studies* 89 (1996): 180.

7. William Dow, "Paul Auster's *The Invention of Solitude:* Glimmers in a Reach to Authenticity," *Critique* 39.3 (Spring 1998): 279.

8. Susan Sontag, *On Photography* (London: Penguin, 2002), 15.

9. Ibid., 16.

10. Roland Barthes, "The Photographic Message," in *Image Music Text,* trans. Stephen Heath (London: Fontana Press, 1977), 21.

11. Ibid., 19.

12. In an early typescript of "Portrait," Auster consistently refers to his first wife as "Lydia" (Lydia Davis, herself a well-known American writer and translator). In the published version, she becomes "my wife." Just as the grandfather is virtually cut out of family history, so Auster tries his own act of excision, making Lydia both there and not-there by removing her name. Berg Collection, Box 4, Folder 1.

13. Chris Pace, "Unpublished Interview with Paul Auster," *Blue Cricket,* 21 February 1993, http://www.bluecricket.com/auster/links/secret.html.

14. Aliki Varvogli, *The World That Is the Book: Paul Auster's Fiction* (Liverpool: Liverpool University Press, 2001), 11.

15. Carsten Springer, *Crises: The Works of Paul Auster* (Frankfurt am Main: Peter Lang, 2001), 90. Springer may well be drawing on a famous quotation from Ralph Waldo Emerson, with which Auster is undoubtedly familiar—"I am not solitary whilst I read and write, though nobody is with me." Ralph Waldo Emerson, "Nature," in *Selected Writings of Ralph Waldo Emerson,* ed. William H. Gilman (New York: Signet, 2003), 183.

16. Reproduced in Auster and Contat, "Manuscript in the Book," 174.

17. "Zimmer" is the German and "zimer" the Yiddish for "room."

18. "Notebook 1966–67," in Berg Collection, Box 8, Folder 2.

19. "Interview with Edmond Jabès," in Berg Collection, Box 8, Folder 1.

20. Derek Rubin, "'The Hunger Must Be Preserved at All Cost': A Reading of *The Invention of Solitude,*" in *Beyond the Red Notebook: Essays on Paul Auster,* ed. Dennis Barone (Philadelphia: University of Pennsylvania Press, 1995), 61.

21. Ibid.

22. "Secular Jewish Culture / Radical Poetic Practice," at the Center for Jewish History / American Jewish Historical Society, New York, 21 September 2004, http://www.writing.upenn.edu/pennsound/x/AJHS.html.

23. Steven Alford argues that there is a "brave" Auster and a "weak" Auster in his writing. The former accepts meaninglessness; the second looks for patterns and conspiracies. Steven E. Alford, "Chance in Contemporary Narrative: The Example of Paul Auster," in *Bloom's Modern Critical Views: Paul Auster,* ed. Harold Bloom (Philadelphia: Chelsea House, 2004), 123.

24. Springer, *Crises,* 94–95.

Chapter Three: *The New York Trilogy*

1. Charles Baxter, "The Bureau of Missing Persons: Notes on Paul Auster's Fiction," *Review of Contemporary Fiction* 14.1 (Spring 1994) 42.

2. Dennis Porter, *The Pursuit of Crime: Art and Ideology in Detective Fiction* (New Haven, Conn.: Yale University Press, 1981), 245.

3. Paul Auster, "New York Spleen," in Berg Collection, Box 60, Folder 1.

4. Stefano Tani, *The Doomed Detective: The Contribution of the Detective Novel to Postmodern American and Italian Fiction* (Carbondale: Southern Illinois University Press, 1984), 41–42.

5. Marcel Berlins, "Case of the Inner Self," *Times,* 18 February 1988.

6. Dennis Drabelle, "Mystery Goes Post-Modern," *Washington Post Book World,* 15 June 1986, 9. The Nobokov text to which Drabelle refers is most likely *Pale Fire* (1962), a novel in which a poem called "Pale Fire" becomes the main clue in a detective plot to uncover truths about its author.

7. Toby Olson, "Metaphysical Mystery Tour," *New York Times,* 3 November 1985.

8. Brendan Martin, *Paul Auster's Postmodernity* (London: Routledge, 2008), 31.

9. Paul Auster, *The Red Notebook,* in *Collected Prose,* 262, 263.

10. Mark Brown, *Paul Auster* (Manchester: Manchester University Press, 2007), 36.

11. Aphasia is a loss of the ability to produce or comprehend language, usually brought about by brain injury.

12. Varvogli, *World That Is the Book,* 28–29.

13. Paul Benjamin, *Squeeze Play* (London: Faber and Faber, 1991), 16.

14. Arthur Saltzman, *Designs of Darkness in Contemporary American Fiction* (Philadelphia: University of Pennsylvania Press, 1990), 62.

15. Alison Russell, "Deconstructing *The New York Trilogy:* Paul Auster's Anti-detective Fiction," *Critique* 31 (Winter 1990): 77.

16. Ibid.

17. Ibid.

18. Henry David Thoreau, *Walden* (Cambridge, Mass.: Riverside Press, 1882), 98.

19. Ibid., 135.

20. Mark Ford, "Inventions of Solitude: Thoreau and Auster," *Journal of American Studies* 33 (1999): 202.

21. Thoreau, *Walden*, 20.

22. Mark Brown, "'We Don't Go By Numbers': Brooklyn and Baseball in the Films of Paul Auster," in *The Brooklyn Film*, ed. John B. Manbeck and Robert Singer (Jefferson, N.C.: McFarland, 2003), 145.

23. See Richard Swope, "Approaching the Threshold(s) in Postmodern Detective Fiction: Hawthorne's 'Wakefield' and Other Missing Persons," *Critique* 39.3 (Spring 1998): 207–27.

24. Varvogli, *World That Is the Book*, 49.

25. John Dickson Carr, "The Locked-Room Lecture," in *The Three Coffins* (New York: Harper Brothers, 1935), 220–37.

26. Stephen Bernstein, "Auster's Sublime Closure: *The Locked Room*," in Barone, *Beyond the Red Notebook*, 91.

27. Springer, *Crises*, 122.

28. Varvogli, *World That Is the Book*, 51.

Chapter Four: Last Chances

1. Paul Auster, *In the Country of Last Things* (New York: Viking, 1987), 2. All parenthetical citations are from this edition.

2. Elaine Feinstein, "*In the Country of Last Things*, by Paul Auster," *Times*, 11 August 1988, 23.

3. Berg Collection, Box 43, Folder 4. Other early drafts in Box 6, Folder 2.

4. Queen Isabella I of Castile and King Ferdinand II of Aragon, the "Catholic King and Queen," were the fifteenth-century monarchs who approved the expedition of Cristobal Colon (Christopher Columbus) to the New World. By using these names, Auster suggests that the city is in the New World (America).

5. Padgett Powell, "The End Is Only Imaginary," *New York Times,* 17 May 1987, 11.

6. Austin MacCurtain, "Paperbacks; Books," *Sunday Times Books,* 25 June 1989, 7.

7. David Colker, "Paul Auster Explores Survival 'In the Country of Last Things,'" *Los Angeles Herald Examiner,* 24 May 1987.

8. Varvogli, *World That Is the Book,* 90. Varvogli also mentions the work of Emmanuel Ringelblum, the historian who collated the writings of inhabitants of the Warsaw ghetto.

9. Auster, *Collected Poems.* All parenthetical citations are from this edition.

10. Elisabeth Wesseling, "Parable of the Apocalypse," *Neophilologus* 25 (1991): 498.

11. "The Art of Hunger" is Auster's essay on Knut Hamsun's novel *Hunger.* In this essay, Auster describes the art of hunger as "the direct expression of the effort to express itself . . . an art of need, of necessity, of desire" (18).

12. Paul Auster, *The Music of Chance* (New York: Viking, 1990), 12. All parenthetical citations are from this edition.

13. Paul Auster, interview by author, Brooklyn, N.Y., 27 March 2005; "Interview with Larry McCaffery and Sinda Gregory," 294.

14. Christopher Bigsby, "In Conversation with Paul Auster," in *Writers in Conversation,* 22.

15. Robert Nye, "The Malice of Chance," *Guardian,* 21 March 1991, 28; Madison Smartt Bell, "Poker and Nothingness," *New York Times,* 4 November 1990.

16. Octavio Roca, "Wit, Quick Prose Keep Philosophical 'Chance' Rolling," *Washington Times,* 31 October 1990; Matthew Gilbert, "Auster's Intriguing *The Music of Chance,*" *Boston Globe,* 8 October 1990.

17. Tim Woods, "*The Music of Chance:* Aleatorical (Dis)harmonies within 'The City of the World,'" in Barone, *Beyond the Red Notebook,* 146.

18. Jack Kerouac, *The Dharma Bums* (London: Penguin Books, 2000), 11.

19. Bernd Herzogenrath, *An Art of Desire: Reading Paul Auster* (Amsterdam: Rodopi, 1999), 163.

20. Eyal Dotan, "The Game of Late Capitalism: Gambling and Ideology in *The Music of Chance*," *Mosaic: A Journal for the Interdisciplinary Study of Literature* 33.1 (March 2000): 161–76.

21. Ibid., 161.

22. Brown, *Paul Auster*, 141.

23. Auster, interview.

24. Early in the novel, Pozzi compares Flower and Stone to Laurel and Hardy (30). In *Laurel and Hardy Go to Heaven* (1976–77), reproduced in *Hand to Mouth,* Auster creates an absurd scenario worthy of Samuel Beckett, in which Stan and Ollie procrastinate over the building of a wall from eighteen huge stones. Earlier versions of this play exist—one is called *Eclipse* and stars Brahms and Liszt instead of Laurel and Hardy, and one is called *The Stones* and features Marx and Freud. The constants are the stones. Berg Collection, Box 15, Folder 1.

25. John Calvin (1509–64) was a Protestant theologian and one of the most influential developers of Reformation theology. His works, particularly *Institutes of the Christian Religion,* were touchstones for groups such as the New England Puritans.

26. Franz Kafka, *The Great Wall of China and Other Pieces,* trans. Edwin Muir (London: Martin Secker, 1933).

27. Varvogli, *World That Is the Book,* 114.

Chapter Five: Auster's Frontier Novels

1. Frederick Jackson Turner, "The Significance of the Frontier in American History," in *Does the Frontier Experience Make America Exceptional?* (Boston and New York: Bedford / St. Martin's, 1999) 19.

2. Ibid., 20.

3. Ibid., 35.

4. Ibid., 20.

5. Ibid., 21.

6. Patricia Nelson Limerick, Clyde A. Milner II, and Charles E. Rankin, preface to *Trails: Toward a New Western History* (Lawrence: University Press of Kansas, 1991), xi.

7. Ibid.

8. Paul Auster, "The Surveyor's Letter," in Berg Collection, Box 9, Folder 4, 11.

9. Ibid., 8.

10. Ibid., 9.

11. Ibid., 12.

12. See R. W. B. Lewis, *The American Adam: Innocence, Tragedy, and Tradition in the Nineteenth Century* (Chicago: Chicago University Press, 1955), for a seminal exploration of Adam in the New World Eden.

13. Austin MacCurtain, "*Moon Palace* by Paul Auster," *Sunday Times Books,* 15 April 1990, 3.

14. Joyce Reiser Kornblatt, "The Novelist Out of Control," *New York Times Book Review,* 19 March 1989, 9; Gary Indiana, "Pompous Circumstance: Paul Auster Indulges Himself," *Village Voice,* 4 April 1989, 45.

15. Steven Weisenburger, "Inside *Moon Palace,*" in Barone, *Beyond the Red Notebook,* 133.

16. Varvogli, *World That Is the Book,* 125.

17. Weisenburger, "Inside *Moon Palace,*" 138.

18. "Manifest destiny" is an extremely influential phrase in U.S. history and culture that was first coined by the journalist John L. O'Sullivan in 1845. It refers to the conception of America's divine right to expand across the continent provided for the people "by Providence." "Annexation," *United States Magazine and Democratic Review* 17.1 (July–August 1845): 5–10. Critics of the idea argue that it attempts to justify subjugation of Native peoples and the aggressive annexation of land.

19. Varvogli, *World That Is the Book,* 120.

20. Edwin Fussell, *Frontier: American Literature and the American West* (Princeton, N.J.: Princeton University Press, 1965), 14.

21. In Gérard de Cortanze, *La Solitude du labyrinthe: Essai de entretiens* (Paris: Actes Suds, 1997), 75. Translation by Sheena Kalayil.

22. Paul Auster, *Mr. Vertigo* (New York: Viking, 1994), 15. All parenthetical citations are from this edition.

23. Joan Smith, "Flight Fancy," *Financial Times Books,* 16 April 1994, xxi; Danny Calegari, "Back to Earth, with a Crash," *Sunday Age Agenda,* 10 April 1994, 8.

24. Phil Edwards, "*Mr. Vertigo,*" *New Statesman and Society,* 8 April 1994, 37.

25. Jay Cantor, "Some People Just Know How to Fly," *New York Times Book Review,* 28 August 1994, 1.

26. Brendan Martin, *Paul Auster's Postmodernity* (New York: Routledge, 2008), 23.

27. Brown, *Paul Auster,* 106.

28. Ibid., 108.

29. "Remember how the LORD your God led you all the way in the desert these forty years, to humble you and to test you in order to know what was in your heart, whether or not you would keep his commands" (Deut. 8:2).

30. Springer, *Crises,* 178.

31. Catherine Storey, "The Heights of Achievement; *Mr. Vertigo* by Paul Auster," *Independent,* 17 April 1994, 36.

Chapter Six: *The Book of Illusions*

1. Jonathan Lethem, "Jonathan Lethem Talks with Paul Auster," *Believer* 3.1 (February 2005): 55.

2. Ibid.

3. Brown, *Paul Auster,* 118.

4. Lethem, "Jonathan Lethem Talks with Paul Auster," 51–52.

5. Ibid., 54–55.

6. Paul Auster, *The Book of Illusions* (New York: Henry Holt, 2002), 15. All parenthetical citations are from this edition.

7. Max, "Professor of Despair."

8. John Crowley, "Flickering Images," *Washington Post,* 8 September 2002.

9. Janet Maslin, "A Novel's Actor More Real Than Many Made of Flesh," *New York Times,* 5 September 2002.

10. F. Scott Fitzgerald, *The Great Gatsby* (Harmondsworth, U.K.: Penguin, 1973), 8.

11. T. J. Lustig, *Henry James and the Ghostly* (Cambridge: Cambridge University Press, 1994), 1.

12. The name also references the Hölderlin poem "To Zimmer," quoted in Auster, *Invention of Solitude* (99).

13. Eve Kosofsky Sedgwick, *The Coherence of Gothic Conventions* (London: Routledge, Kegan and Paul, 1986), 4.

14. There are other examples in Auster's writing of people who blur the boundary between life and art. In the introduction to his translation of the French high-wire walker Philippe Petit's *On the High Wire,* Auster says, "the experience of the high wire is direct, unmediated . . . the art is the thing itself, a life in its most naked delineation," suggesting that the art and the life are synonymous. Paul Auster, "On the High Wire," in *The Red Notebook* (London and Boston: Faber and Faber, 1995), 92.

15. Auster's grandparents emigrated from Stanislav, another instance of fiction and biography overlapping.

16. See Judith Butler, *Excitable Speech: A Politics of the Performative* (London: Routledge, 1997).

17. Nicci Gerrard, "Dead Men Do Tell Tales," *Observer,* 29 September 2002, 13.

18. Brown, *Paul Auster,* 126.

Chapter Seven: Other Works

1. Berg Collection, Box 1, Folder 2. This prose resembles the poetry in tone: "What is seen, here, in the voice, falling, that which falls, a soft liquid, in the voice, falling, to a bowl, filled with, in the voice, filled of, moistened flames, the voice, faintly falling to silence."

2. Gerard Woodward, "The Stones Speak," *Guardian*, 17 March 2007, 18.

3. Eric McHenry, "Collected Poems, by Paul Auster," *New York Times*, 25 January 2004.

4. Auster interview.

5. Paul Auster, "Truth, Beauty, Silence," in *Collected Prose*, 341.

6. Norman Finkelstein, "In the Realm of the Naked Eye: The Poetry of Paul Auster," in Barone, *Beyond the Red Notebook*, 56.

7. The comparison is not only valid for the poetry. In *The Music of Chance* Jim Nashe explicitly compares the wall he and Pozzi are about to start building with the Wailing Wall (86).

8. Bill Goldstein, "Audio Special: Paul Auster," *New York Times on the Web*, 5 May 1999, http://www.nytimes.com/books/99/06/20/specials/auster-audio.html.

9. Eileen Battersby, "*Timbuktu* by Paul Auster," *Irish Times*, 8 July 2000, 70.

10. Jonathan Yardley, "It's a Dog's Life," *Washington Post Book World*, 23 May 1999, X01.

11. Jim Shepard, "This Dog's Life," *New York Times*, 20 June 1999.

12. Russell Celyn Jones, "Novelist Gone to the Dogs," *Times*, 27 May 1999.

13. Steven G. Kellman, "Austerity Measures: Paul Auster Goes to the Dogs," in *Bloom's Modern Critical Views: Paul Auster*, ed. Harold Bloom (New York: Chelsea House, 2003), 226.

14. Brown, *Paul Auster*, 112.

15. Sean O' Hagan, "Abstract Expressionist," *Observer*, 8 February 2004, 30.

16. Slavoj Žižek, "Welcome to the Desert of the Real," in *Re:constructions: Reflections on Humanity and Media after Tragedy*, 15 September 2001, http://web.mit.edu/cms/reconstructions/interpretations/desertreal.html.

17. Paul Auster, *Man in the Dark* (New York: Henry Holt, 2008), 175. All parenthetical citations are from this edition.

18. The novel takes its name from Thomas Hobbes's work of 1651. Written during the English Civil War, Hobbes's treatise advocates the rule of strong centralized government. The implementation of that "great LEVIATHAN called a COMMONWEALTH, or STATE, in Latin CIVITAS" is necessary in order to stave off the default condition of humankind, which is chaos and conflict. Thomas Hobbes, *Leviathan: On the Matter, Forme and Power of a Commonwealth Ecclesiasticall and Civil,* ed. Michael Oakeshott (New York: Collier Books, 1973), 19, 100.

19. Paul Auster, *Leviathan* (New York: Penguin 1993), 244, 1. All parenthetical citations are from this edition.

20. Hobbes, *Leviathan,* 127.

21. In an interview on BBC Radio 4's *Front Row,* 31 May 2004, Auster reveals that the story about the prostitute and the dead baby was a real news story.

22. Peter Conrad, "Blasts from the Past," *Observer,* 8 February 2004, 15.

23. Lethem, "Jonathan Lethem Talks with Paul Auster," 53.

24. Jeff Turrentine, "Try a Little Tenderness," *Washington Post Book World,* 15 January 2006, T07.

25. Paul Auster, *The Brooklyn Follies* (New York: Henry Holt, 2006) 1, 2. All parenthetical citations are from this edition.

26. Eric Grunwald, "Uncomfortably Adrift with the Bewildered Mr. Blank," *Boston Globe,* 25 February 2007.

27. Paul Auster, *Travels in the Scriptorium* (New York: Henry Holt, 2006) 22, 20, 33. All parenthetical citations are from this edition.

28. Gurria-Quintana, "Haven't We Met Before?" 40.

Selected Bibliography

Primary Sources

Books by Paul Auster

Unearth. Weston, Conn.: Living Hand, 1974. Book of poetry.
Wall Writing. Berkeley, Calif.: Figures, 1976. Book of poetry.
Effigies. Paris: Orange Export Ltd., 1977.
Fragments from Cold. New York: Parenthèse, 1977. Book of poetry.
Facing the Music. Barrytown, N.Y.: Station Hill Press, 1980. Book of poetry.
White Spaces. Barrytown, N.Y.: Station Hill Press, 1980. Prose poem, nonfiction.
Editor, *The Random House Book of Twentieth Century Poetry*. New York: Random House, 1982. Poetry selection, various authors.
As Paul Benjamin, *Squeeze Play*. London: Alpha and Omega, 1982. New York: Avon Books, 1984. Novel.
The Invention of Solitude. New York: Sun Press, 1982. London: Faber and Faber, 1988. Autobiographical memoir.
City of Glass. Los Angeles: Sun and Moon Press, 1985. Novel.
Ghosts. Los Angeles: Sun and Moon Press, 1986. Novel.
The Locked Room. Los Angeles: Sun and Moon Press, 1986. Novel.
The New York Trilogy. New York: Penguin, 1987. London: Faber and Faber, 1987. Novel.
In the Country of Last Things. New York: Viking, 1987. London: Faber and Faber, 1988. Novel.
Disappearances: Selected Poems. Woodstock, N.Y.: Overlook Press, 1988. Poetry anthology.
Moon Palace. New York: Viking, 1989. London: Faber and Faber, 1989. Novel.
Ground Work: Selected Poems And Essays, 1970–79. London: Faber and Faber, 1990. Poetry and essay collection.

The Music of Chance. New York: Viking, 1990. London: Faber and Faber, 1991. Novel.

Leviathan. New York: Viking, 1992. London: Faber and Faber, 1992. Novel.

The Red Notebook: True Stories. London and Boston: Faber and Faber, 1992. Prose anthology.

The Art of Hunger: Essays, Prefaces, Interviews. Los Angeles: Sun and Moon Press, 1992. New York and London: Penguin, 1993. Prose anthology.

Mr. Vertigo. New York: Viking, 1994. London: Faber and Faber, 1994. Novel.

Hand to Mouth: A Chronicle of Early Failure. New York: Henry Holt, 1997. London: Faber and Faber, 1997. Autobiographical memoir.

Selected Poems. London: Faber and Faber, 1998. Poetry anthology.

Timbuktu. New York: Picador, 1999. London: Faber and Faber, 1999. Novel.

Editor, *I Thought My Father Was God, and Other True Tales of American Life from NPR's National Story Project.* New York: Henry Holt, 2001. As *True Tales of American Life.* London: Faber and Faber, 2001.

The Story of My Typewriter. New York: Distributed Art Publishers, 2002. Autobiographical memoir, with illustrations by Sam Messer.

The Book of Illusions. New York: Henry Holt, 2002. London: Faber and Faber, 2003. Novel.

Oracle Night. New York: Henry Holt, 2003. London: Faber and Faber, 2003. Novel.

3 Films: Smoke, Blue in the Face, Lulu on the Bridge. New York: Picador, 2003. Screenplays and interviews.

Collected Prose: Autobiographical Writings, True Stories, Critical Essays, Prefaces, and Collaborations with Artists. London: Faber and Faber, 2003. New York: Picador, 2005. Prose collection, includes *The Invention of Solitude* and *Hand to Mouth.*

City of Glass. Adapted by Paul Karasik and David Mazzucchelli. New York: Picador, 2004. Graphic novel.
Collected Poems. Woodstock, N.Y.: Overlook Press, 2004. London: Faber and Faber, 2007. All of Auster's published poems.
The Brooklyn Follies. New York: Henry Holt, 2005. London: Faber and Faber, 2005. Novel.
Travels in the Scriptorium. London: Faber and Faber, 2006. New York: Henry Holt, 2007. Novel.
The Inner Life of Martin Frost. New York: Henry Holt, 2007. Screenplay.
Man in the Dark. New York: Henry Holt, 2008. London: Faber and Faber, 2008. Novel.

Translations by Paul Auster

A Little Anthology of Surrealist Poems. New York: Siamese Banana Press, 1972.
Fits and Starts: Selected Poems of Jacques Dupin. Weston, Conn.: Living Hand, 1974.
Arabs and Israelis: A Dialogue, by Saul Friedlander and Mahmoud Hussein. New York: Holmes and Meier, 1975. With Lydia Davis.
The Uninhabited: Selected Poems of André de Bouchet. Weston, Conn.: Living Hand, 1976.
The Notebooks of Joseph Joubert: A Selection. San Francisco: North Point Press, 1983.
A Tomb for Anatole, by Stéphane Mallarmé. San Francisco: North Point Press, 1983.
On the High Wire, by Philippe Petit. New York: Random House, 1985.
Joan Miró: Selected Writings and Interviews. Boston: Hall, 1986. With Margit Rowell.
Jacques Dupin's Selected Poems. Newcastle-upon-Tyne: Bloodaxe, 1992.
Translations. New York: Marsilio, 1997. Translations by Paul Auster of works by Philippe Petit, Joseph Joubert, and others.

Chronicle of the Guayaki Indians, by Pierre Clastres. New York: Zone Books, 1998.
If There Were Anywhere but Desert: The Selected Poems of Edmond Jabès. New York: Station Hill, 1998. With Keith Waldrop.
The Station Hill Blanchot Reader. Barrytown, N.Y.: Station Hill Press, 1998. With Lydia Davis.

Selected Articles and Book Contributions by Paul Auster

"The Poetry of William Bronk." *Saturday Review* (8 July 1978): 30–31.
"A Few Words in Praise of George Oppen." *Paideuma: A Journal Devoted to Ezra Pound Scholarship* 10 (1981): 49–52.
Gould, Eric, ed. *The Sin of the Book: Edmond Jabès.* Lincoln: University of Nebraska Press, 1985. Auster has an interview with Jabès entitled "The Book of the Dead: An Interview with Edmond Jabès," 3–25.
"Moonlight in the Brooklyn Museum." *ARTnews* 86 (September 1987): 104–5. Auster discusses the Ralph Blakelock painting *Moonlight,* featured in *Moon Palace.*
Calle, Sophie. *Double Game and Gotham Handbook.* London: Violette Editions, 1992. Auster collaborated with the conceptual artist Sophie Calle, the inspiration for Maria Turner in the novel *Leviathan,* on a project entitled "How to Improve Life in New York City."
"Thinking of Rushdie." *New York Times,* 1 July 1993.
Hamsun, Knut. *Hunger.* New York: Farrar, Straus and Giroux, 1995. Auster wrote the introduction, "The Art of Hunger," in 1970.
Lyons, Deborah, Adam D. Weinberg, and Julie Grau, eds. *Edward Hopper and the American Imagination.* New York: W. W. Norton, 1995. Auster contributed an extract from *Moon Palace* to the book, which accompanied the Whitney Museum retrospective on Edward Hopper.
Leach, Terry. *Things Happen for No Reason: The True Story of an Itinerant Life in Baseball.* Berkeley, Calif.: Frog, 2000. Auster wrote a preface.

Spiegelman, Art, and Françoise Mouly, ed. *Little Lit: Strange Stories for Strange Kids.* New York: RAW Junior, 2001. Auster contributed a story, illustrated by Jacques Loustal, called "The Day I Disappeared."

Hawthorne, Nathaniel. *Twenty Days with Julian and Little Bunny by Papa.* New York: New York Review of Books, 2003. Auster wrote the introduction to this autobiographical memoir.

Selected Interviews and Conversations with Paul Auster

Auster, Paul. "Interview with Larry McCaffery and Sinda Gregory." In *The Art of Hunger: Essays, Prefaces, Interviews,* 287–326. New York: Penguin, 2001.

Auster, Paul, and Michel Contat. "The Manuscript in the Book: A Conversation." Trans. Alyson Waters. *Yale French Studies* 89 (1996): 160–87.

Begley, Adam. "Case of the Brooklyn Symbolist." *New York Times Magazine,* 30 August 1992, 41, 52–54.

Bigsby, Christopher. "Paul Auster." In *Writers in Conversation: Volume Two,* 17–31. Norwich: EAS Publishing, 2001.

Bone, James. "Dem Old Bush Blues." *Times,* 17 April 2004, 4–5.

Bremner, Charles. "A Brooklyn Identity." *Times,* 16 March 1991, R18–19.

Campbell, James. "The Mighty Quinn." *Guardian Review,* 12 November 2005, 11.

Irwin, Mark. "Memory's Escape: Inventing *The Music of Chance*—A Conversation with Paul Auster." *Denver Quarterly* 28.3 (Winter 1994): 111–22.

Lethem, Jonathan. "Jonathan Lethem Talks with Paul Auster." *Believer* 3.1 (February 2005): 49–57.

Lewis, Tim. "An Audience with Paul Auster." *Esquire,* December 2005, 125–30.

Lorberer, Eric, and Xandra Coe. "Paul Auster." *Rain Taxi* 4.3 (Fall 1999): 16–18.

Marcus, James. "Auster! Auster!" *Village Voice,* 30 August 1994, 55–56.

McCrum, Robert. "Once Upon a Time in America." *Observer,* September 2004, 22–33. Auster is interviewed, along with a number of other contemporary American authors, about 9/11 and the Bush administration.

O'Hagan, Sean. "Abstract Expressionist." *Observer,* February 2004, 30.

The South Bank Show: Paul Auster. Pres. Melvyn Bragg. ITV Granada. 7 July 1996.

Books about Paul Auster

Bibliographies and Checklists

Drenttel, William. *Paul Auster: A Comprehensive Bibliographic Checklist of Published Works 1968–1994.* New York: William Drenttel, 1994. Thorough checklist, including interviews, periodical publications, theater adaptations, and audio readings.

Giles, James Richard, Wanda H. Giles, and Gale Group, eds. *American Novelists since World War II.* Sixth Series. Dictionary of Literary Biography, Vol. 227. Detroit: Gale Group, 2000.

Shatzky, Joel, and Michael Taub, eds. "Paul Auster." In *Contemporary Jewish-American Novelists: A Bio-critical Sourcebook,* 13–20. Westport, Conn.: Greenwood Press, 1997. Chapter outlines major works and critical reception.

Springer, Carsten. *A Paul Auster Sourcebook.* New York: Peter Lang, 2001. Lists literary allusions and includes a bibliography for reviews and articles up to *Timbuktu.*

Critical Books

Barone, Dennis, ed. *Beyond the Red Notebook: Essays on Paul Auster.* Philadelphia: University of Pennsylvania Press, 1995. Critical essays on poetry and prose up to *Leviathan.* Highlights include Derek Rubin's essay on hunger in *The Invention of Solitude* and Jewish literature generally (60–70); Steven Weisenburger's excellent essay "Inside *Moon Palace,*" which explores how Auster's novel disrupts genealogical lines (129–42); and Motoyuki

Shibata's essay on translating Auster into Japanese, which becomes a meditation on translation itself (183–88). Also very useful are Madaleine Sorapure's essay on detectives and authors in *City of Glass* (71–87) and Tim Woods's superb analysis of Stone's "City of the World" in *The Music of Chance* (143–61).

Bloom, Harold, ed. *Bloom's Modern Critical Views: Paul Auster.* Philadelphia: Chelsea House, 2004. Aimed primarily at undergraduate students. As well as an introductory essay by Bloom, it includes a biography of Auster and a number of short critical essays on novels up to and including *Timbuktu*. Most of them are essays and reviews that previously appeared in journals and newspapers (see, for example, entries above and below for Baxter, Fredman, Dow, Weisenburger, Lavender, Russell, Powell, Washburn, and Fleck). Aliki Varvogli's "Exploding Fictions" (191–206) is an excellent article on *Leviathan,* and Bruce Bawer's "Doubles and More Doubles" (183–90) is a useful introduction to Auster's use of the doppelganger motif in various novels.

Brown, Mark. *Paul Auster.* Manchester: Manchester University Press, 2007. Sees in Auster's work a gradual opening out from confined spaces in early poems to wider landscapes and increasing inclusivity in later work.

Herzogenrath, Bernd. *An Art of Desire: Reading Paul Auster.* Amsterdam: Rodopi, 1999. The first full-length study of Auster's novels up to *The Music of Chance*. Leans heavily on psychoanalytical theory.

Martin, Brendan Peter. *Paul Auster's Postmodernity.* London: Routledge, 2008. Argues that *The New York Trilogy* sets the pattern for subsequent work.

Springer, Carsten. *Crises: The Works of Paul Auster.* Frankfurt am Main: Peter Lang, 2001. Argues that the connecting theme of all Auster's work, movies included, is identity crises.

Varvogli, Aliki. *The World That Is the Book: Paul Auster's Fiction.* Liverpool: Liverpool University Press, 2001. Looks at Auster's novels in relation to European and American literary influences.

214 / Selected Bibliography

Journal Issues Wholly or Partly Dedicated to Paul Auster

Critique: Studies in Contemporary Fiction 39.3 (Spring 1998)

Dow, William. "Paul Auster's *The Invention of Solitude*: Glimmers in a Reach to Authenticity," 272–82. Suggests that *The Invention of Solitude* is an autobiography, but one that challenges the idea of a coherent or preexisting, unified self.

Segal, Alex. "Secrecy and the Gift: Paul Auster's *The Locked Room*," 239–57. A challenging but nonetheless useful article that sees the idea of a paradox of the gift—a gift given is no longer a gift, so a gift must remain secret—as lying at the heart of *The Locked Room*.

Swope, Richard. "Approaching the Threshold(s) in Postmodern Detective Fiction: Hawthorne's 'Wakefield' and Other Missing Persons," 207–27. Examines Nathaniel Hawthorne's "Wakefield" (1835) as an important literary ancestor of metaphysical detectives, including Auster's.

Zilcosky, John. "The Revenge of the Author: Paul Auster's Challenge to Theory," 195–206. Uses *The New York Trilogy* to explore the issue of authorship, arguing that the author is still very much a creative presence in the text.

Critique: Studies in Contemporary Fiction 49.2 (Winter 2008)

Markku, Salmela. "The Bliss of Being Lost: Revisiting Paul Auster's Nowhere," 131–46. Explores the idea of being "nowhere" in Auster's fiction, a nonspace in which creativity can occur.

Patteson, Richard F. "The Teller's Tale: Text and Paratext in Paul Auster's *Oracle Night*," 115–28. Argues that alternate texts within the main narrative participate in the series of deaths and resurrections that happen to the main characters.

Shostak, Debra. "Under the Sign of *Moon Palace*," 131–46. Explores the tension in Auster's third novel between a reality constructed only through language and a real, material reality.

Review of Contemporary Fiction 14.1 (Spring 1994)

Baxter, Charles. "The Bureau of Missing Persons: Notes on Paul Auster's Fiction," 40–43. Argues that Auster's work since *The Invention of Solitude* has been about trauma and consequent lost identities.

Bray, Paul. "The Currents of Fate and *The Music of Chance*," 83–86. Suggests that chance is such a strong influence in the novel that it assumes a logic of its own

Tysh, Chris. "From One Mirror to Another: The Rhetoric of Disaffiliation in *City of Glass*," 46–52. By "disaffiliation" Tysh means a tearing away from former certainties such as genealogy, objective truth, rigid genre boundaries, and narrative closure.

Washburn, Katherine. "A Book at the End of the World: Paul Auster's *In the Country of Last Things*," 62–65. Argues that Anna Blume's nightmarish world is not a hellish future but a recognizable present.

Selected Critical Articles and Chapters on Paul Auster

Adams, Timothy Dow. *Light Writing and Life Writing: Photography in Autobiography.* Chapel Hill: University of North Carolina Press, 2000. Looks at Auster's reproduction of family photographs in *The Invention of Solitude*.

Alford, Steven E. "Mirrors of Madness: Paul Auster's *The New York Trilogy.*" *Critique: Studies in Contemporary Fiction* 37.1 (Fall 1995): 17–33. Examines the fragmented nature of identity in the trilogy.

———. "Spaced-Out: Signification and Space in Paul Auster's *The New York Trilogy.*" *Contemporary Literature* 36.4 (1995): 613–32. Argues that spaces in the trilogy can be characterized as "neither-here-nor-there": they are always in-betweens.

Amidon, Stephen. "The Promise of Happiness." *Sunday Times Culture,* 20 November 2005, 53. Review of *The Brooklyn Follies*.

Austan, Jacqueline. "The Invention of Solitude." *American Book Review* 6.1 (November–December 1983): 23. Review of *The Invention of Solitude*.

Barone, Dennis. "Chinese Boxes." *American Book Review* 25.6 (September–October 2004): 24. Review of *Oracle Night*.

———. "Travels in the Scriptorium." *Rain Taxi* 12.1 (Spring 2007): 48. Review of *Travels in the Scriptorium*.

Battersby, Eileen. "*Timbuktu* by Paul Auster." *Irish Times*, 8 July 2000, 70. Review of *Timbuktu*.

Begley, Adam. "Mutt from New York." *Guardian*, 29 May 1999, 10. Review of *Timbuktu*.

Bell, Madison Smartt. "Poker and Nothingness." *New York Times Book Review*, 4 November 1990, 1. Review of *The Music of Chance*.

Berlins, Marcel. "Case of the Inner Self." *Times*, 18 February 1988, 17. Review of *The New York Trilogy*.

Bernstein, Stephen. "'The Question Is the Story Itself': Postmodernism and Intertextuality in Auster's *New York Trilogy*." In *Detecting Texts: The Metaphysical Detective Story from Poe to Postmodernism*, ed. Patricia Merivale and Elizabeth S. Sweeney. Philadelphia: University of Pennsylvania Press, 1999. Examines the way texts in Auster's fiction often refer not to reality, but to other texts.

Bewes, Timothy. "Against the Ontology of the Present: Paul Auster's Cinematographic Fictions." *Contemporary Literature* 53.3 (Fall 2007): 273–97. Bewes is interested in the relationship between cinema and literature, and suggests that Auster's recent work seems to aspire to the immediacy of the movies.

Birkerts, Sven. "Paul Auster." In *American Energies: Essays on Fiction*. New York: William Morrow, 1992. Art, Birkerts says of Auster's work, is about finding the self and its relation to others.

———. "Postmodern Picaresque." *New Republic*, 27 March 1989, 36–40. Review of *Moon Palace*.

Blake, Peter. "A State of Willing Suspension." *Times Literary Supplement*, 8 April 1994, 20. Review of *Mr. Vertigo*.

Bleiler, E. F. "Almanacs of Urban Decay." *Washington Post Book World*, 29 March 1987, X11. Review of *The Locked Room*.

Bradbury, Malcolm. *The Modern American Novel*. Rev. ed. Oxford: Oxford University Press, 1992. Bradbury calls Auster's work "experimental realism" and suggests that his Jewish origins may have something to do with the displacement techniques seen in *The New York Trilogy*.

Briggs, Robert. "Wrong Number: The Endless Fiction of Auster and Deleuze and Guattari and . . ." *Critique* 44.2 (Winter 2003): 213–24. Argues that Auster's fiction is frequently open-ended.

Brooker, Peter. *New York Fictions: Modernity, Postmodernism, the New Modern*. London: Longman, 1996. Asserts that Auster's work is not mere aesthetic playfulness, but is more in tune with lived social relations.

Brown, Mark. "'We Don't Go By Numbers': Brooklyn and Baseball in the Films of Paul Auster." In *The Brooklyn Film*, ed. John B. Manbeck and Robert Singer. Jefferson, N.C.: McFarland, 2003. Argues that Brooklyn and baseball provide positive models of microcommunities in a globalizing world.

Burnside, John. "Be Careful What You Wish For." *Scotsman Weekend*, 17 January 2004, 7. Review of *Oracle Night*.

Byrnes, Paul. "Ad Libbing About Life in Brooklyn." *Sydney Morning Herald*, 4 April 1996. Review of *Blue in the Face* (film).

Cantor, Jay. "Some People Just Know How to Fly." *New York Times Book Review*, 28 August 1994, 1. Review of *Mr. Vertigo*.

Coe, Jonathan. "Moon Madness." *Guardian*, 14 April 1989, 30. Review of *Moon Palace*.

Cohen, Josh. "Desertions: Paul Auster, Edmond Jabès, and the Writing of Auschwitz." *Journal of the Midwest Modern Language Association* 33.3 (Fall 2000): 94–107. Examines those aspects of Auster's writing most expressive of his Jewish heritage.

Conrad, Peter. "Blasts from the Past." *Observer,* 8 February 2004, 15. Review of *Oracle Night.*

Coren, Giles. "Trifles Well Considered." *Times,* 20 April 1995, 36. Review of *The Red Notebook.*

Crowley, John. "Flickering Images." *Washington Post,* 8 September 2002. Review of *The Book of Illusions.*

Danto, Ginger. "All of This Might Never Have Happened." *New York Times Book Review,* 20 September 1992, 1. Review of *Leviathan.*

De Botton, Alain. "Down and Out in New York." *Sunday Telegraph,* 14 December 1997. Review of *Hand to Mouth.*

D'Erasmo, Stacey. "Noir Like Me." *New York Times,* 30 November 2003. Review of *Oracle Night.*

Deveson, Tom. "At Cross Purposes." *Sunday Times Books,* 1 February 2004, 52. Review of *Oracle Night.*

Dimovitz, Scott A. "Public Personae and the Private I: De-compositional Ontology in Paul Auster's *New York Trilogy.*" *Modern Fiction Studies* 52.3 (Fall 2006): 613–33. Argues that Auster's trilogy exploits the "already exhausted" genre of antidetective fiction in order to reinstate chance as the overriding factor of existence.

Dirda, Michael. "Marvels and Mysteries." *Washington Post Book World,* 26 March 1989, 3. Review of *Moon Palace.*

Donovan, Christopher. *Postmodern Counternarratives: Irony and Audience in the Novels of Paul Auster, Don DeLillo, Charles Johnson, and Tim O'Brien.* New York: Routledge, 2005. Argues that Auster's work strives to find a middle ground between postmodern irony and solidarity with the world of others, and between experimentation and realism.

Dotan, Eyal. "The Game of Late Capitalism: Gambling and Ideology in *The Music of Chance.*" *Mosaic: A Journal for the Interdisciplinary Study of Literature* 33.1 (March 2000): 161–76. Argues that increased gaming and gambling is a symptom of late capitalism.

Drabelle, Dennis. "Mystery Goes Post-Modern." *Washington Post Book World*, 15 June 1986, 9. Review of *City of Glass* and *Ghosts*.

Edwards, Thomas R. "Sad Young Men." *New York Review of Books*, 17 August 1989, 52. Review of *Moon Palace*.

Felperin, Leslie. "Smoke Opera." *Sight and Sound* (April 1996): 6–9. Review of *Smoke* (film).

Fleck, Linda. "From Metonymy to Metaphor: Paul Auster's *Leviathan*." *Critique* 39 (Spring 1998): 258–71. Argues that this novel is dominated by chance and contingency.

Ford, Mark. "Brooklyn Has It All." *Times Literary Supplement*, 26 April 1996, 14. Review of *Smoke* (film).

———. "Citizens of Sinister City." *Times Literary Supplement*, 13 March 1991, 11. Review of *The Music of Chance*.

———. "Inventions of Solitude: Thoreau and Auster." *Journal of American Studies* 33 (1999): 201–19. Discusses Auster's relationship with Henry David Thoreau, both writers interested in the idea of creative solitude.

Fox, Sarah. "*I Thought My Father Was God and Other True Tales from NPR's National Story Project*." *Rain Taxi* Online Edition (Winter 2001/2002). http://www.raintaxi.com/online/2001winter/auster.shtml. Review of *I Thought My Father Was God*.

Fredman, Stephen. "'How to Get Out of the Room That Is the Book?' Paul Auster and the Consequences of Confinement." *Postmodern Culture* 6.3 (May 1996). http://muse.jhu.edu/cgibin/access.cgi?uri=/journals/postmodern_culture/v006/6.3fredman.html. Explores images of masculine creativity, memory, and the Holocaust in *The Invention of Solitude*.

Gach, Gary. "Magna Civitas, Magna Solitudo." *American Book Review* 8.5 (September–October 1986): 23. Review of *City of Glass*.

Gerrard, Nicci. "Dead Men Do Tell Tales." *Observer*, 29 September 2002, 13. Review of *The Book of Illusions*.

Gressor, Megan. "Element of Magic Requires a Deft Hand." *Sydney Morning Herald Spectrum*, 2 April 1994, 7. Review of *Mr. Vertigo*.

Grunwald, Eric. "Uncomfortably Adrift with the Bewildered Mr. Blank." *Boston Globe*, 25 February 2007. Review of *Travels in the Scriptorium*.

Gurria-Quintana, Angel. "Haven't We Met Before?" *Financial Times*, 7 October 2006, 40. Review of *Travels in the Scriptorium*.

Hensher, Philip. "Repeatedly Falling." *Guardian*, 20 October 1992, 28. Review of *Leviathan*.

Homberger, Eric. "Happy Accidents." *Independent*, 9 December 2005, 25. Review of *The Brooklyn Follies*.

Indiana, Gary. "Pompous Circumstance: Paul Auster Indulges Himself." *Village Voice*, 14 April 1989, 45. Review of *Moon Palace*.

Jahshan, Paul. "Paul Auster's Specters." *Journal of American Studies* 37.3 (December 2003): 389–406. Looks at the figures of the mirror and the double in *Ghosts*, and argues that the text addresses the challenges of a virtual age, in which information and identity become increasingly spectral.

Jarvis, Brian. *Postmodern Cartographies: The Geographical Imagination in Contemporary American Culture*. London: Pluto Press, 1998. Suggests that *City of Glass* obsesses on waste and the underclass, but shies away from a specific political engagement.

Kakutani, Michiko. "A Memoir of Too Much Money, Then Too Little." *New York Times*, 2 September 1997. Review of *Hand to Mouth*.

Kirn, Walter. "The Music of Chance." *New York Times*, 8 January 2006. Review of *The Brooklyn Follies*.

Lavender, William. "The Novel of Critical Engagement: Paul Auster's *City of Glass*." *Contemporary Literature* 34 (1993): 219–39. Argues that Auster uses aspects of literary theory in *The New York Trilogy* to break down the idea of a conventional novel.

Lindgren, Michael. "*Man in the Dark*." *Rain Taxi* 13.3 (Fall 2008): 8. Review of *Man in the Dark*.

Little, William G. "Nothing to Go On: Paul Auster's *City of Glass.*" *Contemporary Literature* 38.1 (Spring 1997): 133–63. Asks why nothing happens, in the conventional plot sense, in *City of Glass*.

Mallon, Thomas. "Caught in the Waltz of Disasters." *Washington Post Book World*, 6 September 1992, X5. Review of *Leviathan*.

Malmgren, Carl D. "Detecting/Writing the Real: Paul Auster's *City of Glass*." In *Narrative Turns and Minor Genres in Postmodernism*, ed. Theo D'haen and Hans Bertens. Amsterdam: Rodopi, 1995. Observes that although a character called "Paul Auster" appears in *City of Glass*, complete with wife, Siri, and son, Daniel, this can still only be called a representational gesture in the text; it is not "real."

Maslin, Janet. "Cigars and Conversation in the Course of Revelation." *New York Times*, 9 June 1995. Review of *Smoke* (film).

———. "In Hip Brooklyn, Take 2 on That Old Cigar Store." *New York Times*, 13 October 1995. Review of *Blue in the Face* (film).

———. "A Novel's Actor More Real Than Many Made of Flesh." *New York Times*, 9 May 2002: 7. Review of *The Book of Illusions*.

Max, D. T. "The Professor of Despair." *New York Times*, 1 September 2002. Review of *The Book of Illusions*.

McHenry, Eric. "Collected Poems, by Paul Auster." *New York Times*, 25 January 2004. Review of *Collected Poems*.

Merlob, Maya. "Textuality, Self, and World: The Postmodern Narrative in Paul Auster's *In the Country of Last Things*." *Critique* 49.1 (Fall 2007): 25–45. Looks at the use of fractured and discontinuous spaces in Auster's novel.

Merwin, W. S. "Invisible Father." *New York Times*, 27 February 1983: 10. Review of *The Invention of Solitude*.

Millard, Kenneth. *Contemporary American Fiction: An Introduction to American Fiction since 1970*. Oxford: Oxford University Press, 2000. Millard's analysis of *The New York Trilogy* treats it as an essentially solipsistic, self-referential set of linguistic and allusive games without a clear political agenda.

Müller, Monika. "From Hard-Boiled Detective to Kaspar Hauser? Masculinity and Writing in Paul Auster's *The New York Trilogy*." In *Subverting Masculinity: Hegemonic and Alternative Versions of Masculinity in Contemporary Culture*, ed. Russell West and Frank Lay. Amsterdam: Rodopi, 2000. Argues that Auster plays with the notion of the masculine detective, torn away from domesticity by his work.

Nealon, Jeffrey T. "Work of the Detective, Work of the Writer: Paul Auster's *City of Glass*." *Modern Fiction Studies* 42 (1996): 91–110. Explores the relationship between the writer and the detective, figures who both create narratives.

Norfolk, Lawrence. "On the Brink of Decay." *Times Literary Supplement*, 22 July 1988, 802. Review of *In the Country of Last Things*.

Norman, Howard. "The Strange Hours of Mr. Blank." *Washington Post*, 4 March 2007. Review of *Travels in the Scriptorium*.

Nye, Robert. "The Malice of Chance." *Guardian*, 21 March 1998, 28. Review of *The Music of Chance*.

Oberman, Warren. "Existentialism and Postmodernism in Paul Auster's *The Music of Chance*." *Critique* 45.2 (Winter 2004): 191–206. Sees in the novel a confrontation with freedom in a late capitalist historical context.

Olson, Toby. "Metaphysical Mystery Tour." *New York Times*, 3 November 1985. Review of *City of Glass*.

Parrinder, Patrick. "Tall Storeys." *London Review of Books*, 10 December 1987, 26. Review of *The New York Trilogy*.

Peacock, James. "Carrying the Burden of Representation: Paul Auster's *The Book of Illusions*." *Journal of American Studies* 40.1 (April 2006): 53–70. Takes the character of Alma as central to the novel, her birthmark being a symbol of the endless representation of the individual by others.

———. "Signs of Grace: Paul Auster's *Oracle Night*." *English* 55.211 (Spring 2006): 65–78. Proceeds from the name of the wife, Grace, and argues that the novel has a very Puritan concern with grace and salvation.

Powell, Padget. "The End Is Only Imaginary." *New York Times Book Review,* 17 May 1987, 11–12. Review of *In the Country of Last Things.*

Rafferty, Terence. "Brooklyn Miscellany." *New Yorker,* 23 October 1995, 96–98. Review of *Blue in the Face* (film).

Rowen, Norma. "The Detective in Search of the Lost Tongue of Adam: Paul Auster's *City of Glass.*" *Critique* 32.4 (Summer 1991): 224–34. Argues that the detective's quest is to restore language to its paradisiacal state, when words and things matched up.

Royle, Nicholas. "Being Paul Auster: A Trip through the Teeming Brain of the Author." *Independent Extra,* 30 October 2006, 20. Review of *Travels in the Scriptorium.*

Russell, Alison. "Deconstructing *The New York Trilogy:* Paul Auster's Anti-Detective Fiction." *Critique* 31 (1990): 71–84. Rowen's article, above, follows on from Russell's. The latter sees the "crime" in *The New York Trilogy* as essentially linguistic.

Saltzman, Arthur. *The Novel in the Balance.* Columbia: University of South Carolina Press, 1993. Saltzman explores the relationship between chaos and order in *The Music of Chance,* suggesting, like Paul Bray, that Pozzi relies on fate and chance to the extent that they attain their own kind of arcane logic.

Scurr, Ruth. "Attempts to Sleep Alone." *Daily Telegraph Books,* 23 August 2008, 26. Review of *Man in the Dark.*

Seidl, Christian. "'Regeneration through Creativity': The Frontier in Paul Auster's *Moon Palace.*" *PhiN* 31 (2005): 60–78. Plays into frontier mythology by arguing that it is in the novel's frontier locations, rather than the urban settings, that the characters can achieve creative rebirth.

Shepard, Jim. "This Dog's Life." *New York Times,* 20 June 1999. Review of *Timbuktu.*

Shiloh, Ilana. "A Place Both Imaginary and Realistic: Paul Auster's *The Music of Chance.*" *Contemporary Literature* 43.3 (Autumn 2002): 488–517. Explores the relationship between chance, power, and money in *The Music of Chance.*

Smiley, Jane. "Enough to Keep You Up at Night." *Los Angeles Times Sunday Calendar,* 24 August 2008. Review of *Man in the Dark.*

Taylor, John. "The Red Notebook." *Times Literary Supplement,* 28 April 1995, 21. Review of *The Red Notebook.*

Turrentine, Jeff. "Try a Little Tenderness." *Washington Post,* 15 January 2006. Review of *The Brooklyn Follies.*

Uchiyama, Kanae. "The Death of the Other: A Levinasian Reading of Paul Auster's *Moon Palace.*" *Modern Fiction Studies* 54.1 (Spring 2008): 115–39. Uses the work of the philosopher Emmanuel Levinas to explore the physical aspects of the novel, including sleep, eating, aging, and death.

Walker, Joseph S. "Criminality and (Self) Deception. The Case of Paul Auster." *Modern Fiction Studies* 48 (Summer 2002): 389–421. Argues that many Auster narratives begin with a criminal act (for example, Auggie Wren's stealing of the camera in *Smoke*), followed by periods of intense self-discipline (for example, Auggie's decision to take a photograph in the same place at the same time every day).

Wall, Stephen. "Cityscapes." *London Review of Books,* 1 September 1988, 21–22. Review of *In the Country of Last Things.*

Walters, Michael. "Life's Punning Plots." *Times Literary Supplement,* 17 February 1989, 158. Review of *The Invention of Solitude.*

Wesseling, Elisabeth. "Parable of the Apocalypse." *Neophilologus* 25 (1991): 496–504. Argues that although the idea of apocalypse is evoked in *In the Country of Last Things,* an absolute ending is never offered.

Woodward, Gerard. "The Stones Speak." *Guardian,* 17 March 2007, 18. Review of *Collected Poems.*

Yardley, Jonathan. "Above the Fruited Plain." *Washington Post Book World*, 28 August 1994, X3. Review of *Mr. Vertigo*.

———. "It's a Dog's Life." *Washington Post*, 23 May 1999. Review of *Timbuktu*.

———. "Under Auster's 'Music' Spell." *Washington Post Book World*, 10 October 1990, D2. Review of *The Music of Chance*.

Index

Alcott, Bronson, 71
American Dream, 132, 134, 139, 143, 144, 145, 178
antidetective fiction, 44–48, 58, 79
Auster, Anna (grandmother), 12, 24–26
Auster, Daniel (son), 28, 35, 36
Auster, Harry (grandfather), 12, 24–26
Auster, Paul: childhood, 24; grandparents, 24-26; Jewish heritage of Paul Auster, 12–14, 26, 34–35, 37–38, 41, 95–96, 99–100, 139, 156, 171–73; WORKS—*Blue in the Face* (movie), 3, 147, 185; *The Book of Illusions*, 146–67; *Collected Poems*, 88, 175; *Effigies*, 168; *Facing the Music*, 168; *Fragments from Cold*, 173–75; *I Thought My Father Was God* (edited by Auster), 9, 185, 186; *In the Country of Last Things*, 84–99; *Inner Life of Martin Frost* (movie), 3, 146–47; *The Invention of Solitude*, 15–41; *Lulu on the Bridge* (movie), 3, 147; *Man in the Dark*, 180, 181; *Moon Palace*, 119–31; *Mr. Vertigo*, 131–46; *The Music of Chance*, 99–115; "New York Spleen," 46; *The New York Trilogy*, 42–83; "Prolusion: The Clown's Universe," 168; *Red Notebook*, 48; *Smoke* (movie), 3–5, 147; *Squeeze Play* (as Paul Benjamin), 2, 42–43, 55, 70; *Timbuktu*, 175–79; *Unearth*, 169–71; *Wall Writing*, 172; *White Spaces*, 175
Auster, Queenie (mother), 1
Auster, Samuel (father), 1, 7, 15–28, 43
Auster, Sophie (daughter), 147

Babel, Isaac, 28
Barthes, Roland, 23
Baudelaire, Charles, 60–61
Beckett, Samuel, 2
Beecher, Henry Ward, 65
Bellow, Saul, 121
Benjamin, Paul (Paul Auster's pseudonym), 10
Berlin Wall, 113, 115
bildingsroman, 121, 122, 131
Blakelock, Ralph, 126–28, 146
Blanchot, Maurice, 29
Blue in the Face (movie), 3, 147, 185
Book of Jonah, 32, 35–38

Brooklyn, New York, 5, 14, 64–65, 70, 184–86, 187
Brown, Mark, 10, 134, 146, 166–67, 177
Bush, George W., 189, 190
Byrne, David, 2

Carr, John Dickson, 74
Carroll, Lewis, 60
Cervantes, Miguel de, 59–60, 62
Chandler, Raymond, 42, 47, 51
Chateaubriand, François-René de, 149–51, 157, 165
Christie, Agatha, 45
Cody, Buffalo Bill, 137–38
Coen brothers, 116
Columbus, Christopher, 119
Cooper, James Fenimore, 116, 135

Davis, Lydia, 1
DeLillo, Don, 180, 181
Dickens, Charles, 121
Dupin, Jacques, 1

Emerson, Ralph Waldo, 8, 55
exile, 13–14, 34, 126, 139, 172

Fitzgerald, F. Scott, 149
Forster, E. M., 4
Frank, Anne, 7, 30, 87–88

Great Wall of China, 114

Haas, Philip, 99
Hammett, Dashiell, 42
Hartley, Hal, 147
Hauser, Kasper, 53
Hawthorne, Nathaniel, 2, 10, 71, 75, 149, 150, 157, 161–64, 191
Herzogenrath, Bernd, 103
Hobbes, Thomas, 183
Hölderlin, Friedrich, 7, 30
Holmes, Sherlock, 46
Holocaust, 12, 34, 37, 45, 172, 181
Humpty Dumpty, 58
Hustvedt, Siri, 1, 10, 59

I Thought My Father Was God (edited by Auster), 9, 185, 186
Inner Life of Martin Frost (movie), 3, 146–47
Iraq War, 181, 188, 190

Jabès, Edmond, 2, 33–35, 37
Jacob, Irène, 147

Kafka, Franz, 2, 13, 186–87
Keitel, Harvey, 2
Kerouac, Jack, 103
Kierkegaard, Sören, 29

Lake Havasu, Arizona, 110
language, 6–9, 13, 16, 26–27, 29, 32–33, 34, 38–40,

52–56, 64, 66–67, 68, 86, 88–91, 95, 111, 152, 168–69, 171, 174–75,
Leibniz, Gottfried Wilhelm von, 2
Lethem, Jonathan, 146, 184
Lulu on the Bridge (movie), 3, 147

McCarthy, Cormac, 116
McEwan, Ian, 180
McInerney, Jay, 180
Mallarmé, Stéphane, 1, 170
Manhattan, New York, 49, 65
Melville, Herman, 71
Milton, John, 55
Mitchum, Robert, 70
Moran, Thomas, 128

Nabokov, Vladimir, 47
New Western Historians, 118
"New York Spleen" (Auster), 46

Oppen, George, 170

Pascal, Blaise, 30
Patinkin, Mandy, 99
Pinocchio (Carlo Collodi), 35–36
Pirandello, Luigi, 189
Poe, Edgar Allan, 2, 10, 46, 50, 54, 60, 74, 153
"Prolusion: The Clown's Universe" (Auster), 168

Proust, Marcel, 28, 29
Pynchon, Thomas, 46

Red Notebook (Auster), 48
Reed, Lou, 3
Reznikoff, Charles, 13, 170
Robinson, Jackie, 70
Roth, Philip, 11, 12
Rowling, J. K., 121

Sayers, Dorothy L., 45
September 11, 2001 (9/11), 14, 180–91
Smoke (movie), 3–5, 147
Sontag, Susan, 20
Spader, James, 99
Spillane, Mickey, 44–45
Springer, Carsten, 29, 41, 76, 140
Squeeze Play (as Paul Benjamin), 2, 42–43, 55, 70
Statue of Liberty, 182
stock market crash of 1929, 132, 134

Thewlis, David, 147
Thoreau, Henry David, 2, 10, 65–67, 70–71
Tower of Babel, 54–56, 57–58
Tsvetayeva, Marina, 35
Turner, Frederick Jackson, 116–7, 120, 121, 130, 136
Twain, Mark, 120

Updike, John, 180

Van Gogh, Vincent, 30
Varvogli, Aliki, 29, 55, 82, 87, 115, 121, 128

Warsaw Ghetto, 86
Western Wall (Wailing Wall), 113, 171–72
Walpole, Horace, 150
Wang, Wayne, 3

Whitman, Walt, 65, 71, 174
Wild West, 13, 38, 117, 119, 120–21, 123, 126, 128–29, 135–36, 143, 144
Wizard of Oz, 135
Wolfson, Louis, 55

Zukofsky, Louis, 170

CPSIA information can be obtained
at www.ICGtesting.com
Printed in the USA
FFOW04n1614060217
32046FF